D1260093

ArtScroll Judaica Classics®

A Treasury of Chassidic

by

Rabbi Shlomo Yosef Zevin

Translated by Uri Kaploun

ספורי חסידים על התורה

VOLUME TWO

ויקרא / Leviticus
במדבר / Numbers
דברים / Deuteronomy

tales on the torah

A COLLECTION OF INSPIRATIONAL CHASSIDIC STORIES RELEVANT TO THE WEEKLY TORAH READINGS

Published by
Mesorah Publications, ltd / *New York*
in conjunction with
HILLEL PRESS / *Jerusalem*

FIRST EDITION
First Impression ... July, 1980
Second Impression ... November, 1980
Third Impression ... August, 1981
Fourth Impression ... January, 1984

Published and Distributed by
MESORAH PUBLICATIONS, Ltd.
1969 Coney Island Avenue
Brooklyn, New York 11223
In conjunction with
HILLEL PRESS, Jerusalem

Distributed in Israel by
J. GROSSMAN / MESORAH MAFITIZIM
Rechov Bayit Vegan 90/5
Jerusalem

Distributed in Europe by
J. LEHMANN HEBREW BOOKSELLERS
20 Cambridge Terrace
Gateshead
Tyne and Wear
England NE 8 1RP

ISBN:
0-89906-902-9 (Hardcover)
0-89906-903-7 (Paperback)

סדר במסדרת
חברת ארטסקרול בע"מ

Typography by Compuscribe at ArtScroll Studios, Ltd.
1969 Coney Island Avenue / Brooklyn, N.Y. 11223 / (212) 339-1700

Printed in the United States of America by Moriah Offset

Table of Contents

ספר ויקרא
Leviticus

סדר ויקרא
Sidra Vayikra

◆§ A Man Like Any Other

וַיִּקְרָא אֶל מֹשֶׁה *And He called to Moshe (1:1)*

וַיִּקְרָא: the first word of this Book appears in the Torah with a small *aleph (Mesorah).*

At a tender age Reb Menachem Mendel of Lubavitch, who is known as the Tzemach Tzedek, lost his mother, the daughter of Reb Shneur Zalman of Liadi, and was brought up thereafter by his illustrious grandfather, who on the day after Yom Kippur, 1792, brought the child to the *cheder* to begin his Torah lessons. Reb Shneur Zalman had prayed at daybreak, which was not his custom, and had led the prayers and read the Torah himself. It was a Thursday, in the week in which the Portion of *Haazinu* was read from the Torah, and he read the passage "Remember the days of old" in a way that stirred the minds and hearts of all his listeners. When he came to the verse — "He led him about, he instructed him, he watched over him like the apple of his eye" — his eyes brimmed over with tears, and a shudder passed through the congregants.

After prayers he had the toddler enveloped in a *tallis* so that he could see nothing around him, and asked to have him carried to his mother's burial place. They arrived at the cemetery together with the child's father, Reb Shalom Shachna, and approaching the gravestone the rebbe said in a loud and cheerful voice: "*Mazel Tov* to you, Devorah Leah the daughter of Sterna! Today I am introducing your son, Menachem Mendel the son of Devorah Leah, to the study of the Torah. Give him your blessing that just as he has been brought to the study of the Torah, so too should he be led to the *chuppah* and to the performance of good deeds; and bless him too with long life."

And all those who stood with them responded warmly: "Amen!"

When they came home the child was brought to the courtyard of the synagogue, where the rebbe asked the boy's *melamed* to teach him the opening passage of *Vayikra,* the chapter of *Leviticus* with which young children traditionally begin their Torah studies. Throughout the lesson the rebbe leaned his head on his arms in the wordless ecstasy of *dveikus,* and when it came to an end he asked that the child be given a cake of oil and honey and a hard-boiled egg, on both of which verses from the Torah were inscribed.

At this point the youngster asked his grandfather: "Why is the *aleph* of the word *Vayikra* small?"

For some time the rebbe remained silent in a state of *dveikus,* then he opened his eyes and said: "Adam was created by God's hands, and in understanding he surpassed the ministering angels. He was aware of his own stature, and thereby erred in the sin of the Tree of Knowledge. Moshe Rabbeinu was also aware of his own stature, but not only did this not cause him to wax proud: on the contrary, he was humble of spirit, thinking that any other man — who was not the son of Amram, nor seventh in direct line of descent from the Patriarch Avraham — if he were granted a soul like his, and the spiritual advantages of an ancestry like his, would have been far greater than he. The Torah itself testifies to his modesty: 'And the man Moshe was very humble, more so than all the men on the face of the earth.' Now the Torah is comprised of large letters, letters of intermediate size, and small letters. This is to teach us that every man should strive through the study and practice of the Torah to attain the spiritual level of a *beinoni* [the so-called "intermediate" man, whose consistently successful struggle for mastery over his Evil Inclination is described in Reb Shneur Zalman's classic *Tanya,* which is also known as the *Sefer shel Beinonim*]. The name of Adam, who stumbled because of his awareness of his own greatness, appears in the Book of *Chronicles* with a large *aleph;* Moshe Rabbeinu, who was led by this awareness to an unparalleled degree of humility, is addressed in the Torah by the word *Vayikra,* which is written with a small *aleph*".

The rebbe then delivered a chassidic discourse based on the verse: "If any man among you brings an offering to God," and asked all those present to partake of the *seudas mitzvah*. He left the synagogue, and those remaining washed their hands in preparation for the festive meal, and took their places at the table. Some of the elder chassidim sat the child on a chair, placed it on the table, and asked him to repeat the answer which his grandfather had given to his question. This he did, in the unfaltering voice of a little boy who had just turned three.

Hearing his words, one of the oldest chassidim present rose and said: "May the Almighty fulfill all the blessings with which our rebbe blessed his grandson, Menachem Mendel the son of Devorah Leah!"

And all his friends responded: "Amen! Amen!"

◆§ *Guard Your Tongue*

וְנֶפֶשׁ כִּי תֶחֱטָא וְשָׁמְעָה קוֹל אָלָה

And if a person sins, and hears the voice of an oath (5:1)

When he was a young man, recalled Reb Yitzchak of Vorki, he suffered a great deal of anguish from his wife, but no matter how bitterly she berated him he bore everything in silence. When he saw, however, that she was making life a misery for their servants as well, he was unable to decide whether for the sake of peace he should make no comment, or whether he was under a moral obligation to speak up — not, indeed, for himself, but in defense of the downtrodden servants. He decided that this was a question for his rebbe, Reb David of Lelov.

The tzaddik, listened, and said: "Why do you tell me? Tell yourself!"

Reb Yitzchak was baffled by this response — until after some time he came across a teaching of the Baal Shem Tov: If a person is remiss in the realm of action, he suffers anguish caused by his cattle and his servants; if he does not rule his tongue, he has to undergo distress caused by the harsh words and curses of his wife and other people; and if he is careless as to what kinds of thoughts are allowed to occupy his mind, his children will be the cause of his heart-ache. Moreover, taught the

Baal Shem Tov, if a person succeeds in setting aright these three areas of his life — his thought, speech, and action — then the three corresponding sources of distress are transformed to sources of happiness. Pondering over this teaching of the Baal Shem Tov, Reb Yitzchak of Vorki came to understand his rebbe's sharp reaction: "Tell yourself!"

A certain scholar saw a hint of this teaching in the verse: "And if a person sins, and hears the voice of an oath." If a person sins, he said, then he is bound to hear oaths and curses from his wife and from others.

◆§ *Exchange of Energy*

וְלֹא אֹתִי קָרָאתָ יַעֲקֹב כִּי יָגַעְתָּ בִּי יִשְׂרָאֵל

You have not called on Me, O Yaakov, for you have been weary of Me, O Yisrael (Haftarah)

Ridden by illness and pain, Reb Yisrael of Koznitz was confined to his bed for long periods, but when the time came for prayer, or for the study of the Torah, or for the performance of a mitzvah, he rallied with the strength of a lion, and appeared to be perfectly fit and robust.

One of his chassidim took the liberty of asking him for an explanation of this phenomenon, and the Maggid answered: "We read in the Book of *Isaiah*, וְקוֵֹי ה' יַחֲלִיפוּ כֹחַ — 'Those who trust in God will renew (literally: *exchange)* their strength.' Now we often see laborers who work hard as porters and the like for six days of the week, and when *Shabbos* comes they are so exhausted that they almost fall asleep during their prayers. Where has their strength disappeared to? Simple — during that time they exchange their strength with those who trust in God, so that the latter will have the strength to serve their Maker in prayer and study. And when their prayers are over, those who trust in God return the strength to those who lent it, thus enabling them to resume their new week's hard work."

סדר צו
Sidra Tzav

☙ Dressed for the Occasion

וּפָשַׁט אֶת בְּגָדָיו וְלָבַשׁ בְּגָדִים אֲחֵרִים
And he shall take off his garments, and put on other garments (6:4)

Reb Uri of Strelisk was once told of the seemingly pretentious conduct of Reb Yisrael of Ruzhin, who used to have musical instruments played before him. The Saraph of Strelisk wanted to know what the tzaddik of Ruzhin looked like when he was listening to his musicians, and was given a picture of inspired ecstasy.

"Concerning the Prophet Eliyahu," he said, "we are told that 'the girdle of his loins was a girdle of leather.' This really means that in his case his very loins, his very body, was like a leather girdle, which he could put on and take off at will. And so it is with the tzaddik of Ruzhin: when he so desires, he can divest himself of his body, and when he wills it otherwise, he can clothe himself in his body."

☙ In Another Man's Shoes

It once happened that Reb David Zvi Chein, the *rav* of Chernigov, arrived late for his *yechidus* with his rebbe, Reb Shmuel of Lubavitch. He decided to wait in the room adjoining the rebbe's study, and to ask a certain question of the rebbe as he passed, for he had to return home within a short time. He was joined there by the rebbe's attendant, who had brought the change of clothing which the rebbe would soon need, for by the time he had received a long series of chassidim for private interviews he always perspired heavily.

"Would you happen to know," the attendant asked Reb David Zvi, "why he perspires so much when he grants *yechidus* in there? The whole thing lasts only an hour, but does he perspire!"

The chassid remained silent, so the attendant asked again: "Why, in heaven's name, does he perspire so much?"

The door to the study opened at once, and the rebbe addressed the questioner: "I am dismissing you as of today. Please go home, and I will send you your wages there every week. And by the way, why is it so hard to understand why I perspire? In the course of this past hour I received twenty-five people for *yechidus*. If I am to counsel each man well, then I must experience his distress exactly as he himself experiences it: I must divest myself of my own garments and clothe myself in his. When the time comes for me to offer him advice, I cannot do this while I am still dressed in his spiritual garments — just as he was unable to advise *himself* while in that condition. I therefore have to get out of his clothes and dress myself again in my own. In brief, for every person who comes in with a question, I have to undress and dress twice. Now work it out for yourself: if in the course of one hour a man has to undress and dress fifty times over, how can he not perspire?"

◆§ *A Prayer by Any Other Name*

לֹא יֵחָשֵׁב לוֹ פִּגּוּל יִהְיֶה
It shall not be accounted to him; it shall be an abomination (7:18)

Prayer substitutes for the sacrificial offering. Let the worshiper therefore take heed not to admit any alien thought — just as an improper thought renders a sacrifice invalid *(Shulchan Aruch)*.

On their way through Ruzhin, a group of *misnagdim* from Sanik decided to call on Reb Yisrael of Ruzhin in order to enjoy a little argument with him on the ideology of Chassidism.

"We, at least, walk in the path of God," they began. "We set aside times for the study of Torah; we pray with a *minyan* at daybreak; and when prayers are over, while we are still wearing our *tallis* and *tefillin*, we settle down to learn *Mishnayos*. But the chassidim — not only do they pray after the statutory time, but when they have done with their prayers they sit down to drink vodka together. And then they call themselves chassidim, which means 'pious ones,' and us they call *misnagdim*, their antagonists. Why, it should be the other way round!"

The rebbe's *shammes*, who happened to be present,

could not contain himself, and came out with his own jocular reply: "You *misnagdim* serve the Creator frigidly — you are as lacking in warmth as a corpse, God forbid. And everyone knows that after a death the traditional custom is to study *Mishnayos*. But when chassidim serve their Maker, be it ever so little, at least they do it with enthusiasm, and their heart is on fire, just as a living man is full of warmth — and doesn't a living man need a drop of vodka now and again?" י

The tzaddik commented: "This answer, of course, was not to be taken seriously. But the fact is that from the day on which the Temple was destroyed, it is prayer that substitutes for the sacrifices which can no longer be offered, as it is written: וּנְשַׁלְּמָה פָרִים שְׂפָתֵינוּ — 'And our lips will compensate for oxen.' Moreover, the Sages teach us that the daily prayer services were timed so as to correspond to the daily sacrifices. Just as a sacrifice is rendered invalid by an improper thought, and becomes an abomination which is not acceptable On High, so too is a man's prayer invalidated by the admixture of an alien thought. The Evil Inclination therefore devises various stratagems by which to introduce all manner of alien thoughts into the mind of the worshiper in order to distract him. And that is why the chassidim invented a counter-strategy of their own. After their prayers they sit down to drink vodka together, and wish each other *LeChaim*; and as each man gives expression to what he most needs, his friend says: 'May God grant your request!' Now according to the law of the Torah, prayer may be uttered in any language, so these informal words are of course reckoned in heaven as prayer. Here, however, the Evil Inclination has no say, for when he sees people eating and drinking and speaking in their everyday language, he thinks that this is a mere bodily activity and does not even realize that this is prayer!"

☙ *Enemy Aliens*

A man called on Reb Yaakov Yitzchak, the Chozeh (or Seer) of Lublin, and complained that alien thoughts bothered him during prayer.

"*Alien* thoughts?!" queried the Chozeh. "Concerning

 tzaddikim, whose thoughts are always holy and revolve around the Torah, one may describe the thoughts that seek admission to their minds as alien. But with you — why, these unholy thoughts are not *alien:* they are all your very own!"

סדר שמיני
sidra sh'mini

☙ *Smiling Through One's Tears*

וַיִּדֹּם אַהֲרֹן
And Aharon held his peace (10:3)

The son-in-law of Reb Shlomo of Radomsk, a chassid by the name of Reb Lipman of Radomsk, once came to visit Reb Menachem Mendel of Kotsk, who asked him to repeat some teaching of his famous father-in-law. Reb Lipman obliged, and said: "The tzaddik once pointed out that when Aharon was rebuked, the Torah records in his praise, וַיִּדֹּם אַהֲרֹן — 'And Aharon held his peace' — and this shows what a high spiritual level he had attained. But King David surpassed him and reached a yet higher rung: לְמַעַן יְזַמֶּרְךָ כָבוֹד וְלֹא יִדֹּם — 'In order that my soul may sing praise to You, *and not be silent'* — for even in times of distress he would still sing God's praises."

Reb Menachem Mendel was delighted with this *vort* and thanked his guest warmly for conveying it to him.

☙ *All Ears and Eyes*

וַיִּשְׁמַע מֹשֶׁה וַיִּיטַב בְּעֵינָיו
And Moshe heard, and it was good in his eyes (10:20)

Reb Yaakov Yitzchak, the Yid HaKadosh ("the holy Jew") of Pshischah, was a tutor in his younger days in a certain household. After some years the son of his former employer was stricken by some eye ailment, and no doctor was able to help him. When the boy's father heard, therefore, that the former *melamed* had in the meantime acquired a name as a tzaddik, he took his son, who was called Moshe, to visit him.

On their arrival the tzaddik discussed various Torah subjects with the boy, and then said: "Moshe, do you hear?"

"Yes," answered the sightless boy.

שמיני

Said the Yid HaKadosh: "It is written, וַיִּשְׁמַע מֹשֶׁה וַיִּיטַב בְּעֵינָיו — 'And Moshe heard, *and it was good in his eyes*.' "

And the boy immediately regained his vision.

Of Hosts and Guests

מִמַּעֲלֵי הַגֵּרָה וּמִמַּפְרִסֵי הַפַּרְסָה
Of those that chew the cud, or that divide the hoof (11:4)

Two chassidim whose rebbe had passed away traveled to visit Reb Meir of Premishlan in order to decide whether or not to choose him as rebbe for themselves and for their fellow chassidim. They arrived at Premishlan just in time for candle-lighting, on the eve of a *Shabbos* on which the weekly Portion of *Shemini* was read. They did not even have enough time to order meals for *Shabbos* at a hotel, but went straight to the *beis midrash* of the rebbe. After prayers each of them was invited to the home of one of the local householders. One of the hosts was accustomed to eating very little, so his guest, though ravenously hungry, could hardly bring himself to eat a square meal in his presence. The other host ate, but did not slice the *challah* that was on the table, and since his guest did not take the liberty of slicing it for himself, he too remained hungry. After the meal they both came to the *tish* of the tzaddik at which he presided until after midnight. When it was over, they went to one of the local hotels and asked the proprietor if he had anything for them to eat. He explained that he only had a place for them to sleep, but since they were hungry he would give them some leftovers that required no preparation.

After *Shacharis* prayers in the morning they went home with the same hosts, and exactly the same story repeated itself. In the afternoon they came to the *beis midrash* of the rebbe for *Minchah*, but Reb Meir was not yet there. Assuming that he was doubtless studying Torah in his room, they went to his house, but his *gabbai* told them that he was out in the courtyard. They went out and, sure enough, Reb Meir was there — telling his attendant to feed the geese and chickens. When that was done, he said: "Let us go and *davven* the *Minchah* prayer."

The guests were stupefied: throughout the entire

Shabbos they had not heard a solitary word of Torah from his mouth. To make things worse, they had now seen what kind of spiritual preparations he made for his afternoon prayer. Besides, they were hungry, so they decided not to go to the *Seudah Shlishis* of the rebbe, and to try their luck once again at the homes of their respective hosts. Their hosts were not at home, though: they had gone to the *tish* of the rebbe, so their would-be guests had no option but to go there too.

As soon as they arrived the rebbe said: "Where are the two young men who are seeking a rebbe who is possessed of the holy spirit?"

There was no answer.

Again the rebbe asked: "Where are they? Why are they hiding from me?"

Not a word in reply.

The third time he said: "If they don't come before me at once, they will regret it."

The two guests approached him shamefacedly, and he greeted them and asked: "Where did you eat your *Shabbos* meals?"

When they named their hosts, Reb Meir called them to him and said: "The Torah gives us a mitzvah of hospitality — but one has to know how to conduct oneself when one has guests. When one invites a guest, the host should slice bread generously on the table so that his guest should not be obliged to do so or be too embarrassed to help himself. And even if a host does this, if he himself does not eat, his guest will not feel comfortable eating in his presence. There is a hint of this in today's Portion of the Torah: אֶת הַחֲזִיר כִּי מַפְרִיס פַּרְסָה הוּא — the pig, for he does slice the bread [actually, "divide the hoof," but here punningly mistranslated: פַּרְסָה means "hoof"; פְּרוּסָה means "slice"]; וְהוּא גֵּרָה לֹא יִגָּר — but he does not chew the cud, that is, he himself does not eat; טָמֵא הוּא לָכֶם — he is unclean unto you; אֶת הַגָּמָל כִּי מַעֲלֵה גֵרָה הוּא וּפַרְסָה אֵינֶנּוּ מַפְרִיס טָמֵא הוּא לָכֶם — the camel does chew the cud, but does not 'slice the bread'; he is likewise unclean unto you. Only one that does *both* is a kosher creature!

"And now," added the tzaddik, "these two young men are no doubt very hungry. We should really give them something to eat."

With that, he gave each of them a slice of *challah* with a piece of fish on it.

He went on to deliver a discourse, in the course of which he intimated to the two guests the mystical explanation for his having fed the poultry during the afternoon. None of those present understood his references to the cloven hoof and the chewed cud, nor his abstruse discourse — except for the two hosts and their guests.

And on *Motzaei Shabbos,* when the holy day had drawn to a close, the two visitors to Premishlan recounted the whole story, and concluded: "Here we have found a rebbe on whom rests *ruach hakodesh,* the spirit of God."

❧ *Sensitivity*

וּבֵין הַחַיָּה הַנֶּאֱכֶלֶת וּבֵין הַחַיָּה אֲשֶׁר לֹא תֵאָכֵל

Between the creature that may be eaten and the creature that may not be eaten (11:47)

Reb Yitzchak Meir of Ger, the author of *Chiddushei HaRim,* was possessed of a remarkable ability to identify whether any item of food that was placed before him was tainted by the merest suspicion of a prohibition, even if strictly speaking it was legally kosher. It once happened that a *she'elah* arose in the kitchen of his household, so the maid duly took along the chicken involved to the local *rav* to have the query clarified, and he ruled that it was kosher. The *rebbitzin,* who knew that her husband was accustomed not to eat of any food over which such a query had arisen, was not at home, and since the maid was new and unaware of this, she saw no reason to report to anyone what had happened. When the *shammes* served the rebbe the cooked chicken, he looked at it and asked to have it removed from the table without so much as tasting it. The *shammes* went to the *rebbitzin* to find out what had happened; then the two of them went to see the maid, who told them of her visit to the local *rav.*

This kind of story repeated itself quite frequently, and the tzaddik once said: "You no doubt think that this is some special prerogative of a rebbe. This is not so, for every Jew who so desires can develop the sensitivity to discern whether his heart allows him to eat a particular dish or not. And this is hinted at in the verse: וּבֵין הַחַיָּה

הַנֶּאֱכֶלֶת — 'between the creature that allows itself to be eaten' (literally, 'that may be eaten'), וּבֵין הַחַיָּה אֲשֶׁר לֹא תֵאָכֵל — 'and the creature that does not allow itself to be eaten' (literally, 'that may not be eaten')."

On another occasion he told his chassidim: "You should realize that this is not a feat that demands any great spiritual achievements. In fact any one of you can easily attain this sensitivity, by following the tried and tested advice which Reb Simchah Bunem of Pshischah taught us: before a person takes any food or drink into his mouth, let him undertake, decisively and wholeheartedly, that if (God forbid) it is forbidden in any way, he would prefer to choke on it rather than swallow it. And then, if need be, they tell him from heaven, in a way that he feels clearly, that he should not swallow a particular mouthful."

◆§ *Secrets from an Unknown Land*

When Reb Meir of Premishlan was a child of about ten, he was taught by a chassid by the name of Reb Dov of Podheits. Every Thursday, which was market day in Podheits, the boy would collect donations and distribute them to the poor in time for them to buy their provisions for *Shabbos.* In the course of his rounds he once came to a butcher by the name of Shimon and asked him for his weekly donation of one *kreutzer* for the poor.

"I'll give you two," said the butcher, "on condition that you tell me whether this ox that I want to buy is going to turn out to be kosher or not."

"Very well," replied the boy. "If you give me half a *fertziger* — that is, ten *kreutzer* — then I'll tell you."

The butcher thought it over for a moment, and gave it to him, whereupon the boy told him: "This ox cannot be eaten; it is *trefah.*"

Pointing to another ox, the butcher asked: "And what about this one?"

"If you give me another half-*fertziger,*" said the boy, "then I'll tell you."

And when he received the coin, he said: "About this ox there aren't even any queries about possible blemishes in its lungs: it is *glatt* kosher."

The butcher had his doubts as to whether there was any substance to all this, but he paid up his two half-*fertziger* all the same, because the boy was born of holy parents, and he was a likable child — and besides, everyone knew that the alms he collected was for the paupers. And so it was that Shimon bought the second ox, while the first was bought by some other butcher. Sure enough, Shimon's ox was in fact *glatt* kosher, and the other was found after slaughtering to be *trefah.*

The following Thursday, when the boy came to the ox market to collect his donations from the dealers, Shimon the butcher called him aside and said: "Meir'che, I will give you a whole *fertziger* if you tell me whether each one of the oxen up for sale is kosher or not."

"If you give me half a *fertziger* for each ox," said the boy, "I'll tell you."

The butcher paid in full without hesitation, and the boy told him: "This one is kosher, this one is *trefah*" — and so on.

Young Meir was of course delighted with the way things had worked out, for he now had a considerable sum to distribute to the poor without having to lose valuable study time in trudging for hours from one donor to the next.

The butcher, for his part, seeing that the child never missed his target, approached him on the third week with a new proposition: "I would like to make a contract with you, and I will pay you weekly for each ox according to your request — provided that our little transaction remains a secret."

"I am not interested in contracts and secrets," said the boy, "but if you give me half a *fertziger* for each ox, I'll give you the answer."

This went on for a few months, and no one knew of it. Week by week the butcher paid in advance for his information, as a result of which he prospered exceedingly, because he bought nothing but kosher animals, while the other butchers grew poorer. His competitors banded together and brought their bitter complaint to the local *rav:* it was clear that the *shochatim* were receiving bribes from Shimon in exchange for which they pronounced his animals kosher, while in the course of slaughtering they either caused or pronounced *their* animals to be *trefah.*

"But you can see for yourselves in the slaughterhouse," said the *rav,* "that all of Shimon's cattle are in fact *glatt* kosher, without any room for the slightest doubt — and what is to be done if he has such good fortune?"

To this the butchers had no answer. Nevertheless, they started watching Shimon's movements very closely: what could he be doing to ensure that all his animals without exception were in fact kosher? The following Thursday they watched him walking the length of the market place in the company of little Meir, who was pointing at each of the oxen in turn. When Shimon finally left him, they approached the child and said: "Meir'che, pray for us, too, just like you pray for Shimon; or please do for us whatever you do for Shimon."

"I don't do anything," he assured them. "If you give me half a *fertziger* I'll tell you what I tell him."

"Well, what is it that you tell him to do?" they asked. "Tell us, too, and then we'll do whatever he does."

"He asks me which ox is kosher and which is not," said Meir, "and I tell him."

So they gave him a half-*fertziger,* and pointed at an ox that stood near them.

"That one is *trefah,*" said the boy.

When they pointed at another ox, he said: "But you have given me only one half-*fertziger,* and Shimon gives me that much for every single ox."

"So *that's* his secret!" said the butchers to each other. And from that Thursday on, they gave Meir in partnership the amount he stipulated for charity, and walked with him up and down the market place, while he told them which oxen were kosher and which were not.

When word of this reached the boy's *melamed,* Reb Dov, he scolded him and told him that in future he should not tell anyone things revealed to him through *ruach hakodesh.*

Now Reb Dov was a chassid of Meir's father, Reb Aharon Leib of Premishlan, and when he went to visit him he told him the whole story, adding that he had scolded the rebbe's son.

"Well done," said the father. "A boy must learn not to divulge privileged information."

◆§ *The Bear and the Ballroom Dance*

וְדָוִד מְכַרְכֵּר בְּכָל עֹז לִפְנֵי ה׳
And David leaped about before God with all his might (Haftarah)

After the Friday evening prayers of welcome to the Sabbath Queen, Reb Aryeh Leib of Shpola, who is known as the Shpoler Zeide, would often dance in ecstasy, wheeling and turning at a remarkable speed, while his chassidim sang their rhythmic accompaniment.

One *Shabbos* he had as a guest the son of the Maggid of Mezritch, Reb Avraham, who because of his piety was nicknamed "the *Malach*" ("the angel"). Reb Avraham observed every dance-step closely, then approached his host and said: "Sir, you certainly dance well! Until now I did not know how one dances before the Bride, the *Shabbos* Queen — but in every single dance-step tonight I saw a heavenly *yichud*, a sublime feat of divine worship."

"This ability," returned the Shpoler Zeide, "I have by virtue of a blessing I received from the Baal Shem Tov."

Reb Avraham was not satisfied: "But even as far as plain dancing and rhythm are concerned you dance like an expert. Where did you learn this?"

"It was the Prophet Eliyahu who taught me how to dance like this," answered the Shpoler Zeide, "and there is a story behind it all. Listen!

"In the days when I used to wander about in remote regions, it came to my ears that in a certain village a Jew had been arrested by the local squire because he had been unable to pay him what he owed on his lease. The squire, who held the title *graf*, was not a particularly villainous type, but the manager of his estates, who had the last word on everything that went on in the village, was a great anti-Semite, and he incited the *graf* to imprison the Jew who had defaulted. Now in those days each squire ruled his village like an absolute monarch, even sentencing people to death, and in cases like this one they would cast a Jew into a deep dungeon, and once a week lower him his provisions of bread and water. There he would languish until the squire's birthday, when he would make a raucous feast for all his cronies, and when they were tipsy with wine they would drag out the Jew to entertain them. Their tradition was to prepare a bearskin which they would dry on a wooden dummy, until when it was ready it almost looked like a live beast. They would dress the hapless Jew in this bearskin and lead him into the ballroom where the landlords tippled and made merry, and there he was told to dance to whatever tune the musicians played. One of the servants was appointed to lead in the fearsome creature by the kind of iron chain that is used for real bears, and to take charge of him during the dancing. The servant would dance to the music, and the Jew in the bearskin was obliged to keep up to the pace of his dancing partner. But before they started, someone would announce in a loud voice: 'Listen, bear! If you dance nicely before us and keep up with your partner, you will be freed today; if you dance better than he does, you will be allowed to attack him and beat him up, just like a bear attacks a cow; but if you don't dance well, then your partner will lead you off to dance with the dogs!'

"The squires in those days used to keep large numbers of big, ferocious dogs, and when they were thrown a man who had been sentenced to death, they would tear him to pieces.

"After all that time in the dungeon, with his wretched rations of bread and water, the Jew of course could barely walk straight, let alone dance in a bearskin.

"At this point I was given the order by the Prophet Eliyahu to go to that village, where I was to hire myself out as a *melamed* in the household of one of the local Jews, so that I would able to find out all the details of how to go about saving that poor fellow from the teeth of the squire's hounds. For I was to replace him in the bearskin, and dance better than my partner, and eventually attack him and beat him up.

"So I said to Eliyahu: 'But I don't know the first thing about dancing. I don't even know the names of the dances!'

"And he answered: 'I shall teach you how to dance.'

"So it was that every time we met he taught me some other kind of dance, until I became quite an expert. In the meantime, while I worked as a tutor in the village, I investigated all the ins and outs of the garden in which the dungeon was located. I found out, among other things, that it was possible for a man to lower himself down into the dungeon by a rope through an aperture at the top, though it would be very difficult to climb out of there by rope.

"One night before the night of the birthday party, I crept stealthily through a hole under the fence into the garden, and found the dungeon. With the aid of a rope, several staves, an iron peg, and a sledge-hammer that I brought with me, I managed to lower myself down into the pit.

"The poor Jew was of course alarmed. 'Have no fear!' I reassured him. 'I have come to save you.'

"I revived his spirits with a drop of vodka that I had brought, and with words of encouragement: God would surely come to his help. We then exchanged clothes. I put on his moldy and foul-smelling rags, and he dressed in my clothes. Then I told him that when the iron trap-door covering the dungeon would be opened, I would go out instead of him. Only after I was at some distance from the garden was he to climb out; the door would probably be left open, because he was the only prisoner there.

"Around midnight we heard rude laughter resounding over our heads. The iron trap-door creaked open, and a half-drunk voice bellowed out the name of my companion, and ordered him to get out. I clambered out on all fours in order that I should not be recognized, and groaned and tottered as if I was unable to walk. They immediately threw the bearskin over me and tied it firmly around my body, put an iron chain around my neck, and led me along to the tune of their loud guffaws. Before they had opened the door the prisoner had told me that he recognized the laughter up there as belonging to the manager of the squire's estates, the same man who had persuaded his master to imprison him. I asked him to describe his appearance precisely, which he did.

"When they led me into the ballroom, all that merry crew laughed and clapped their hands with glee. I could tell at once by the prisoner's description that the man designated to be my dancing partner was none other than the manager of the squire's estates, who was now looking forward to seeing his project through to the finish by personally throwing his victim to the dogs.

"A voice was now heard, asking all the guests to take their places and to listen to the sentence which was to be read out. A man dressed from head to foot in red, like a hangman, duly stepped forward in front of me and read from a sheet of paper. He announced what was promised me if I equalled my partner or bettered him, and warned me that if I did not perform well enough he would lead me straight out to the kennels, where the dogs would soon teach me how to dance. This was greeted by an outburst of laughter. When it subsided, the signal was given to the musicians to start playing a Cossack dance.

"My partner immediately pranced into action, then they motioned me to join in as his opposite number. Seeing that I was outshining him, the audience laughed and clapped. The band was told to stop playing. I could clearly tell that my partner was terror-stricken: he had never thought such a defeat possible. The master of ceremonies then announced that the band was to play a mazurka, and as it started, my partner took me by the hand. As I twirled my way through the steps of the dance, I sensed that my drunken partner was about to fall — which he did. I at once jumped upon him, and gave him a choking bearhug and a sound beating. There was an immediate uproar from all sides. Some of the guests egged me on, for I was doing what the rules of the game entitled me to do, but two squires ran up and begged that I spare the man's life. Since I was now free, I had better go home and gladden the hearts of my wife and family. I took their advice, and released my hold. They hurried to do whatever they could for the estate manager who lay in a faint on the floor; and I, bearskin and all, ran as fast as I could to the house of the prisoner. There, as you may well imagine, I found a household bursting with joy."

Having come to the end of his story, the Shpoler Zeide turned to his guest and said: "Well, Reb Avraham, do you understand now how it is that I can dance so well?"

"After such a story," replied the *Malach*, "it is clear that your dances are loftier than my prayers."

An Opportunity for Joy

וְשִׂחַקְתִּי לִפְנֵי ה׳ וּנְקַלֹּתִי עוֹד מִזֹּאת *I will play before God, and be even less esteemed than this (Haftarah)*

Looking through the window, Reb Zusya of Hanipoli once saw a wedding procession passing his house. He went straight out, and danced in the street before the bride and groom with the greatest of joy. When he came in again, his family remarked that it was neither seemly nor dignified for him to dance out there in the street for some wedding or other.

"Let me tell you a story," said Reb Zusya. "In my youth I was a pupil of Reb Yechiel Michel, the Maggid of Zlotchov, and it once happened that he scolded me severely. He later came around to clear up any hard feelings, and said: 'Reb Zusya, forgive me for my harsh words.'

" 'Rebbe,' I answered, 'I forgive you.'

"Before I went to sleep he came again, and said: 'Reb Zusya, forgive me!'

"I reassured him again: 'Rebbe, I forgive you.'

"And when I lay down to sleep, but was still awake, my rebbe's father, Reb Yitzchak of Drohovitch, appeared to me from the World Above, and said: 'One only son I left after me in the World Below, one precious son — and do you want to destroy him because he insulted you?'

" 'Rebbe!' I protested. 'But I have already forgiven him with all my heart and soul! What else should I do?'

" 'This is not yet a perfect forgiveness,' he said. 'If you come along with me, I will show you how to forgive.'

"I got out of bed and followed him, until we came to the local *mikveh*. There he told me to immerse myself in it three times, and to say each time that I forgave his son. Coming out of the *mikveh*, I saw that Reb Yitzchak's face radiated a light so bright that I could not look at him. When I asked him what it came from, he said that all his life he had been careful to observe the three things to which the Talmudic sage Rabbi Nechunyah ben HaKanah attributed his longevity: 'I never gained honor at the expense of the degradation of my fellow; I never went to sleep without forgiving everyone for the day's vexations; and I have been generous with my money.'

Reb Yitzchak added that what he had attained through these three things could also be achieved through joy.

"Therefore," concluded Reb Zusya, "when I saw the wedding procession passing by our house, I hurried out in order to participate in the joy of a mitzvah."

◆§ *Verses and Curses*

In 1777 a large group of chassidim settled in *Eretz Yisrael,* and Reb Shneur Zalman of Liadi established the Rabbi Meir Baal HaNess Fund for their support. One of his chassidim, Reb Yitzchak Aizik of Homil, thereupon began to hire himself out as a jester at weddings, where he would entertain the guests, according to the old custom, by improvising jocular verses. All the earnings he would give to the Fund.

It so happened that there was once a wedding involving a well-known chassidic family from Homil, and a respected family from Slutsk, which was an uncompromising center of hard-boiled *misnagdim.* The *mechutan* from Slutsk watched Reb Yitzchak Aizik versifying happily away, and commented: "Woe is to accursed Belorussia! Where *we* come from, a wedding like this is an occasion for scholars to vie with each other in the complexity of their learned discourses; here, people fill their heads with doggerel ... "

His chassidic counterpart from Homil sought to correct him. "*Mechutan,*" he said, "would you perhaps like to discuss Torah scholarship with this jester of ours?"

The *misnaged* did so, and was stupefied to discover that the jester — better remembered as the author of *Chanah Ariel* — was in fact a scholar of repute. He turned to his chassidic *mechutan,* and exclaimed: "Villains, *that's* what you are! Here you have such a sage in your midst, and you allow him to earn his living as a jester!"

And he was appeased only when he was told that this was not the jester's occupation: he was simply doing a good deed to benefit charity.

סדר תזריע
Sidra Tazria

◆§ *A Hidden Tzaddik*

וּבַיּוֹם הַשְּׁמִינִי יִמּוֹל
And on the eighth day shall he be circumcised (12:3)

When the Baal Shem Tov was a young man, soon after his marriage, and his saintliness was still known to no man, he used to eke out a meager livelihood by the toil of his hands. With his horse and cart he would bring loads of mortar and sand which would be sold in town. His pious wife, having been brought up in a wealthy household, was unused to the rigors of harsh labor; nevertheless, feeling sorry for her husband, she too went out with him with a spade and helped him load his cart. Sometimes they traveled from town to town for weeks on end, but no one took much notice of them, taking them for just another couple of itinerant beggars.

In time the Baal Shem Tov's horse grew so weak that it was unable to draw a load. The tzaddik was distressed: he could not afford a new horse, yet without one he had no way of earning his daily bread. He mentioned his plight to some other poor folk whom he met on the road. They advised him to set out for a certain village near Uman, to the home of a Jewish landowner called Reb Baruch who was known for his hospitality. Whenever a pauper drove his wagon into his estate in order to buy bones or rags or whatever, Reb Baruch always offered to exchange his guest's old hack for one of his spare horses that was no longer capable of drawing a plow, but could still be useful for lighter work. And so it was that the Baal Shem Tov and his wife undertook the long and arduous journey to that village.

Reb Baruch had fled to Russia from the pogroms in his native Bohemia. He was certainly no Torah scholar: just an ordinary householder, but he was upright and God-fearing, as was his wife Rachel. Of all their many charitable and neighborly acts, they exerted themselves in particular for the mitzvah of hospitality. For this purpose they set aside a separate house which was made up of many small rooms, each furnished with two beds and a table. Here any needy wayfarer was welcome to stay for a week. He was given two meals daily, and on *Shabbos* joined all the other paupers at Reb Baruch's table. When a poor man came together with his wife and children, the couple was assigned a separate room; if a man and a woman came without children Reb Baruch would not give them a room together, for fear that they were not man and wife. And before any of their penniless guests left, their hosts gave them gifts of money — Reb Baruch to the men, Rachel to the women.

It was in this house that the Baal Shem Tov and his wife rested when they finally arrived at their destination. After they had been offered a meal the Baal Shem Tov told his host about his horse, and Reb Baruch immediately instructed his servants to replace it. The gift was of course much appreciated, but since the tzaddik and his wife were exhausted after their journey, most of which they had been obliged to make on foot, they stayed to rest for a few days until after *Shabbos*. Reb Baruch nevertheless did not give his guests a joint room, and explained that this was a principle of his, unless he knew for sure that his guests were a married couple. The Baal Shem Tov was pleased with his answer. And throughout the entire *Shabbos* there was nothing about his conduct that could suggest that here was a man who was somewhat different from the general run of paupers.

On *Motzaei Shabbos*, after the holy day had come to a close and Reb Baruch was preparing to retire for the night, he was surprised to see a bright light shining through his window. He got up to see where it came from, and observed that its source was one of the rooms occupied by the paupers. Bestirred by wonderment and the fear of fire, he dressed in haste and went out to investigate. He tiptoed stealthily to the door of the room, peeked through the keyhole, and saw the new arrival sitting on the floor, and reciting in holy dread the midnight lament on the Destruction of the Temple and the exile of the Divine Presence — *Tikkun Chatzos*. He strained and heard the piteous words: "Why do You forget us for all eternity, and forsake us for so long?" The arms of the supplicant were stretched out toward heaven, his countenance was radiant, and tears were in his eyes. Nor was he alone, for by his side there stood a white-garbed figure, tall and gaunt, a long beard flowing from his luminous countenance. Terror struck at the heart of the man at the keyhole; he tottered, and collapsed on the floor in a faint.

Hearing the thud at his door, the Baal Shem Tov quickly rose to open it, and saw his host prostrate before him. He massaged him until he came to, then brought him into his little room to rest. Realizing by now that his guest was no ordinary man, Reb Baruch fell at his feet, and with tears in his eyes begged forgiveness for not having given him one of the rooms for married couples. The Baal Shem Tov raised him up to his feet, and solemnly adjured him never to breathe a word of what he had seen, all the days of his life. He then blessed him that he should be granted a son who would grow up to be a tzaddik, and added that his wife should take care to nurse this child herself, instead of hiring a wetnurse, as she had done for each of her infant daughters in turn. Reb Baruch listened to the blessing and responded fervently: "Amen! May this be His will!"

Ever so humbly, he then added: "Pardon me, Sir, for my daring, but I have one question. Who was that aged one, robed in white?"

"Since it was granted you to see him," said the Baal Shem Tov, "I shall reveal this secret to you. This was the soul of the saintly Maharal, Rabbi Yehudah Leib ben Bezalel of Prague, from whom you are descended. The time has come for his soul to live another life in This World, in order to set it right by accomplishing awesome *tikkunim*, and it is your privilege to have this lofty soul find its new abode in the body of the son whom you will beget. To this infant you are therefore to give the name 'Leib'. I am certain that I will see him, and I will then bless him."

Reb Baruch wept for joy, for he had never had a son.

"My saintly master," he said. "I beg you not to be angry with me, but I have one more question. I would dearly love to know your name and where you hail from, and I ask you earnestly to allow me throughout my life to provide for all your needs, so that you will no longer know the pain of privation."

"Pray do not ask me these questions," responded the Baal Shem Tov, "for the time for me to be known in the world has not yet come. Your son likewise will not be known early in life. He will first live a life of poverty and want, and his righteousness will later shine forth like the radiance of the sun. Further than this ask me no questions and reveal to no man what you have seen and spoken of with me. Show me no special honor in anyone else's presence, but treat me exactly as you do all the other poor folk. And tomorrow I will be on my way."

Reb Baruch took his leave and went home, and the next day the Baal Shem Tov drove off in his wagon which was now harnessed to the new horse that he had been given. Not a soul knew a word of what had transpired that night, but Reb Baruch recorded every detail of it in his diary.

In due course the blessing of the tzaddik was fulfilled: Reb Baruch's wife gave birth to their first son, and their joy was boundless. The father sent word to all the neighboring townships inviting all their poor to attend the circumcision, and because, as the Talmud says, "Your friend too has a friend," the message spread in no time, and throngs of eager paupers converged on his village, often accompanied by their wives and little ones. Nor were any disappointed, for each needy visitor was provided with a warm bed and ample meals.

The great day arrived, and the faces of hundreds of friends were beaming with joy — all faces, in fact, except for the face of Reb Baruch himself, which divulged a hint of anxiety. He walked back and forth among the crowds of poor people, earnestly looking for that hidden tzaddik whose blessing was the fount of everyone's joy that day. And there he was indeed, with his staff and knapsack, in the thick of that same crowd. Reb Baruch ran to greet him, but did not manage to give expression to his joy before the Baal Shem Tov motioned him to remain silent, adding: "Please take care not to speak to me, nor to honor me in any way. Simply treat me like all the other poor people here."

The circumcision was carried out after morning prayers, and the infant was named Aryeh Leib. According to the custom then current, the *kvater*, followed by the father, carried the baby past the standing guests, each of whom would lay his hand on the infant's head and bless him and his father. Reb Baruch made sure that the godfather carried the baby all the way through the crowds of poor folk, too, because he was eager to have the baby receive their blessings — in particular, the blessings of one unknown stranger who stood obscurely in their midst ... Slowly, silently, they neared his presence. The Baal Shem Tov placed his two hands on the baby's head, and said in a loud and happy voice: "Look, I'm only an ignoramus, and don't know how to give blessings in the Holy Tongue. But I do remember what my father taught me about the verse in the *Chumash:* וְאַבְרָהָם זָקֵן — 'And Avraham was old.' He said that the Hebrew word אָב *(av)*, which is the beginning of the name Avraham, means 'father,' and the second word — זָקֵן — means *'zeide'* (Yiddish for 'grandfather'). That is to say, the Patriarch Avraham became the grandfather of us all. And now I would like to give this baby my blessing that he grow up to be a grandfather for all Israel, just as Avraham Avinu was."

Many were amused by this commentary and blessing, and the child was called thereafter Zeide — first jokingly, then affectionately. "How's your Zeide?" people would ask his parents, and they themselves would call him "our little Zeidele."

Indeed, this nickname stayed with him throughout his entire life. Reb Aryeh Leib became known as a tzaddik who helped his brothers through acts of kindness in This World and through intercession in the World Above. But he was loved in his time, and is remembered to this day, as the Shpoler Zeide — may his memory be a blessing!

◆§ *No Questions Asked*

At the festive meal following a circumcision, Reb Yitzchak Meir of Ger once asked a certain chassid to tell a story he knew concerning Reb Levi Yitzchak of Berditchev.

"One of the disciples of Reb Levi Yitzchak," began

 the chassid, "was a dealer in oxen. It so happened that the price once dropped at a time when he had many head of cattle to sell, so, anticipating heavy losses, he traveled to Berditchev to ask Reb Levi Yitzchak for advice and a blessing.

" 'Is there one particular mitzvah that you especially engage in from time to time?' asked the rebbe.

" 'Yes,' answered the dealer, 'I am a *mohel.*'

" 'And what do you do,' resumed the rebbe, 'if (God forbid) the bleeding does not stop after you have circumcised an infant?'

"The *mohel* duly enumerated the various kinds of medication he used.

" 'I will give you a certain herb,' said the tzaddik. 'If (God forbid) you should again be confronted by such a situation, then apply this herb to the source of the bleeding and, with the Almighty's help, it will heal at once.'

" 'And what shall I do about the cattle business?' asked the merchant.

" 'But I've already told you,' answered the tzaddik, 'that whenever a newly circumcised child bleeds profusely you should apply this herb, and with God's help the incision will heal immediately.'

"The merchant took his leave and traveled home."

At this point in the chassid's story Reb Yitzchak Meir stopped him for a moment, and said: "From this it is clear that this merchant was a chassid, for he did not persist with his query about the oxen, believing instead that his rebbe's words no doubt included an answer to the question that had brought him there, even though he did not understand how this could be the case."

The chassid continued with his story. "Now on his way home this dealer stopped at an inn, and found out incidentally that the innkeeper's infant son was not circumcised. He therefore approached him and asked: 'Why have you not yet had your son circumcised?'

"The father answered that two earlier sons of his had died as a result of their circumcision (Heaven forfend!), because the bleeding could not be stopped. Recalling the words of the tzaddik of Berditchev, the merchant asked his host: 'What would you give if a solution were to be found to this problem?'

" 'If it were possible to circumcise my son without danger,' he answered, 'I would be prepared to pay four hundred silver rubles.'

" 'I will circumcise him on my responsibility,' said the merchant, 'and will deposit with you four hundred silver rubles of my own, to be forfeited in case (God forbid) of misfortune.'

"The innkeeper agreed, provided the *mohel* remained on the premises for four weeks, until the child was sure to be out of danger. The circumcision in fact caused the infant to bleed heavily, but the *mohel* applied the herb which he had been given, and the bleeding stopped immediately. After some days news reached the village that the price of oxen had risen, and the *mohel* wanted to hurry home to sell his livestock, but his host held him to his promise to stay in the village for four weeks. Several days later he heard that the price was soaring even higher, but the innkeeper ignored his pleas. Only after the full four weeks had reluctantly moved on did he allow the merchant to get back to his business, not forgetting to pay him first his fee of four hundred silver rubles and to return him his deposit of another four hundred. Arriving home, the merchant sold his oxen for a price that exceeded his wildest hopes and made a handsome profit.

"It was now time to visit his rebbe. He rode off to Berditchev, and said to Reb Levi Yitzchak: 'Rebbe, the fee of four hundred rubles belongs to you without a question, and a certain proportion of the profit I made on the sale of my livestock rightly belongs to you likewise.' "

Reb Yitzchak Meir of Ger turned to the storyteller: "Why tell that part too?"

☙ *Who Wants to be Cured?*

נֶגַע צָרַעַת כִּי תִהְיֶה בְּאָדָם וְהוּבָא אֶל הַכֹּהֵן

If the plague of tzaraas is in a man, he shall be brought to the kohen (13:9)

Reb Asher of Stolin disapproved of those chassidim who, when visiting their rebbe, would give prominence to their more commendable traits, and conceal their less attractive side.

"When I used to visit my rebbe," he recalled (that is, Reb Shlomo of Karlin, and he kissed his own fingers at the mention of the cherished name), "I would hide whatever good there was in me — for did the rebbe have God's task of handing out reward and punishment? — and would show him the evil that was in me. For what the Torah commands a man to show the kohen is the symptoms of the *plague* within him ..."

סדר מצורע

SIDRA METZORA

✥ Speaking Up

וּבָא...וְהִגִּיד לַכֹּהֵן...: כְּנֶגַע נִרְאָה לִי בַּבָּיִת

And he shall come...and tell the kohen...: Something like a plague seems to be in the house (14:35)

With three daughters to marry off, and not one wretched kopek in the cottage with which to begin to put together dowries and weddings, the wife of Reb Mordechai of Pintchov nagged him incessantly to describe their woeful situation to his rebbe, the Chozeh of Lublin. Time after time he would travel to Lublin, but never once did he mention his troubles to the rebbe, because on arriving there he would forget them completely. Being a practical woman his wife decided to say nothing more, but to make the journey there by a separate wagon immediately after he had left home. When Reb Mordechai arrived at Lublin, he was confronted by the fact of his wife's presence. There was no way out — and he told the rebbe what the state of affairs was at home.

"Why did you never mention this until now?" asked the Chozeh.

"Rebbe," answered the chassid, "I assumed that my situation would be known to you through *ruach hakodesh*, through the holy spirit that rests upon you."

"Not so," answered the rebbe. "In the case of plagues of the soul the Torah says: 'A man in the skin of whose flesh there shall be ... a plague of *tzaraas* shall be brought to Aharon the *kohen* ... and the *kohen* shall see the plague.' That is to say: As soon as the ailing man is brought before him, the *kohen* will discern the malady himself, without being told. In the case of plagues that affect houses, however, the Torah teaches us otherwise: 'And he who owns the house shall come and tell the *kohen*, saying: Something like a plague seems to be in the house.' From this we see that with plagues affecting houses — the needs of a household — one is obliged to come to the *kohen* and speak up and *tell* him of them ..."

סדר אחרי
Sidra Acharei

☙ *In Good Company*

הַשֹּׁכֵן אִתָּם בְּתוֹךְ טֻמְאֹתָם *That dwells with them in the midst of their impurity (16:16)*

Two lodging places were prepared in a certain city for the forthcoming visit of Reb Avraham Yehoshua Heschel of Apta, who is known as the Ohev Yisrael ("the lover of his fellow Jew"). On arrival he was to choose between them. The two hosts were both wealthy, their kitchens were both impeccably kosher, and their houses were both spacious enough to accommodate the prominent guest comfortably. The reputation of one of them, however, was marred by whispers about certain indiscretions of his, and he, acknowledging the truth to himself, was of a humble spirit and a complaisant temperament. The other host was not only far removed from sin, but was one of those who are known in Yiddish as *"a sheiner Yid"* (a fine, dignified Jew) — and he was not a little proud of the fact. The Ohev Yisrael chose to stay in the home of the former.

When his closest chassidim asked him later to explain his choice, the tzaddik answered: "It is perhaps true that the other host is free from sin. But if he is conceited — why, we learn in the Talmud, regarding the arrogant man, that the Almighty says: אֵין אֲנִי וְהוּא יְכוֹלִים לָגוּר בָּעוֹלָם — 'He and I cannot dwell together in the world.' And if the Almighty, as it were, cannot find any room in such a house, then surely I cannot. But this fellow, even though he has certain transgressions on his account, is not arrogant, and about such folk we read in the Torah, in connection with the Sanctuary: הַשֹּׁכֵן אִתָּם בְּתוֹךְ

 טֻמְאֹתָם – 'that dwells with them in the midst of their impurity.' And seeing that the Divine Presence, as it were, was able to find a lodging place in the home of such a man, I moved in too."

◂§ *Unwarranted Pride*

In the course of a stroll with his son in the Zaksi Gardens in Warsaw, Reb Yechezkel of Kozmir once asked him whether he felt anything special. Surprised that the answer was negative, the father said: "Whoever wants to feel the taste of sanctity has better prospects here than elsewhere, for in a place of impurity, holiness finds no nook in which to rest; and since in truth 'The whole world is full of His glory,' and it must find a place *somewhere,* anyone who wants to cleave to the sanctity of the Divine Presence can do so most readily in this very place. Here, let me tell you a story.

"In the days before Reb Simchah Bunem of Pshischah became known as a tzaddik, whenever he came back from seeing to his affairs in Danzig, he would spend the first *Shabbos* with the Chozeh, Reb Yaakov Yitzchak of Lublin. On one occasion he arrived at Lublin, but the rebbe did not give him the usual greeting of *Shalom.* Taking this for an oversight, he returned to see him some hours later, but again the same thing happened. There must be something in it. So he scrutinized in retrospect every detail of his conduct in Danzig, but could recall nothing in which he could be found wanting. If anything, he noted with satisfaction that this visit was definitely of the kind that he liked to nickname 'a good Danzig', for he had brought many of the assimilated German Jews there back to the path of the Torah.

"After Reb Simchah Bunem had puzzled over his cool reception for some time, a familiar teaching of the Talmud came to mind. The Sages of the Talmud, as you know, advise a person beset by tribulations of unexplained source to scrutinize his actions. They then go on to say: פִּשְׁפֵּשׁ וְלֹא מָצָא, יִתְלֶה בְּבִטּוּל תּוֹרָה – 'If he sought and did not find, then let him ascribe his woes to the sin of losing time from Torah study.' Taking this advice to heart, Reb Simchah Bunem recalled that in the course of his travels he had in fact lost time from Torah study. This he now decided to set right. Opening his Talmud, he sat down and studied earnestly all that day and all that night. At this point, a novel light on that familiar Talmudic teaching dawned on him. He turned the words over in his mind once more: פִּשְׁפֵּשׁ וְלֹא מָצָא, יִתְלֶה בְּבִטּוּל תּוֹרָה. Perhaps what the Sages really meant by their advice was that if a person examined his past and failed to find any blemish in himself, he should *ascribe this failure* to his inadequate study of the Torah. For surely, if a man immersed himself in this as he should, he could not overlook his faults. And what of himself? ... Now that he had once again steeped his mind in the Torah, Reb Simchah Bunem became aware of his sin: he must have been a little *too* pleased with what he had accomplished in the course of his 'good Danzig.' It was time to repent.

"And when in due course he went to see the Chozeh once again, the rebbe greeted him warmly, and said: 'Danzig, as you know, is an impure place. There the Divine Presence is in exile, and clings to any man who desires to cleave to it. If, while you were there, the Divine Presence rested upon you, this was no great feat accomplished by your efforts. You see, there was no justification for your pride."

סדר קדושים
sidra kedoshim

◆§ Chassidic Logic

לֹא תָלִין פְּעֻלַּת שָׂכִיר *You shall not withhold the laborer's wages overnight (19:13)*

Penniless as always, patient as always, Reb Zusya of Hanipoli knew no rest — and now his wife was nagging him for a new dress. In the end he had no option but to somehow put together the money needed; he bought the material, and handed it to his wife to give to the tailor. Now, surely, he would enjoy some peace and quiet. But when Friday came, he saw clouds gathering over the features of his *rebbitzin*.

"What is troubling you?" he asked. "After all, you now have a new dress, thank God, haven't you?"

The *rebbitzin* told him that when the tailor had brought her the finished garment, he had let out a deep sigh. When she asked him what lay behind it, he had told her that when the young man who was to marry his daughter had seen him sewing a dress he had assumed that it was for his bride; when he had discovered that it was not, he was so angry that the poor tailor was sorely distressed.

"So," concluded the *rebbitzin,* "I immediately took the dress and gave it to the tailor as a gift for the bride, poor thing."

"But did you pay him for his work?" asked Reb Zusya.

"No," answered his wife, "but I gave the whole dress as a gift!"

"How on earth could you ever consider cheating the man of his wages?" protested Reb Zusya. "The whole week long this pauper has been working for you, and for you alone, not for his daughter. He has been waiting anxiously, eagerly, to finish this job, so that he will be able to receive his payment and buy bread for his little ones. What is the poor man going to do now? Is it *his* fault that you decided to give the dress to his daughter?"

And the *rebbitzin* set out at once, borrowed a little money, and paid the tailor his wages.

☙ *Where There Is Smoke*

לֹא תֵלֵךְ רָכִיל
You shall not go about talebearing (19:16)

The chassidim of Reb Baruch of Mezhibuzh were ill at ease: their rebbe was marrying off one of his daughters to the son of a man whose name was often whispered by the local gossipmongers. Since none of them would dare proffer advice to the rebbe, they decided to ask his jester, Herschele Ostropolier, to drop him the hint jokingly. Being a resourceful young man, Herschele contrived to refer to the tzaddik and to his apparently mismatched counterpart by borrowing two nicknames from the prayer book: וְהוּא רַחוּם ("And He is compassionate") and עַל חֵטְא ("For the transgression"), respectively. Walking straight into the rebbe's study, he quipped: "They say that וְהוּא רַחוּם has just made a match with עַל חֵטְא ... "

In response to this jest, Reb Baruch called for his chassidim and asked them what they had heard about his *mechutan*, whereupon they repeated the not very moral episode that was being passed around behind his back in Zhitomir.

"And would one of you happen to know what comment Reb Ze'ev of Zhitomir made on this story at the time?" asked Reb Baruch.

At this point one of them indeed recalled seeing Reb Ze'ev standing at his window when this story reached his ears, and he had said: "If this is a lie, he will make a match with the family of the greatest man in this generation."

These words brought reassurance to the chassidim of Reb Baruch, and whatever doubts they may have harbored about their rebbe's judgment were dispelled.

How To Stand Corrected

הוֹכֵחַ תּוֹכִיחַ אֶת עֲמִיתֶךָ
You shall surely rebuke your neighbor (19:17)

Reb Hillel Lichtenstein of Kolomya used to travel about among the Jewish towns and villages, rebuking his listeners, and exhorting them to live their lives piously. Arriving at Zanz one day, he was greeted warmly by Reb Chaim of Zanz, who exchanged Torah thoughts and chassidic insights with his honored guest, and then turned to him with the following remark: "You seem, sir, to be rebuking the whole world. Why don't you rebuke me, too?"

"Quite so," answered Reb Hillel. "The fact is that I am surprised that in this house I do not see the area of a cubit square which is left unpainted in many Jewish houses, in commemoration of the Destruction of the Temple."

His request granted, Reb Chaim asked for a ladder, climbed up, marked off the requisite area on the wall opposite the entrance, as the law requires, and with a knife peeled off all the paint from that square. When that was done, he thanked Reb Hillel for being so candid.

◆§ Take It from a Friend

As he walked up and down the *beis midrash* of Reb Yehudah Aryeh Leib of Ger, all that could be heard from his mouth was an uncomplimentary barrage of rebukes, all of which were addressed at no less a personage than — himself, Reb Pinchas Eliyahu of Piltz. Words like these one would hardly hurl at the most unworthy individual, and when they were heard by the speaker's uncle, Reb Avraham of Parisov, he approached him and said: "Young man, if you don't mind, please don't say such harsh things about our Reb Pintchi, for round these parts we consider him to be a man of some stature. In particular, I would advise you to watch out for the wrath of our younger chassidim, because if they get to hear you saying unpleasant things about our Reb Pintchi, they'll want to break your bones ... Besides, if *I* were to say this kind of thing about you, you would no doubt be angry with me, so who gives *you* the right to talk this way about yourself?"

"True enough," said Reb Pintchi. "If anyone else were to say these things about me, I would probably regard him as an enemy. But when *I* talk about myself this way — why, I'm my own friend."

◆§ Forgive and Beget

וְלֹא תִשָּׂא עָלָיו חֵטְא
Nor cause sin to come upon him (19:17)

Bustling throngs of chassidim were crowded just outside the door of the study of Reb Yitzchak Meir of Ger, and it was the task of Reb Bunem the *shammes* to try to keep order. There was one individual there who impatiently refused to take notice of him. He tried to force his way in ahead of his turn, and when he was refused admission, he slapped the *shammes* across the cheek. Those around him were shocked by his shameful conduct, and the poor *shammes* went straight in and put his complaint before the rebbe: "If I serve you so faithfully, why do I deserve this?"

But he did not give the rebbe the name of the man who had struck him.

The chassidim continued to take their turns at their

private interviews with the rebbe, and when this individual entered for his *yechidus* the tzaddik sensed at once who it was who stood before him. Instead of listening to him, the rebbe addressed him sharply: "Why did you do it?"

The man shed bitter tears, not only because he regretted his action, but also because, being childless, he had come to ask for a blessing, and now, instead of awakening the rebbe's compassion, he had aroused his ire. And the tzaddik was adamant: he would hear no word from him until he had made amends with the injured party and been granted forgiveness.

Off he went to speak to the *shammes*, and when they then entered the rebbe's study together, the *shammes* said: "Rebbe, I am willing to forgive this man, but only on one condition."

"And what is that?" asked the tzaddik.

"My condition, rebbe, is that you give this man your blessing that he be blessed from Above with children."

The rebbe was agreeable, and in due course his blessing was fulfilled.

◈ *Mine and Thine*

וְאָהַבְתָּ לְרֵעֲךָ כָּמוֹךָ
Love your neighbor as yourself (19:18)

"How can you claim that I am a tzaddik," Reb David of Lelov used to say to his chassidim, "when I know that I still love my children and grandchildren more than I love my other fellow Jews?"

It once happened that his son fell seriously ill. Anxious for his welfare, all the townsfolk assembled in the local synagogue to pray for his recovery, visited his bedside frequently, and spared no exertion in securing the services of the most expert physicians and apothecaries. When in due course he recovered, they of course expected to see their rebbe rejoicing — instead of which they found him weeping bitterly.

Reb David sensed their amazement, and said: "When my son fell ill, everyone was concerned, and prayed, and did whatever could be done until he was well. And if any other person is sick, no one makes such a stir about it, and people do not pay nearly that much attention to him. Now isn't that something to weep over?"

◆§ As Yourself

It once entered the head of one of the chassidim of Reb Menachem Mendel of Kotsk to hide behind his rebbe's door in order to hear how he read through the weekly Portion of the Torah when alone. It was the *Shabbos* on which the *Sidra Kedoshim* was to be read — the passage which includes the words וְאָהַבְתָּ לְרֵעֲךָ כָּמוֹךָ: "Love your neighbor as yourself." As he listened, the rebbe came to this phrase, which he read as follows: וְאָהַבְתָּ לְרֵעֲךָ־הָא? כָּמוֹךָ?! ("Love your neighbor — how? *As yourself?!*"). And after a few moments the rebbe repeated the conclusion of the phrase, not as a startled question, but as a placid statement: כָּמוֹךָ ("as yourself").

This query and its response threw the chassid into a turmoil. He hastened to consult Reb Hirsch of Tomashov, an elder chassid who was close to the rebbe, and he explained the incident as follows: "The rebbe asked himself, 'How can the Torah command a man to love his neighbor *as himself?* Why, is a person allowed to love *himself?'* Surely you know that Kotsk teaches that self-love brings on dishonesty, and deception, and intellectual sloth, and so on and on. Then he answered his own question: 'As yourself. Just as you are obliged to hold yourself in unqualified disfavor, so are you obliged to love others with unqualified love.' "

◆§ Loving the Unlovable

Before he left This World, Reb Shlomo of Karlin told his disciples that after his passing they should visit Reb Mordechai of Neshchiz and accept him as their rebbe. Reb Uri ("the Saraph") of Strelisk arrived soon after in Karlin, and learning there of the passing of the tzaddik, asked his colleagues what instructions he had left. He then set out by foot on the long trek to Neshchiz.

Of all the many guests who were standing about in the rebbe's antechamber there, waiting to receive his blessing, the individual who caught Reb Uri's eye was a certain prosperous merchant who had come to consult the rebbe on some forthcoming transaction and to request his blessing for its success. Reb Mordechai soon came out, and greeted this individual warmly — as was his wont with all comers, for in this direction his divine service was in fact outstanding. But Reb Uri, as he looked upon the face of this merchant, could tell that only recently he had sinned, seriously, vulgarly. He was incensed: why should the tzaddik of Neshchiz extend such a cordial welcome to such a creature?

Quick to read his thoughts, Reb Mordechai walked over to Reb Uri: "Please leave this place right away. What do you want here in my room?"

Weary, distressed and disappointed, Reb Uri found his way to the local *beis midrash.* But no sooner had Reb Mordechai concluded his conversation with the merchant than he went out to seek his visitor from Strelisk, found him, and said: "What you knew, brother, I also knew — but do you know why your rebbe of Karlin sent you here? In order to learn that the man in whom the love of a fellow Jew is not so entrenched in his heart that he is unable to love and embrace even a grievous sinner — such a man has not accomplished even half of his divinely appointed lifelong task. For if you bring such a sinner close to your heart, then without a doubt he will return to God with all his heart, and, being a *baal teshuvah,* a sincere penitent, he will rank higher than a perfect tzaddik — that is, unless you know him to be one who transgressed wilfully."

Reb Uri stood silent: he had found a rebbe from whom he would have much to learn in the years to come.

◆§ *Where It Really Hurts*

> *Love your neighbor as yourself:* Let your love and solicitude for your brother be like your love and compassion for yourself *(Maimonides, Sefer HaMitzvos).*

The doctors had decided that there was no other way to treat the painful sore on the back of Reb Mordechai Dov of Hornisteipl than to cauterize it — and the tzaddik gave his consent. In keeping with the medical techniques of those days they heated three metal rods, and prepared to apply them. On the rare occasions when the patient did not react to the first, they would apply a hotter one, and if he appeared not to feel even this, they had a yet hotter one in readiness.

Having accustomed himself to accepting all suffering in silence, the tzaddik gave no indication of what he was going through, so the doctor proceeded to apply the second instrument. Again the same, and the doctor went on to the third. Even now the tzaddik accepted his agony with uncomplaining love. Stupefied, the doctor exclaimed: "I don't know whether this is an angel or a demon!"

Reb Mordechai Dov hardly understood Russian, and asked a bystander: "What did the doctor say?"

When he was told, he answered: "Please tell him that if a fellow Jew comes along and presents me with a *kvitl* on which his woes are recorded, and asks me to pray on his behalf, and I see that I won't be able to bring him help, — it hurts much more, and then too I have to keep silent ..."

◆§ *Someone Else's Child*

While Sarah, the daughter of Reb Menachem Mendel of Vizhnitz, was newly married, and still living with her young husband at the home of his father, Reb Yehoshua of Belz, she fell seriously ill. One day, when for the first time her father received neither letter nor telegram informing him of her condition, he was exceedingly distressed. His son, Reb Baruch, reassured him that there was no cause to fear the worst: there was no doubt simply a postal delay. Sure enough, a telegram arrived that very afternoon from Belz, informing them that Sarah had recovered.

Seeing his father's joyful spirits returning, Reb Baruch asked: "How is it, father, that a man of your stature should allow his spiritual equilibrium to be jarred simply because he has not had news of his daughter for a few hours? What, then, is to be expected of humbler folk?"

"My son," answered Reb Menachem Mendel, "one by one, without great difficulty, I have managed to elevate ınd sanctify all the traits and attributes of my nature. Γhe one task which I found harder than all the rest was o bring myself to fulfill the commandment to love my ıeighbor *as myself,* literally. And there came a time vhen it seemed to me that I had in fact reached the level ıt which I did not distinguish between that which affected me personally and that which affected any other ew in the world. This morning, however, when the ısual mailtime passed without news, I was alarmed — ınd realized at once that I had in fact not reached that evel. For how many notes and letters reach me daily, ıourly, bearing news of all the maladies and misfortunes :hat burden the People of God! But does my heart quite ɔleed for them as it did for my own daughter? My failure :o fulfill the mitzvah in its entirety was twice as hard to ɔear as my daughter's illness, and that explains why I was so downcast."

◆§ *The Food was Heavenly*

לֹא תֹאכְלוּ עַל הַדָּם
You shall not eat anything with the blood (19:26)

You shall not eat anything with the blood (הַדָּם also implies *lifeblood):* You shall not eat before you pray for your lives *(Talmud, Tractate Berachos).*

Bereft of his rebbe, an elderly chassid was unable to decide whom to accept in his place. At this time he happened to be visiting a relative who was the aunt of the *rav* of Torchin, the same who was later to be renowned as the saintly Reb Yechiel of Alexander.

"My nephew is due to be here today," she told him one morning, "and if you see him, that will suffice to put an end to your search."

The old man did not take her assurance seriously, for the *rav* of Torchin was still a very young man, and certainly not yet a rebbe. In the meantime he arrived, greeted the other guest, and embarked on the morning prayers — until nightfall. The elder chassid, listening all those hours, was touched by the sanctity that warmed the words that welled from this young man's heart. When the prayers were over, he approached the younger man and said: "Does the Torah not command us to guard our health? Why do you pray at such length that you are unable to eat all day long, at the expense of your physical well-being?

"You can look at it either way," replied the *rav*. "If with God's help one manages to pray the way one should, who needs to eat? And if not, God forbid, who *can* eat?"

Hearing these innocent words, the chassid thought: "The time will come when thousands will flock here to learn Torah from this young man's mouth!"

סדר אמור
Sidra Emor

The Tzitzis-Jew

אֱמֹר...וְאָמַרְתָּ
Speak...and say (21:2)

Speak ... and say: The adults are obliged to instruct the young *(Rashi).*

The custom in the household of Reb Yisrael of Ruzhin was to clothe each baby boy in a tiny four-cornered garment fringed with *tzitzis* from the age of thirty days. It once happened that one of his infant sons — famous decades later as Reb David Moshe of Chortkov — worried his mother by crying without end, refusing to suck, and being unable to fall asleep, despite all her motherly efforts at soothing her baby by fondling and dandling him. She did not want to call a physician without first telling her husband, but Reb Yisrael only laughed: "Someone has no doubt forgotten to put on the baby's *tzitzis*," he said.

The *rebbitzin* hastened to check. She clothed him in his little garment, the baby stopped crying — and from that day his brothers nicknamed him "the *tzitzis*-Jew."

וּפְאַת זְקָנָם לֹא יְגַלֵּחוּ
They shall not shave off the corners of their beard (21:5)

For the Sake of a Principle

Polish Jewry was in turmoil. The year 5611 (1851) was approaching, by the advent of which — so the government had ordained — all Jews were to divest themselves of their distinctive garb, and were to shave off their earlocks and their beards. The decree was to apply in the first instance to Warsaw, and only later to the rest of the country. Seeing that it was for the most part ignored, the municipal police were ordered to seize any Jews in the street and to shave off their beards and *peyos* by force. They often encountered stout resistance, which led to blows and imprisonment, and the streets echoed with the wailing of the wives and children of those who had been dragged off brutally to jail.

The rumor now spread that the government had designs to lay hands on Reb Yitzchak Meir of Ger, who then lived in Warsaw, for certain *Maskilim* — Jewish advocates of the "Enlightenment" movement — had advised the authorities that if they could impose the requirements of the new law on this distinguished leader of men, the rest of Warsaw Jewry would conform without objection. Word of this conspiracy reached the tzaddik in time to allow him to find a temporary haven in the house of a sympathizer. At the same time, a delegation of local worthies succeeded in securing a promise from the minister in charge of the police force that no harm would befall the rebbe. Though Reb Yitzchak Meir now returned home, he changed his name for good measure from Rothenburg to Alter, which has remained the name of his descendants to this day.

As the decree was gradually proclaimed in more and more Polish cities, the rabbis who were consulted for guidance pointed in either of two opposite directions. Those who took the more stringent view argued that in times of religious persecution — when the aim of the authorities is clearly to stamp out Judaism — the Torah obliges every Jew to be prepared to surrender his life for any observance which is distinctively Jewish, be it ever so peripheral, even a distinctive way of tying one's shoestraps. Other rabbis argued that the government's intention was not necessarily anti-religious, in which case a person would be obliged to give his life for three prohibitions only: idolatry, incest and murder.

The first party was headed by Reb Avraham of Chechanov, who made his view known in all the synagogues of the town, and instructed the scholars in his own *beis midrash* to prepare themselves for the imminent self-sacrifice of *Kiddush HASHEM* by carefully studying all the learned sources on the subject. For, throughout the ages, have Jews not always prepared themselves for the Pessach festival by studying all the laws relating to *that* religious obligation?

The authority of Reb Avraham, however, was questioned by certain reputed scholars of Chechanov, who approached him as follows: "Is it proper that questions of life and death should be decided by one person, singlehanded? For we hear that other respected scholars take a more lenient view on the subject."

Reb Avraham answered that his was not a solitary view, for he had heard from Warsaw that Reb Yitzchak Meir took the same stand.

"But does hearsay suffice for a question like this?" one of them objected.

"Granted," said Reb Avraham. "I will set out at once for Warsaw in order to consult with Reb Yitzchak Meir, after which we will be able to issue a clear statement jointly."

His *rebbitzin* and family implored him to change his mind: the journey to Warsaw was plainly dangerous, since policemen now loitered about the streets unrestrained, waiting for the opportunity to abuse any Jewish bypasser. The worthies of Chechanov likewise entreated him not to leave his flock without a shepherd at such a time, but his answer was clear: he simply had to travel to Warsaw. Then he added: "After all, I am not going to settle [the Yiddish *avekzetzen-zich* could also mean 'to sit'] in Warsaw; I'll be coming straight back home, with God's help."

Accompanied by a chassid by the name of Reb Abba, he set out the same day for Warsaw, where Reb Yitzchak Meir greeted him warmly and offered him a chair. The guest refused the offer once, twice, and again, to the wonderment of all those present, and out of respect for him the host remained standing too.

"I have come here," opened Reb Avraham, "to hear your respected view on the new decree. What do you think is the government's intention?"

"It appears to me," replied his host, "that they simply

want our brethren to desert their Judaism."

"Thank God!" exclaimed Reb Avraham. "The conclusion at which I arrived coincides with your own learned view."

After discussing the laws governing *Kiddush HASHEM* for some two hours, Reb Yitzchak did his guest the courtesy of seeing him off. On the way back to Chechanov, when Reb Avraham spoke highly of Reb Yitzchak Meir, his traveling companion seized the opportunity, and took the liberty of asking the obvious question: "If you think so highly of Reb Yitzchak Meir, why did you not accede to his repeated request that you seat yourself? Does the Talmud not teach us that 'It is not proper to stand on ceremony in the presence of one's superior'?"

"Before I left home," explained Reb Avraham, "I assured my family that I was not going to *avekzetzen-zich* in Warsaw. What I meant, of course, was that I had no intention of *settling* in Warsaw, and would not tarry there. At the same time, however, I did not want to go back on my word, even in its literal sense."

❦ ❦ ❦

Rumor had it that Reb Menachem Mendel of Kotsk took the lenient view on the burning question of the day. Reb Abba was due to leave now for Kotsk, and on the assumption that on his arrival there he would be asked what stand Reb Avraham took, he asked his rebbe for a prepared answer when he went to receive his farewell blessings.

"As you no doubt recall," said Reb Avraham, "Reb Yitzchak Meir and I agreed in Warsaw that the Torah prescribes that in these circumstances a Jew is obliged to give his life rather than submit."

In Kotsk, as expected, the first question from Reb Menachem Mendel was: "What is news in your district as regards the new law? And what does your *rav* have to say on the halachic question involved?"

"Our *rav*," answered Reb Abba, "traveled to Warsaw for the express purpose of discussing this issue with Reb Yitzchak Meir."

"And if two such great scholars met to confer on this

 halachah," said his host, "then we may be certain that they arrived at some conclusion. What then, did they decide?"

When the chassid quoted their joint view, Reb Menachem Mendel grasped his beard in consternation and cried out: "And is that how they decided the *halachah?* Do you mean to say that they studied the subject, and then decided the law *this* way?! I, too, have opened a book on odd occasions; I, too, have some familiarity with the scholarly small print. But I have certainly not come across the law that says that in this case our brethren are obliged to surrender their lives rather than submit! Is it not unthinkable that two great men should treat their people's blood so cheaply? Better by far if great men like themselves were to exert all their influence on our fellow Jews, so that they should all repent wholeheartedly, and in that way bring about the Messianic Redemption! ... "

❦ ❦ ❦

As the months passed, the policemen of Warsaw realized that most of the Jews of the city would not observe the requirements of the law without the application of brute force. Growing weary of violence, the police force gradually became lax in the execution of its duties. Such a situation could not be tolerated — by sundry Jewish assimilationists and *Maskilim.* They presented themselves promptly before the Russian commissioner, and drew his attention to the fact that certain officials on the government's payroll were turning a blind eye to the recent decree, and thereby making a laughing-stock of it; they were no doubt receiving bribes from certain wealthy chassidim. His best course of action, therefore, would be to force Reb Yitzchak Meir to issue a manifesto instructing his fellows to conform to what was required of them, and explaining that this was their religious duty, under the circumstances. They led him further to believe that Reb Yitzchak Meir, alone among all the rabbis, held this intransigent view — a view which could no doubt be changed by a brief period of imprisonment.

In order to avert a furor in the middle of the day, the

local police chief and his assistant arrested Reb Yitzchak Meir at midnight, and took him in their carriage to the lock-up which adjoined the town hall. The high officials who were waiting for him there proposed that he issue a manifesto, and when he refused, they threatened that if he did not oblige within a day or two, they would shave off his own beard.

"Not a hairsbreadth will I give in," he said. "You are wasting your words, for in my view the Torah forbids every Jew to obey this order. Even if you do to me whatever it is in your power to do, I will not cause others to transgress."

Realizing that words alone would achieve nothing, the officials decided to have the tzaddik transferred to a cell which was occupied by coarse-grained criminals of every description. And the indignities which he there underwent for the sake of his principles are recounted by Gerer chassidim to this day.

❦ ❦ ❦

Who in all of Warsaw could sleep that night? The news of the rebbe's imprisonment spread in the darkness like wildfire, and the city was seething with shock and indignation. The chassidim of Reb Menachem Mendel dispatched a delegation to Kotsk, but the rebbe received the news with equanimity, instructing his faithful elder chassid, Reb Hirsch of Tomashov, to write in his name to the chassidim in Warsaw, reassuring them that there was nothing to worry about. Not only would the police officers not be able to touch the beard and *peyos* of the tzaddik, but by virtue of his righteousness all of Jewry would find their salvation, and the decree would be rescinded.

In Warsaw, in the meanwhile, the uproar was growing by the hour, and daybreak found the streets crammed with groups and crowds of distraught Jews, including as well many *Maskilim* and assimilationists who deplored what had been done, seeing it as an insult to Jewry at large. Tens of thousands of Jews, some shouting, others weeping, jostled in the vast square that fronted the town hall, where they were joined in their protest by a number of Polish citizens. Passing government officials saw it as their duty to report what they saw to the responsible ministers, until the message even reached the ears of the Russian commissioner. His advisers warned him that this could well spark off a popular revolt. A moment later he was confronted by a delegation of leading Jewish citizens, accompanied by a few Polish nobles, who pointed out that Warsaw had never seen treatment of this kind meted out to a man of such stature as Reb Yitzchak Meir. The commissioner gave them his word that he would be freed at once, and indeed the rebbe was back at home before midday.

This arrest nevertheless left a somber imprint on the lives of Warsaw's Jews. People were already pointing their fingers at certain *Maskilim* who were known to be the informers, and there were those who made it their task to track them down and wreak vengeance on them. They, for their part, flew to the government for protection, and the populace was splintered by disputants and informers on all sides.

Reb Yitzchak Meir came to the conclusion that the only way for him to bring some peace to the city was to leave it. His followers and admirers begged him not to go, especially since the Pessach festival was only two weeks away, but he left nevertheless for Novidvor, leaving word with his distressed chassidim that he would not return until the decree was annulled. After baking *matzos* in readiness for the festival he wrote a letter to his chassidim in Warsaw, entreating them not to engage in disputes for his sake, nor to speak harshly with any man — "for we are all the sons of Avraham, Yitzchak and Yaakov; and there would be no need for the Torah to exhort us to love our neighbors, nor to warn us against harboring hatred in our hearts, with regard to those who are our loving friends and brothers ... "

Over a week later, after *Shabbos HaGadol,* the decree was rescinded. The leading lights of Warsaw hastened to bring the good news to Novidvor, and soon after, Reb Yitzchak Meir joined them in their carriage for the joyful homeward journey. It was one day before the eve of Pessach when he neared the outskirts of Warsaw, where he was given a hero's welcome by jolly, jubilant crowds of bearded chassidim.

◆§ A Guide for Gourmets אמור

וטְרֵפָה לֹא יֹאכַל
He shall not eat ... trefah (22:8)

Watching the pranks of Reb Shmuel Munkes, you would take him for a rather light-headed chassid, something of a jester. His rebbe, however, Reb Shneur Zalman of Liadi, who knew of his rich spiritual life, respected him highly.

One day he and his friends were sitting around a table *farbrengen* together, as chassidim are accustomed to do — discussing the teachings of their rebbe, exchanging stories of great men, and now and again sipping vodka and nibbling whatever refreshments happened to be on the table. One of the brotherhood, a *shochet,* now came in with a dish of cooked meat which he had brought from home for all those present. Reb Shmuel promptly took it and held it firmly under his arm, allowing no one else at the table to touch it. They demanded that he place it within reach of anyone who wished to help himself, and when he refused to oblige, some of them even tried to snatch it from him by force. Seeing that they would soon succeed, he raised the platter aloft, danced around with it to the corner of the room where a garbage pail stood, and threw it right in.

The other chassidim were dumbfounded by his odd behavior, and would have given him a piece of their mind — but at that moment they were interrupted by the arrival of a breathless messenger from the house of the *shochet:* they were not to eat from that dish! The meat that had been brought by mistake was *trefah!*

The elder chassidim now turned on Reb Shmuel with a different complaint altogether: "Tell us, our budding young tzaddik! Since when has the voice of divine inspiration been whispering secrets in *your* ear?"

Seeing that he would have no respite from their good-natured teasing, he was forced to explain: "Years ago, during the period when I was preparing myself to enter the rebbe's study for my first *yechidus,* I resolved that I would abstain from any physical thing that I desired unduly. Today, when I took this meat dish in my hands, I felt a strong urge to eat it — and that is why I didn't. Then when I saw with what eager eyes our little brotherhood looked upon it, I threw it out."

◈§ Worth the Sacrifice

And I will be sanctified amongst the Children of Israel: Surrender your life and sanctify My name *(Rashi).*

וְנִקְדַּשְׁתִּי בְּתוֹךְ בְּנֵי יִשְׂרָאֵל
And I will be sanctified amongst the Children of Israel (22:32)

This story used to be told by Reb David Zvi Chein, a distinguished chassid who was the *rav* of Chernigov.

A rare manuscript book of chassidic philosophy, bound with *two* spines, was kept in the house of Reb Shneur Zalman of Liadi, and its cover bore the inscription: "The ban of Rabbeinu Gershom respecting the secrecy of documents is hereby invoked — in This World and in the Next — on anyone who looks inside this book."

Fire broke out in his home one day, destroying his entire library and all his manuscripts, including this one. With tears in his eyes he asked his son, Reb Dov Ber of Lubavitch, if he had perchance ever glanced at it. Tne answer was of course negative, but the father persisted: "If you were perhaps to recall even one chapter, one discourse, you would restore my spirits!"

"But could I ever have looked at it?" protested Reb Dov Ber. "Didn't you invoke the ban both in This World and the Next?"

Even this explanation did not satisfy his father, who objected: "But isn't the discovery of fresh manuscripts of chassidic philosophy worth the sacrifice?"

◈§ One Moment of Ecstasy

The following account of the passing of Reb Yaakov Yitzchak, the Yid HaKadosh of Pshischah, was given by Reb Avraham of Sochatchov.

Reb Yaakov Yitzchak had always hoped that his life would come to an end while he was at prayer; he yearned to attain such a degree of *mesirus nefesh* that in a moment of ecstasy his soul would fly home and cleave to its Maker. His sons, however, used to see to it that this should not occur. On one occasion nevertheless he was left alone in his room while he was immersed in his morning prayers, and when he came to the verse:

"Redeemers will go up on Mount Zion" — those who were in the adjoining room heard a thud. The Yid HaKadosh had fallen to the floor. They ran in, just in time to hear him whisper the words יְחִידָה לְיַחֲדָךְ — "My soul proclaims Your unity" — and the tzaddik was no more.

◆§ An Honest Epitaph

After the passing of Reb Uri of Strelisk, his son, Reb Shlomo, journeyed to visit Reb Yisrael of Ruzhin. On his arrival, his host asked him to repeat some quotable saying or to tell of some noteworthy practice of his father, who was nicknamed "the Saraph" — the fiery angel — on account of the ecstatic nature of his prayer. Reb Shlomo thereupon told him two things: firstly, every morning before Reb Uri went off to his prayers he used to go to the kitchen in order to exchange farewells with his *rebbitzin* and children, being fearful lest his soul break loose from his body in the ecstatic *dveikus* of prayer; secondly, on each such occasion he used to say: "Keep in mind that the manuscripts in that chest were authored by my teacher, Reb Shlomo of Karlin, and not by me, and the Talmudic novellae appearing there should not be attributed to me."

Reb Yisrael was well pleased, and said that he valued the second statement even more than the first.

◆§ A Boy at a Picnic

It was too much for the simple householder from Tomashov to comprehend.

"This Reb Menachem Mendel of Kotsk," he would declare, "was born right here in Tomashov, and he and I went to *cheder* together when we were little. And do you mean to say that now he is a rebbe?!"

A number of chassidim of Kotsk heard this statement, and made it their business to ply this fellow with questions about the conduct of their rebbe in his childhood. He insisted that there was nothing to tell: their rebbe had been a child like all the other children. But when they persisted further, he recalled one incident: "One day our *melamed* took all the children from his *cheder* to celebrate Lag BaOmer by a picnic in the high mountains beyond the town, as all schoolmasters do. We had all returned home before we realized that one boy — that's the Kotsker rebbe — was missing! We hurried back to look for him, and found him lying with arms and legs outstretched on the mountainside. Someone bent over him, and heard him murmur: לִבִּי וּבְשָׂרִי יְרַנְּנוּ אֶל אֵל חָי — 'My heart and my flesh sing praises to the living God.''

◆§ *The Voice of the People*

אֵלֶּה מוֹעֲדֵי ה׳ ... אֲשֶׁר תִּקְרְאוּ אֹתָם
These are the festivals of God ... which you shall proclaim (23:4)

These are the festivals of God ... which you shall proclaim: Do not read אֹתָם (them) but אַתֶּם (you); by *your* decision shall they be determined, even if you err unwittingly, or misjudge intentionally *(Talmud, Tractate Rosh HaShanah).*

It is the custom among certain groups of chassidim to mark the visit of a tzaddik to their town by omitting the Tachanun prayer from the morning and afternoon service, as is in fact done by all congregations on festive days. So it was that when Reb Yechezkel of Shiniva spent a few weeks in Militz, the whole town took this liberty throughout his entire stay.

''The reason that chassidim omit *Tachanun* when their town is visited by a sage,'' commented Reb Yechezkel, ''is that a *talmid chacham* is akin to the spirit of *Shabbos* and the festivals — days on which one never recites the penitential prayers. This rationale, however, holds good only for you chassidim here, who choose to regard me as a *talmid chacham.* But as for myself, who knows my own real worth, and who know that I am neither sage nor tzaddik, — why do *I* not say *Tachanun?*

''The explanation is as follows: We read: 'These are the festivals of God ... which you shall proclaim.' On this the Sages comment: ''אַל תִּקְרֵי ''אֹתָם'' אֶלָּא ''אַתֶּם — 'Do not read אֹתָם (them) but אַתֶּם (you): by *your* decision shall they be determined, even if you err unwittingly, or misjudge intentionally.' It follows, therefore, that even if the chassidim here are mistaken in their assessment of my worth, I am nevertheless still akin to *Shabbos* and *Yom Tov*, and am hence exempt from reciting *Tachanun*."

סדר בהר
Sidra Behar

❧ No False Pretenses

אַל תּוֹנוּ אִישׁ אֶת אָחִיו
You shall not defraud one another (25:14)

He was the grandson of Reb Avraham of Chechanov, and he was engaged to be married to one of the prominent burghers of Polotzk — but he was an immature youngster, and one day while his celebrated grandfather took off his coat and left the room, he subtracted a few small coins from his pocket and dropped them into his own. As soon as Reb Avraham returned to the room he sensed what had happened, and was pained by the fact that his own flesh and blood had thus faltered. He sat down at once at his desk and dispatched a letter to the *rav* of Polotzk, asking him to instruct the father of the bride to set out immediately for Chechanov. The poor fellow received the message and trembled in apprehension. Was it possible that at this late stage the tzaddik of Chechanov had decided that he was unworthy of being his *mechuten* after all?

He entered the rebbe's study, and Reb Avraham opened exactly as he had feared: "Now you have been thinking all along that you are about to join your family in marriage with the *rav* of Chechanov." But then he went on: "Well, sir, it is my obligation to inform you that such and such has taken place. I would certainly not want our arrangements to be based on a mistaken assumption."

Much relieved, the *mechutan* said: "Rebbe, I'll go ahead with the match, all the same."

The tzaddik repeated his statement again, and again — but the *mechutan* stood by his first answer.

"If that is the case," said the tzaddik finally, "then the responsibility no longer rests on me. I have done my part."

◆§ A Mitzvah for Mortals

וְהֶחֱזַקְתָּ בּוֹ
You shall support him (25:35)

Hundreds of chassidim from all around converged on Kosov for *Shabbos,* for their rebbe, Reb Menachem Mendel of Kosov, was to be visited by his brother-in-law, Reb Uri of Strelisk. Among them was one Reb Moshe, an *arendar* who had been wealthy and generous, but had now fallen from his fortunes to such an extent that his local squire was threatening him with imprisonment and other humiliations if he did not pay up the rent on his leased business.

When *Shabbos* was out the distracted debtor told his story to his rebbe, Reb Menachem Mendel, who recommended that he recount his woes to Reb Uri as well.

"I certainly feel sorry for you in your troubles," said Reb Uri. "I am now going to immerse myself in the *mikveh* for your sake, and the merit of the *mikveh* will no doubt stand you in good stead and protect you."

When the *arendar* reported this reply back to his rebbe, Reb Menachem Mendel advised: "Please go back to my learned brother-in-law, and tell him that you can't pay your creditors with a *mikveh.*"

Reb Uri's reply to this was: "Very well, my son. Then in addition I am prepared to give you the credit of an even greater mitzvah — the *tefillin* that I am about to don this morning."

When Menachem Mendel was told of this answer, he said: "Now tell Reb Uri, please, that you cannot placate your creditors with *tefillin.*"

The *arendar* had no choice but to obey his rebbe. Once again he went off to Reb Uri, who listened, and then reassured him: "If that is the case, then you may have as well the *zechus* of my prayers this morning. Without a doubt, the merit of all these three mitzvos together will bring about the salvation you require!"

This assurance, too, was relayed to Reb Menachem Mendel, but he remained unconvinced. "Go back and tell Reb Uri," he said "that even with all these three mitzvos together you will not be able to pay a single debt."

Reb Uri realized that it was time to clarify what was

going on. He went along himself, and asked his brother-in-law what he was driving at.

"All I am suggesting," said Reb Menachem Mendel, "is that you and I should spend the next few weeks traveling about the countryside, knocking on the doors of our brethren, collecting whatever amount the poor fellow needs. That we can fulfill a mitzvah which is written in the Torah: 'And if your brother grows poor, ... then you shall support him.' "

And so they did. The *arendar* settled all his debts, and soon after the Almighty again gave him the means to become an open-handed philanthropist, just as he had always been in earlier times.

◆§ *Telegraphic Accounting*

An upstanding householder once came to pour out his troubles to Reb Menachem Mendel of Kosov: he needed a large sum with which to marry off his daughter, and did not have a penny to start with.

"The best thing for you to do," advised the rebbe, "is to travel to Jassy, and there you will do well."

"But how can I cross the border to Rumania without a passport?" asked the chassid.

"I will give you a letter to a certain person who lives near the border," said the rebbe, "and he will get you across."

Everything went as planned, and before dawn the chassid was in Jassy. There was no one in sight who could tell him where he could find a hotel, so he stood with his belongings out in the street, waiting for daybreak. One of the first citizens to be seen was an impressive-looking individual who by his modern garb would seem to be an assimilationist, a "Deitsch". He approached the chassid and asked him where he came from, and was told that he had just arrived and did not yet know where he would be lodging.

"Come along with me," said the stranger.

"Why, do you own a good lodging place?" asked the chassid.

"I certainly do," said the stranger. "But it's not for payment: it's for nothing."

The visitor was somewhat surprised. They had never met before, and here was this total stranger inviting him to his home.

"Come along with me," resumed the stranger, "and I'll tell you what it's all about.

"A few years ago we had a visit here from some rebbe from Galicia by the name of Reb Menachem Mendel. Through his intercession and blessing, heaven granted me the gift of a baby boy, and I vowed at the time that I would give him a certain large sum of money. But I didn't have his address over there, so I never repaid my debt to him. I kept on hoping that one day either I would be in Galicia, or else he would visit us again here, and then I would settle my acount once and for all. Then last night he appeared to me in a dream and said: 'Do you recall that debt that you owe me? Well, I'm sending you now a man of such and such a description, and I would like you to hand him the whole amount. You will know that you have found your man if you go out and find him right away in the street.'

"I woke up with my mind in a whirl. I could rest no longer, and at daybreak I went straight out to the street. I looked around until I caught sight of you — and your description tallies exactly with what the rebbe told me."

His story completed, the stranger gave the visitor the whole sum that he had resolved to give the rebbe, and added to it by asking friends to join in the mitzvah. They then exchanged farewells and parted company, each turning to wend his thoughtful way homeward.

◆§ *The Apple-Vendor*

A poor woman of good family once came to Reb Chaim of Zanz and complained that she did not even have the wherewithal to buy food for *Shabbos*.

"But don't you sell apples?" asked the rebbe.

"I do," she said. "But people say my apples are no good, so I haven't sold any."

The venerable tzaddik, resplendent in his fur hat, black silk *kapote* and white stockings, strode immediately out to the market place, took up his stand next to the poor woman's apple-cart, and cried out: "Apples! Beautiful apples! Who wants to buy first-class apples?"

Crowds of customers jostled with each other in their eagerness to buy the apples that the rebbe was selling. The price did not matter: they offered far more than they needed to, and in no time the entire stock was sold out at an enormous profit.

As he turned to leave the market place, the rebbe said to the woman: "You see, your apples are fine! It's only that our townsfolk didn't know it ..."

סדר בחקתי
Sidra Bechukosai

◈ Head and Heart

אִם בְּחֻקֹּתַי תֵּלֵכוּ
If you walk in the way of My statutes (26:3)

If you walk in the way of My statutes: You shall *toil* in the study of the Torah *(Rashi).*

When Reb Avraham of Sochatchov was a very young man, Reb Menachem Mendel of Kotsk once told his father: "Your brilliant son is a great worshiper, with an unusual gift in prayer. I am only afraid lest it impair his intellectual power."

This was not an easy comment to understand. In the first place, no one had observed the young man exert himself particularly in prayer, and secondly, what did that have to do with his intellectual power?

An uncle of Reb Avraham decided to ask the young man himself, and was given the following innocent explanation: "I once had a watch that I was very fond of, for it used to tell me the time for Torah study, prayer, and so on. One day its wheels stopped, but I couldn't afford to have it repaired by a watchmaker. I wept before the Almighty in my distress — and straight away its wheels started to work, even though it had not been repaired. Now when I saw that my tears were heard Above, every time I was confronted in my studies by a particularly problematic passage I would cry again, asking God to illumine my eyes. And each time I found I could immediately solve the problem at hand.

"Now the rebbe of Kotsk evidently sensed this, and that is why he said that I have 'an unusual gift in prayer.' That also explains why he said that he was fearful that my intellectual powers should be impaired, because what is demanded of us is that we should come to master the Torah through toil of the brain, not by means of prayer."

◆§ *By the Sweat of Your Brow*

I encountered this story in a manuscript written by the hand of Reb Raphael Wolf of Skoli, Galicia, who died in Jerusalem early in 1929 at the age of some ninety years. Reb Raphael heard it from a chassid of repute by the name of Reb Alter of Yazlivitz, who heard it from the mouth of the tzaddik Reb Meir of Premishlan (who died in 1850), son of Reb Aharon Leib, the protagonist of this story.

A certain merchant who was a chassid of Reb Aharon Leib of Premishlan had occasion to pass through Lyzhansk in the course of business. It would be a pity, he thought, to be so far away from home and not to utilize this opportunity to visit one of the towering figures of the generation, Reb Elimelech of Lyzhansk. In order to be able to do this in an untrammeled frame of mind, he first settled his various business affairs in the district, and arranged to be back in town for *Shabbos*. On Friday morning, after immersing himself in the *mikveh*, he went to greet the rebbe.

Reb Elimelech welcomed him, and then said: "Are you not one of the chassidim of Reb Aharon Leib of Premishlan? Tell me, now, why is your rebbe so conceited?"

And Reb Elimelech repeated the phrase in the hearing of all those who happened to be present: "So conceited! So conceited!"

And not only then, but again and again at each of the *Shabbos* meals — until the merchant's joy at the privilege of meeting the celebrated personage turned to distress.

Nor did his departure from Lyzhansk lighten his

burden, for when he came to Reb Elimelech to receive his parting blessings, he was told: "When you come home, please tell your rebbe in my name that he should not be so conceited."

His arrival home threw him into a quandary. Reb Aharon Leib was certain to ask him, as he always did whenever his chassidim came home from a journey, whether he had anything of interest to report. He would have to say that he had met Reb Elimelech. Reb Aharon Leib would then ask, naturally enough, whether he had seen or heard anything noteworthy or quotable. He would then have to say ... — but how could he ever bring himself to mouth such words? At length, realizing that there was no way out of fulfilling the explicit instruction of Reb Elimelech, he spoke to his rebbe and withheld nothing.

"Woe is me!" said Reb Aharon Leib. "Who knows how I have sinned in the sight of God, and what blemish the tzaddik has discerned in me? Indeed, I am in such a sorry state that I do not even sense what my sin is, and therefore do not even know how to go about repenting!"

Calling in his *rebbitzin,* he said: "The tzaddik of Lyzhansk sees that I am a sinner. I must journey there at once to find out from him in what way I have transgressed, otherwise I will not know how to repent. But the road to Lyzhansk is a long, long road, and even when I finally arrive there I know I no longer have the strength to look after myself."

The *rebbitzin* assured him that she would share the rigors of the journey with him and see to his needs. They hired a wagon, trundled along for six whole days, and arrived at Lyzhansk just in time for *Shabbos.* A sinner such as himself would certainly not be granted admission to the Friday night table of the tzaddik, so Reb Aharon Leib asked his *rebbitzin* to go out to the market place to buy a bottle of wine and two loaves of *challah,* while he himself went off to find the local *mikveh,* so that he could immerse himself for purity's sake in honor of the holy day.

Entering the rebbe's house, he found himself among hundreds of chassidim who were also waiting to receive his greeting of *Shalom.* He made his way through the crowd and extended his hand to receive the rebbe's handshake, being careful to keep his head bowed so that the tzaddik should not see his face. Reb Elimelech sensed at once that this was Reb Aharon Leib, and wanted to call him back, but the guest had already hurried off to his lodging place. From there he went to a nearby *shul* for evening prayers, then back to his modest little room, there to sing the *Shalom Aleichem* that welcomes the ministering angels who accompany every Jew on his way back from *shul* to whatever nook he calls home.

At the same time, Reb Elimelech asked his *shammes* and his chassidim to search through the whole town until they found the guest from Premishlan. When they returned without having found him, Reb Elimelech stood up and protested: "A guest of the stature of Reb Aharon Leib is here with us in our town, and will I not have him at my table for *Shabbos?!*"

He again gave the order that his chassidim were to search through the whole of Lyzhansk, from house to house, room by room, until they found this same Reb Aharon Leib, and to inform him that he himself would not sit down to conduct his Friday night *tish* until this guest joined him there.

Again they set out, and searched once more, until they found him at his lodgings in the low-roofed cottage of some penniless *melamed* on the outskirts of the town.

They gave him the message and brought him to the rebbe's table, where Reb Elimelech expressed his delight at his arrival by giving him a seat of honor by his side. Surprisingly, though, several times in the course of the meal he said: "Who would believe that Reb Aharon Leib should be so conceited!"

And, as before, not once, but at every one of the *Shabbos* meals he repeated this comment in public.

When the day of rest was over Reb Aharon Leib called on the rebbe in order to take his leave — but first to find out just what was the conceit that he had perceived.

"Why, is there any conceit greater than this?" answered Reb Elimelech. "On many occasions Eliyahu the Prophet has come to me with the complaint that you do not want to learn Torah from his mouth. He, the Prophet Eliyahu, wanted to teach you Torah, and you refuse! Think how many tzaddikim have longed and yearned for this privilege — and you decline the offer! In any case, I promised Eliyahu that I would try to persuade you to change your mind."

"I am afraid that even after your persuasion," answered Reb Aharon Leib, "I cannot agree."

"Why so?" asked his host.

"Because my desire," said the guest, "is to do my own hard work in the study of the Torah. For how does the Psalmist express it? 'When you eat of the labor of your hands, happy shall you be, and it shall be well with you.' And the same lesson we learn in the Talmud: 'The Torah truly becomes the possession only of him who gives his very life in the effort of its study.' For this reason I have not been taught by him, nor will I be taught by him. I will only pray to the Almighty that he give me the strength to toil always in the study of His Torah."

The tzaddik gave him his blessing, and Reb Aharon Leib made his way back to Premishlan, where he continued to serve his Maker by an honest day's labor, day by day.

◆§ Judging by Appearances

וְנָתַתִּי גִשְׁמֵיכֶם בְּעִתָּם
And I will grant your rains in their season (26:4)

A *Chabad* chassid of the Slonim family traveled to White Russia over a hundred years ago to visit his rebbe and relative, Reb Shmuel of Lubavitch. The rebbe was eager to hear news of the welfare of the Jews in *Eretz Yisrael,* and the chassid in the course of his report, commented: "I cannot understand the claim which is made in many sacred books that in *Eretz Yisrael* there are to be found people with lofty souls. I know the Jews over there, and I have not seen amongst them any more individuals with lofty souls than are to be found in other countries."

"And do you understand exactly who it is who has a lofty soul?" queried the rebbe. "Let me tell you a story that I heard from my father, Reb Menachem Mendel, of blessed memory, and you will see to what heights a simple Jew in the Holy Land can sometimes aspire.

"In a village just beyond the outskirts of Jerusalem there lived a very simple peasant, who had studied neither *Chumash* nor Mishnah, and did not even understand the meaning of the words of the daily prayers. Not only that, he could not even find his way around the *Siddur,* so that he was unable to work out for himself which prayers were to be said on any particular day. When he drove his donkey cart up the winding road to Jerusalem once a week to sell his fruit and vegetables, he would call on a certain *rav,* who would jot down for him the order of prayers for the coming week. It might have been simpler to explain the subject in general terms — to tell him that all weekday prayers are identical, except for the Daily Psalm, and except for the additional passages on Mondays and Thursdays, and so on — but this was out of the question. The poor fellow was so utterly ignorant that he would only flounder in all those unmanageable details. The *rav* was therefore obliged to write down each day's order of service in full, day by day.

"Once he came to the *rav* in the rainy month of Cheshvan, and asked him to write out the daily lists that would be needed for several weeks ahead, for the roads were likely to become muddy and impassable. As things worked out, however, a week or so later he found that he had to make the trip to town after all. He arrived in Jerusalem, but was amazed to find that all the Jewish shops were closed. Perhaps he had made a mistake, God forbid, and today was in fact *Shabbos?* As he stood next to his donkey, straining to puzzle this out, he saw a man walk past with his *tallis* and *tefillin* under his arm. That was a relief, for everyone knows that one doesn't don *tefillin* on *Shabbos.* But what kind of day could it possibly be? He asked the same bypasser, who told him that that day was a public fast.

"The villager could not begin to understand how his *rav* could have neglected to note this down in his list. In the first place, he had thus eaten on a fast day; and secondly, he had omitted the special prayers which he should have been told about. He left his donkey and wagon in the market place and ran off to the house of the *rav,* where he was told that the man he sought had gone to the local synagogue. He hurried there in confusion, went straight over to the *rav,* and broke down in bitter tears: 'Tell me, rabbi! Do you think that's fair? How could you ever do such a thing to me?'

"The *rav* was nonplussed, and asked gently: 'What is the matter, my son?'

" 'What do you mean *What is the matter?*' returned the villager. 'Today is a public fast day, and you didn't write down any mention of it. So now I've eaten when I shouldn't have, and I haven't prayed what I should have!'

" 'Do calm down, my son,' the *rav* replied. 'Today is not a regular fast day, but a fast that we decreed just now in Jerusalem especially for today, because of the drought that is threatening. We are all fasting here, and asking the Almighty to send us rain.'

" 'Do you mean to say that for this you have to decree a *fast?*' mused the villager.

" 'Then what, in your opinion, should one do?' countered the *rav*.

" 'Simple,' said the villager. 'I know that when I don't get enough rain on my fields back at home, I go outside, and I say to God: *Father, I need rain!* And the rain starts to fall.'

" 'Very well,' said the *rav*, 'then try to do the same thing here.'

"The simple fellow went out to the courtyard of the synagogue, was overcome with tears, and said: 'Father! Is it possible that Your children in the Holy City should perish of hunger? Can't you see that they need rain?'

"And the Holy City was blessed at once with rain."

❀ ❀ ❀

His story concluded, the rebbe asked his guest: "Tell me, are you still able to judge exactly who in *Eretz Yisrael* is possessed of a lofty soul?"

☙ *Every Custom Tells a Story*

וְחֶרֶב לֹא תַעֲבֹר בְּאַרְצְכֶם *Nor shall a sword pass through your land (26:6)*

The little town of Rimanov, for as long as it survived, had a custom all of its own. Every *Shabbos* eve before the late afternoon prayer the congregants used to chant together the verses of Psalm 144, which opens with the words: בָּרוּךְ ה׳ צוּרִי הַמְלַמֵּד יָדַי לַקְרָב אֶצְבְּעוֹתַי לַמִּלְחָמָה —

 "Blessed be God, my Rock, Who teaches my hands for battle, my fingers for war" — and proceeds to express the gratitude of the Psalmist to Him Who repelled His enemies, leaving His People to dwell unafraid. The custom originated with Reb Menachem Mendel of Rimanov, who died in 1815. This is its story.

The fury of a violent peasants' revolt at the time focused on Rimanov. When the authorities at Dukla heard that even bridges were being smashed, they dispatched troops forthwith in order to restore law and order to the best of their ability. The peasants fled in all directions, and the troops, unwilling to lose valuable time in the dispensation of justice, let loose with their clubs and muskets on whomever happened to be in sight. The townsmen, including the Jews of Rimanov, locked and barred their houses, and no one dared to step out into the terrors of the street.

Before daybreak on Friday morning, Reb Menachem Mendel did not hear the communal *shammes* doing his accustomed rounds of the cobblestoned alleys to wake up the *shomrim* whose turn it was to go to *shul* for early morning devotions. Asking his attendant for the reason, he was told that the militiamen had come to town, and people were afraid to go out of doors.

"They won't spend the night here," said the rebbe. "Of that I am certain."

When sunset was drawing near, and the rebbe went to his *beis midrash* for the afternoon prayers, he found the building deserted, apart from his own family and attendants.

"Where is the holy congregation?" he asked.

And he was told that the worshipers were afraid to leave their wives at home alone, because of the soldiers who were still roaming the streets.

Reb Menachem Mendel stepped forward to lead the *Minchah* service, but before starting it, he began to recite Psalm 144. He had not even managed to read its fifteen verses, when his companions were startled by a raucous clarion call, summoning the militiamen to parade at their colors. And in a matter of minutes, still before nightfall, the unwelcome regiment had galloped out of sight and hearing.

And from that Friday on, Reb Menachem Mendel instituted the custom of chanting Psalm 144 every Friday afternoon before the afternoon prayers, in remembrance and gratitude to Him Who repelled the enemies of His People, leaving them to dwell unafraid.

☙ Real Trust

בָּרוּךְ הַגֶּבֶר אֲשֶׁר יִבְטַח בַּה׳

Blessed is the man who trusts in God (Haftarah)

While traveling in distant parts with the Baal Shem Tov, Reb Mendel of Bar was once parched with thirst.

Said the Baal Shem Tov: "If you will truly trust in God, you will certainly come across water."

And so it was. They encountered a gentile, who asked them whether they had perhaps seen the horses which he had lost and for which he had been searching for three days. They then asked him whether he had any water with him, and he allowed Reb Mendel to drink some.

When he had passed, Reb Mendel asked the Baal Shem Tov: "Since Providence evidently ordained that this gentile should come past here especially for my sake, why, then, should he have spent three days on the road?"

Replied the Baal Shem Tov: "The Almighty had him prepared earlier, so that if you were to have *real* trust in Him, your need would have been satisfied at once."

☙ No Worries

The Baal Shem Tov was once instructed by a voice from heaven to make the journey to a certain village in order to learn a lesson in how to trust in God. Arriving there with his disciples, he took up lodgings with the local *arendar*, an innkeeper who held his hostelry on lease from the squire of that region. Their host was an elderly and dignified gentleman, and was obviously happy to be able to extend a warm welcome to guests such as these.

The next morning, as they were preparing for their prayers, a sheriff in the service of the squire strode into the inn, struck the table three times with a hefty rod, and strode out. The guests asked no questions, but searched the face of their host for an explanation. His cheerful equanimity had not been ruffled in the slightest. Half an hour or so later, after their prayers, they witnessed the same odd visit, repeated exactly.

The Baal Shem Tov asked the innkeeper what was going on, and received the following answer: "This is a warning that today I am obliged to pay his master the annual rent on the inn. He does this three times. If, after the third visit, the squire doesn't get his money, he comes along and throws the leaseholder and his family into his dungeon."

"It is clear, just from looking at you, that you have the necessary sum in hand," said the Baal Shem Tov. "I would therefore suggest that you go along now to the squire, before breakfast, and pay up your lease. We will wait till you return, and then we will all be able to sit at the table at leisure."

"At the moment, though," said the *arendar,* "I haven't even got a single penny — but the Almighty will no doubt bring some money my way. Let us therefore sit down, please, and eat and drink without haste, for I still have three hours grace."

They took their time over their meal, and one would never be able to tell from the host's face whether he needed the money or not. As they finished eating, in came the sheriff on his third visit and hammered his threefold warning into the table — but the innkeeper did not stir. When they had all recited the Grace after Meals with unhurried devoutness, the inkeeper rose from the table, donned his best *Shabbos* coat, belted it with his broad girdle, and said: "Gentlemen, I must now be on my way to pay the squire his lease."

The Baal Shem Tov repeated his earlier question: "But do you have enough money?"

"I haven't got a single penny of it yet," answered the innkeeper, "but the Almighty will no doubt see to that."

Taking his leave of them he went on his way, while the Baal Shem Tov and his chassidim went up to the balcony overlooking the highway, to see him off from afar as he set out on his unpredictable mission. From out of the distance they could discern a wagon rumbling dustily along to meet him. Now it stopped, and they could tell that its driver was exchanging a few sentences with their innkeeper. He then continued walking further away from them as before, and the wagon likewise continued in its own direction, coming towards the inn, but more slowly than before. After a moment or two the wagon stopped, its driver called out to the innkeeper asking him to retrace his steps, and when he reached the wagon they could see that money was changing hands.

The innkeeper thereupon resumed his previous direction and was soon out of sight, but when the wagon finally arrived at the inn, the Baal Shem Tov and his chassidim asked its driver: "Tell us, please, what was this little incident with our host, whom you called back after he had already walked away, and then gave him money?"

"I proposed a business offer," said the driver. "I would buy up the vodka that he is due to make next winter. At first we couldn't agree on a price. But later, when I saw that he stood his ground, and was prepared to wait for his price, and even walked away — and I know him to be an honest man — I had to give him the price he asked. But I couldn't spend much time talking with him, because he said he was on his way to the squire to pay up his lease."

"Just look," said the Baal Shem Tov to his disciples, "how mighty is the power of a man's trust in God!"

◆§ *Faith without Trimmings*

While explaining the beauty of faith and trust to his chassidim, Reb Noach of Lechovitch told the story of a simple Jew who arrived at the level of pure, uncomplicated faith, and prospered thereby.

This simple fellow, Hirschke by name, used to earn his living by bargaining with the gentile farmers over the merchandise that they used to bring to town on market day — hides, honey, wax, milk, boar bristle, and so on. Stallholders at the market, like himself, were accustomed to go out to the countryside two or three hours before daybreak in order to meet the *goyim* on their way to the market, in the hope of clinching their deals before the merchandise arrived in town.

Now one day an itinerant preacher came to spend *Shabbos* in town, and he held forth in the synagogue on the virtues of living with perfect trust in God. He explained the teaching of the Talmud that the world is so ordered that in the final analysis no man ever trespasses on the earnings that have been divinely ordained as the particular livelihood of another. This *darshan* was a God-fearing man, so it is not to be wondered at that his words found their way deep into Hirschke's heart. The next day, Sunday, was market day, but instead of rising hours before daybreak in order to meet the gentile farmers before his competitors did, he decided that this time he was not going to do so. Whatever Providence had set aside for him he would be able to buy at home — for is it not written that "no man ever trespasses on the earnings" and so on? His wife, seeing him lying snugly in bed at a time when he was normally up and about, urged him to get up and start moving.

"I'd like you to know," he answered, "that I myself heard the preacher say that no one can take away the earnings that have been set aside for someone else. Why, then, should I rush out in the freezing snow on the lookout for these *goyim?* For nothing is stopping God from seeing to my needs right here in my house."

His wife was not one to submit meekly. She buried him in abuse, and then declared: "This preacher of yours will be paid for his sermon, that's for sure! And you? You'll sit home idle — and starve!"

Hirschke did not answer a single word — but neither did he step out of the house.

After a little while they heard the loaded wagons of the gentiles creaking past their house. They could even hear Hirschke's friends slapping their hearty handshakes with the gentiles as they settled their deals.

This was too much. "Tell me, Hirschke," she pleaded. "Are you stark crazy, or just a fool? Can't you see that your friends will buy up every last ounce of merchandise?"

"Those uncircumcised *goyim* can jolly well come in here, if they like!" he retorted. "Why should I go out to them in this bitter cold?"

Then, right under their very shutters, they heard the

insistent voice of one of the gentile farmers: "We're not selling any more stuff until Hirschke turns up!"

One of Hirschke's competitors gave a quick reply: "Hirshcke's dead!"

"A bunch of lies!" shouted the gentiles, and began thumping with their fists on the shutters. "Hirschke, get up!"

Hirschke obliged. He got dressed, and opened the door, and the farmers with whom he was accustomed to do business came right inside, and he bought up whatever merchandise he had always bought from them, without even having to bargain. From that day on he never had to leave his house, for the farmers used to bring him their goods, and he made a respectable livelihood to the end of his days.

Reb Noach had finished his story. "Now this worked for him," he added, "because he was a simple fellow whose faith was whole and uncomplicated. Things would hardly be the same for someone who tried to improve on Hirschke's kind of faith by adding the sophistication of reason."

◆§ *From Your Hand*

Before he was known as a rebbe, Reb Yitzchak of Vorki used to live in a village where he was responsible for the timber interests of Tamar'l, a prosperous lady who invested her wealth in acts of charity. He was once asked to use his influence on her for the benefit of a chassid who was related to her, and who was hoping that she would help him bear the expense of marrying off his daughter. At first Reb Yitzchak would not hear a word of the chassid's request, but finally told him to come back the next day.

When he paid his second visit, Reb Yitzchak not only received him warmly, but asked him in a voice loud enough to be heard by Tamar'l, who was standing nearby: "So how much is it that you say you are short of? Was it three hundred gold rubles for a dowry and another two hundred for the wedding? You are related to Tamar'l, aren't you, so I am sure she will help you out."

Tamar' took the hint, and acted on it. But the chassid

could not understand why the tzaddik should have rejected his request so firmly the day before, if in the end he was to consider it so compassionately. He decided to ask him point blank.

"I only wanted to teach you," said Reb Yitzchak, "not to rely on mortals, but only on God alone."

ספר במדבר

NUMBERS

סדר במדבר
SIDRA BAMIDBAR

◆§ A Labor of Love

לַעֲבֹד אֶת עֲבֹדַת הַמִּשְׁכָּן
To do the work of the Sanctuary (3:7)

The story of how Reb Shalom of Belz built his famous synagogue has already been told — but once his older brother, Reb Leibish Rokeach, came to Belz to visit their mother, and encountered the tzaddik working with bricks and mortar together with the construction laborers. This sight rather displeased him, and he sought to correct his brother: "Surely you are familiar with the teaching of our Sages, that 'Once a man is appointed a leader of the community he is forbidden to engage in menial tasks in public.' Why, then, do you do otherwise?"

"My dear brother," answered Reb Shalom, "when I used to live in Skohl I had two close friends with whom I used to study Torah. At that time it was intimated to me from Above that if one were to remain awake for a thousand nights, one could aspire to the level at which Eliyahu the Prophet reveals himself. The three of us resolved to stay awake every night and to study together. One of my friends left us after a few hundred nights, and after eight hundred nights the other friend could manage no more. I remained alone. On the thousandth night there raged such a furious tempest that it shattered all the windows of the *beis midrash* and extinguished all the lamps. Only the violent wind held me back from going home. I staggered in my anguish through the darkness towards the Holy Ark, and wept there. God took pity on me, the storm subsided, and an old man appeared before me. He began to speak and to teach me Torah, and the very last law that I heard from his lips was a law regarding the synagogue. How, then, could I possibly part with this work, and leave it to be done by others? Believe me brother, that if I only had the strength I would build this whole *shul* myself, from the foundations to the rafters — but God knows that I no longer have the strength for such an undertaking. At least what I am able to do, I do myself."

Concerning this *shul* Reb Shalom once said that he had located it at such a point that if one were to draw a straight line between its site and Jerusalem, one would encounter neither symbol nor image of idolatrous worship all the way.

◆§ *Longsightedness*

As a number of merchants were passing through Belz on their way home from Lvov to the nearby town of Krasnopoli, Reb Shalom of Belz sent them a message through his *gabbai* requesting them to stay in his town a little while, and to help the construction workers build the local synagogue. Now these men were not chassidim of his, and besides, they were in a hurry to reach home. Nevertheless, they did not feel easy about ignoring his request, so they went along and helped out as he had asked — though every little while they sent one of their number to ask him whether they could finally be on their way. The answer each time was that they should continue in the meantime; he would inform them himself when it was time for them to leave.

A few hours later, when he had finally released them from their task and they were out on the highway on their way home, they encountered a stranger who told them breathlessly: "The river which you have to cross on your way suddenly flooded over its banks. Only an hour or two ago the parish priest, being unprepared, tried to cross, and was drowned."

The impatient merchants now saw the tzaddik's insistence in a different light.

◆§ *Lifeline*

בְּנֵי אֵל חָי
You are the children of the living God (Haftarah)

Reb Naftali of Ropshitz had spent a year studying at the feet of the aged tzaddik Reb Mordechai of Neshchiz, when his teacher one day told him, suddenly: "It is time for you to return to your home."

Since his own entreaties were ignored, Reb Naftali

decided to ask his teacher's *rebbitzin* to try to persuade her husband on his behalf. His answer to her was brief: "I have always taken your advice, and I shall do so now. I only hope that we shall have no cause for regret."

A few days later, while the tzaddik was at *shul,* a stranger visited his home and entered his study. Reb Naftali was there at the time, and no sooner had he laid eyes on this stranger than he perceived that he was besmirched with sin. He was unable to restrain himself, and blurted out: "Get out, you impure fellow! How dare you step over the rebbe's threshold!"

The stranger fled, but Reb Mordechai, sensing what had happened, hastened home and asked: "Who was here?"

When Reb Naftali described the visitor, the tzaddik rebuked him: "Whatever have you done? Quick, quick! Hurry out and bring him here!"

When the stranger was brought in, Reb Mordechai gave him a warm, smiling welcome, and asked him why he had not called on him for so long. The visitor assured the tzaddik that in future he would come more frequently, offered him gifts of his own farm produce, and took his leave.

The tzaddik then explained to Reb Naftali that this man had once been close to him, and the tzaddik had been able to help him keep his distance from evil. Lately, however, various circumstances had combined to prevent him from visiting Neshchiz, and the link between them had been severed. At first he had become sullied with lesser transgressions, but since, as the Sages teach, "One sin brings on another in its train," he reached the point where he asked himself: "How am I going to end up? After all, I am really neither a Jew nor a *goy.* I can hardly go off to Neshchiz to visit the rebbe, for he will recognize at once that I am utterly enslaved to the Evil Inclination. On the other hand, if I don't go, I will simply become more and more deeply entangled in sin." And so he had continued to ponder the possibilities open to him, until finally he had decided to break his ties with his faith, and to become an apostate, God forbid.

But at that point a new idea had entered his head: "Let me make one more trial. I will make the journey to

Neshchiz, and there I will see: if he receives me warmly, that shows that there is hope for me yet; I'll put my life in order, be a good Jew again, and visit the rebbe often, just like I used to do. But if he doesn't, then I'll make a clean break with him and with Judaism altogether."

The tzaddik, understandably enough, had not wanted all his hard work on behalf of this struggler, in speech and in prayer, to be imperiled by Reb Naftali's impetuous tongue. And that was why, some days earlier, he had asked him to go home.

סדר נשא
SIDRA NASSO

◆§ *Putting in a Good Word*

וְהִתְוַדּוּ אֶת חַטָּאתָם
And they shall confess their sin
(5:7)

The disciples of Reb Yisrael of Ruzhin once told him that one of his outstanding chassidim had passed away. The tzaddik had known him well, for all his life he had been an eager disciple, and those who had now delivered these tidings hoped that the tzaddik would be moved to intercede on his behalf in the Heavenly Court. How great therefore was their surprise when instead of that, he uttered a deep sigh, and said: "Oh, but he was a great sinner!"

Their hair stood on end. What could the tzaddik mean by such talk? Why should he choose to join the prosecution in the World Above?

They sought an explanation from his son, Reb Avraham Yaakov, who in later years succeeded his father as rebbe in Sadigora. He spoke as follows: "The whole of creation, as you know, may be perceived in three dimensions — עולם (literally 'world,' that is, space); שָׁנָה (literally 'year,' i.e. time); and נֶפֶש ('soul,' i.e., the spiritual dimension). The choicest *place* in the world is *Eretz Yisrael;* the loftiest spot within the Holy Land is Jerusalem; within the Holy City, the Temple Mount; on the Mount,the Temple courtyard; within it, the site of the Temple; and within that site, the Holy of Holies. The holiest *times* of the year are the days of *Shabbos* and the festivals; and the most elevated of the holy days is Yom Kippur, the Day of Atonement. The loftiest *souls* are those of Israel; within the House of Israel, the Tribe of Levi; within Levi, the *kohanim;* and of all the priestly clan, the *Kohen Gadol,* the High Priest. Now when this High Priest enters the Holy of Holies on the Day of Atonement, what does he say there? 'Your People, the House of Israel, have sinned and transgressed' — for he is the one chosen to confess on behalf of all Israel.

"Unfortunately, the chassid you spoke of did not manage to confess before he passed away. Who, then, is more fit to confess on his behalf than my father?"

◈ *Returning a Favor*

They had already mounted the wagon for the long-awaited journey to Belz — the village leaseholder, with his daughter and future son-in-law — for it was the custom of Reb Shalom of Belz to reserve his blessings for young women until the day of their marriage. As they were about to set out, the leaseholder's wife called out: "And don't forget! Ask the rebbe to pray that we earn a decent living! And that we should bring up our children without problems!"

The horses were already straining in their harness, but she ran after the wagon and reminded her husband: "And another thing! Don't forget to ask that the cows should give plenty of milk! And the harvest — don't forget to ask him to pray that we sell the next harvest at a good profit!"

The wagon rolled out of sight and they soon arrived in Belz, where the father of the bride began to set out his list of requests — a blessing for the young couple, a request for their own livelihood, and so on — faithful to his instructions word for word.

Said Reb Shalom: "The right thing for a man undertaking a journey would be to confess his sins."

The leaseholder did not allow this remark to disturb him, and proceeded as before — the cows, and the milk, and the harvest, and ...

The tzaddik again reminded him that he should confess his sins, whether committed intentionally or unwittingly. When he saw that even now the leaseholder resumed his list unperturbed, the tzaddik assumed that he did not know what confession meant, so he began to translate for him the words of the *Vidui*, one at a time: "אָשַׁמְנוּ – We have transgressed; בָּגַדְנוּ – We have acted perfidiously" – and so on. Even this did not convince the visitor that it was time to react to the rebbe's words, and he took his leave.

On their way home the travelers lost their way in a dense forest, and eventually slithered – horses, wagon, and all – into a deep swamp. They tried to climb down, but sank in the quagmire up to the waist. The man now recalled the words of the tzaddik and they all confessed, each of them knowing his own account, and "from out of the depths," as the Psalmist says, they cried out to God. Suddenly they heard a gentile wagon-driver urging on his horses, and as soon as he reached them – without saying a word – he dragged them all, with their wagon, out of the mire. When he had brought them to a nearby inn they uttered a prayer of thanksgiving for their salvation, and asked the gentile how it was that he had suddenly come to their help.

"Then let me tell you my story," he said. "I was employed by a squire to drive his carriage and to take charge of his stables. Just my luck, and one day his two favorite horses were stolen. He immediately concluded that I had made off with them and sold them, and threw me in his dungeon for a long time. Then he decided he would do better by freeing me, so that I could search for his horses in all the markets and fairs in the district. Not that he sent me alone. I was trailed everywhere by two of his servants whose job it was to make sure I didn't run away. On the way I asked them to let me go to visit the holy man of Belz, for I had heard that he works miracles. They agreed, and came along with me. When I told him my whole sad story, he said: 'If you promise that you will always be friendly to Jews, then in a few days you will find your horses in next week's fair in such-and-such a town.' I gave him my promise, and sure enough I found my horses, just as he had said. I took them home to my master, and he not only compensated me generously for everything he had put me through, but even freed me! With the money he gave me I bought a wagon and horses of my own, and besides that I do some farming on the side. So altogether I can say that I've definitely come up in the world.

"Now just last night the holy man of Belz came to me in my dream and reminded me of my promise. Then he told me to get up quickly and to save a number of Jews who were sinking in the mud at a certain spot. To tell the truth I was a little lazy, and I didn't feel like getting out of bed in the middle of the night to go and help some Jews. But a little while later I dreamed a second time, and he said: 'Why didn't you go as I told you to? Soon they will perish out there!' So I answered: 'Right away, rabbi! I'll go right away!' But I only curled up under my quilt-cover, even more cozily than before. This time, though, when he appeared to me again in my dream, he seized me by my hair, and didn't let go until I had dressed, and harnessed the horses. I galloped off to the place he told me of, looked around for the mire — and there you were!"

◆§ *For Good Measure*

After lighting the Channukah candles, it was the custom of Reb Chaim of Zanz to take his seat next to the fireplace, where he would sit for some time, motionless, in the rapt state of *dveikus*. In awesome silence his chassidim stood about and waited — and then he would give a discourse on the mystical meanings of the festival, and finally pour wine for each of the listeners.

It once happened that during one such holy trance his son Reb Baruch, being weak, fainted. Those around hastened to splash him with water in order to help him come to, but his father remained unaware of all the excitement in the room. When his son returned to his place, pale and drenched, his father finally saw him and asked what had happened, and was told.

Then, with reference to *Vidui*, the confession which is uttered on the approach of death, Reb Chaim asked: "Did you say the confession? When I was young I also fainted several times, and each time, as soon as I began to feel unwell, I said *Vidui.*"

◆§ *Grand Finale*

A thousand miles south of his native Odessa, the once-famous *chazzan* Betzalel Shulsinger lay waning on his deathbed in Jerusalem for three whole days. As the evening of the third day drew near, he suddenly rallied, opened his eyes, and asked for his student cantors, his choir of *meshorerim.*

"Listen,' he said, "and I will tell you a true story. I was one of the close disciples of Reb Meir of Premishlan. On one occasion I approached him, expecting the usual greeting of *Shalom.* Instead of that, however, he quoted a phrase from a Mishnah — not as quotation, but as an expression of wonderment: בֶּאֱמֶת אָמְרוּ הַחַזָּן רוֹאֶה?. [In its context of the laws of *Shabbos,* this phrase refers to the duties of a schoolteacher, the Mishnaic word for which is *chazzan.* In the way it was spoken by Reb Meir, however, it meant: 'Did the Sages really mean that the cantor can see?!'] I understood what he was hinting at. He had no doubt been told that at one stage I had sung in a theater like a common actor, and had thereby defiled my vision through having used my eyes in undesirable directions. I heard his words, and wept in repentance. So the tzaddik turned to me and said: 'Very well, then, I promise you that you will not die before you repent.'

"It seems that I was unable to die before this incident came to mind. They must be waiting Up There for my confession. In that case, my dear choirboys, please prepare yourselves to sing *Vidui — Ashamnu, Bagadnu* — with me.

And in solemn remembrance of the majestic chords to which the old *shul* in Odessa had echoed on Yom Kippur in years gone by, the *chazzan* sat up to sing his tremulous solo while the choirboys around his bed intoned their hushed harmonies. The last magical cadence rose, and then faded. Reb Betzalel bowed deeply to the great Conductor, and returned his soul in peace.

◆§ One Account to Settle

A simple fellow who lived in Jerusalem suffered such agony while in the prolonged throes of death that he begged his callers to pray that God take his soul, and spare him from his misery. For a moment it would seem that welcome death was near at hand — but then it would withdraw.

Among his visitors was one who asked him to recount the story of his life. There was much that he could not recall, but he mentioned in passing that he had once been in Lyzhansk. This set his questioner thinking.

"And did you go to visit the burial place of Reb Elimelech of Lyzhansk?" he asked.

"And is it possible to visit Lyzhansk and not to go to pray at the grave of that tzaddik?" returned the ailing man.

"If so," said the other, "everything is clear. For Reb Elimelech wrote in his will that whoever passed by his grave to pray there could rest assured that he would not die without first having repented. You would be well advised to say *Vidui*, my friend, and to repent."

The sufferer did so, and died thereafter.

◆§ The Soul Sees what the Law Decrees

וְאִם לֹא שָׂטִית
And if you have not strayed (5:19)

Two men once traded in partnership with the help of their wives, one of whom was more expert and active than the other. One day this woman asked her husband: "Who needs this partnership? I am livelier than that other woman, and I have a better business head than she will ever have. She is the kind who will never succeed in any sort of enterprise. Who needs her kind of help?"

Her husband acted on her advice, the partnership was dissolved, and each couple traded separately from then on.

After some time, the merchant whose wife had assumed that כֹּחִי וְעֹצֶם יָדִי עָשָׂה לִי אֶת הַחַיִל הַזֶּה — "My power and the might of my hand have acquired me this wealth" — found that his income was declining, while his former partner was growing wealthy. His wife became so obsessed with envy that she even went to the length of hiring two witnesses to testify falsely that the other woman had been unfaithful to her husband, in order that he should be obliged by law to divorce her. Everything went according to plan — except that its victim, knowing that the court's ruling was unwittingly founded on a cruel lie, asked her husband to accompany her to visit Reb Avraham Yehoshua Heschel of Apta.

Now the *rav* of Apta — who is known as the Ohev Yisrael, "the lover of his fellow Jew" — saw by divine inspiration that the poor woman who stood before him was telling the truth. But was it possible, on the strength of one's *ruach hakodesh* alone, to undo a ruling arrived at by a duly constituted rabbinical court, after it had accepted testimony which was *prima facie* valid?

He called in his son, Reb Yitzchak Meir, and said: "Working on the assumption that I am a tzaddik, people have always been giving me their *pidyon* contributions for charity. Now go out and announce that they should stop at once. Not one penny more! For my *ruach hakodesh* contradicts the laws of the Torah as laid down by a *beis din* — in which case it is not *ruach hakodesh.*"

Now as soon as he uttered these words, the malicious woman and her false witnesses were seized by such a fearful trembling that they too were moved to make the journey to Apta, where they assured the tzaddik that they had conspired to ruin an innocent woman's life because of spiteful jealousy.

The tzaddik of Apta turned to his son: "Now go out and announce that people may indeed give me their *pidyon* offerings, for my *ruach hakodesh* is in harmony with the laws of the Torah."

☙ *Inspired Efficiency*

וְכִפֶּר עָלָיו
And he shall make atonement for him (6:11)

And he shall make atonement for him: The Nazirite sinned by abstaining from wine. And if such a man is called a sinner, how much more will this be true of one who causes himself anguish by refraining from other things *(Talmud, Tractate Taanis).*

Reb Elimelech of Lyzhansk had come to Nikolsburg to spend some time at the feet of his teacher, Reb

נשא

Shmelke. He was walking down the street on *Shabbos,* when he heard someone studying Torah with the voice of one who experiences both the love and awe of Him Who gave the Torah. Entering the house quietly, he stood and watched for an hour, while the young man who was seated there — it was Reb Mordechai Bennet — was so utterly concentrated on the volume of Talmud before him that he did not even notice the presence of a stranger.

At length he paused, and Reb Elimelech approached him: "Repent, brother, repent! Return to the ways of your Maker!"

The scholar was taken aback, and answered nothing; in fact he knew that his rebbe — Reb Shmelke — was very fond of him. He therefore called on Reb Shmelke a little later, and told him that Reb Elimelech had said this thing even though he had seen him doing nothing but studying Torah.

"Let me explain," said Reb Shmelke. "You fasted this whole week through; this must have weakened you, and in some degree hampered your Torah study. And the task of a scholar such as yourself is to study — unhindered!"

◆§ *A Mission of Peace*

וְיָשֵׂם לְךָ שָׁלוֹם *And grant you peace (6:26)*

David of Lelov, accompanied by his disciple Reb Yitzchak of Vorki, set out for a certain town in order to settle a dispute that had brought discord among the townsmen. The moment they arrived they said their prayers, and as soon as they had concluded, Reb David had the horses harnessed so that they could return home immediately.

"Rebbe!" asked Reb Yitzchak in amazement. "Didn't we come here in order to bring peace to this town? Why are we going home now?"

"In the course of our prayers," answered Reb David, "I said ... עֹשֶׂה שָׁלוֹם בִּמְרוֹמָיו — 'He Who makes peace in His heavens, may He make peace for us and for all Israel.' And that sufficed to bring peace upon this town."

◆§ A Burden to Shoulder

בְּכָּתֵף יִשָּׂאוּ
They shall bear it on their shoulders (7:9)

For several hours Reb Yitzchak of Vorki had been closeted with Reb Yechezkel of Kozmir, and when he came out, tears were streaming down his cheeks — but he revealed the cause to no one. Only after his passing was the following account of this meeting given by his son, Reb Yaakov David of Amshinov.

His father had come to Kozmir to consult with Reb Yechezkel as to the choice of his own final resting place. Should it be Vorki, where for many years he had served his Maker, and fired his brethren with the awe of heaven? — Or Warsaw, which he had frequently visited in the course of his many contacts and intercessions with the authorities on behalf of the Jewish community? They had agreed that when his time came he should be buried at Vorki, leaving Warsaw for his son.

And indeed, in 1868 his second son, Reb Menachem Mendel of Vorki, was stricken by a grievous illness. He was brought to Warsaw for treatment, but died there.

Now the custom in that city was that the deceased were not carried to the cemetery by shoulder, but were brought on a special wagon. Now Reb Yechiel of Alexander, one of the disciples of the tzaddik of Vorki, would not agree to this on any account. He went straight to Rabbi Beirish Maisels, the head of the local rabbinical court, and requested that he sanction the carrying of his rebbe by shoulder. The rabbi at first refused to allow such a departure from the established local custom, but when the tzaddik of Alexander begged him again to change his mind, he asked him at least to offer some hint in the Torah that would affirm that the practice he sought implied respect for a sage.

Reb Yechiel was quick to answer. "With regard to one of the Levite families we read in the Torah: כִּי עֲבֹדַת הַקֹּדֶשׁ עֲלֵהֶם בַּכָּתֵף יִשָּׂאוּ. Literally, of course, this means: 'For the sacred work devolves upon them; they shall bear their burdens by shoulder.' But we could also read these words so as to mean something else: 'Those upon whom the sacred work devolves shall be carried by shoulder...'

And the rabbi of Warsaw granted his request.

סדר בהעלתך
Sidra Beha'aloscha

◆§ Spiritual Symbiosis

עִמְדוּ וְאֶשְׁמְעָה מַה יְּצַוֶּה ה׳ לָכֶם
Stand still and I shall hear what God will command concerning you (9:8)

Each of the prayer services rises to its hushed crescendo in the *Shemoneh Esreh,* and on this prayer the Baal Shem used to linger for hours on end. The other worshipers in his *beis midrash* found it difficult to wait until he completed his inspired meditations, so they used to go home to take some refreshment, and on their return they could be sure to find him standing in the same place as before. But the chassidim of stature — his closest disciples who made up the holy brotherhood which was known as the חֶבְרַיָּא קַדִּישָׁא — would wait in deference for their rebbe.

It once happened, though, that even they felt so weak that they too found it necessary to go home to eat something. They were certain that they would come back in good time — hence their surprise to find on their return that the tzaddik had already concluded his devotions. Some of the elder chassidim allowed themselves the liberty of asking him to explain why that day was so different, and he answered: "I will give you a parable. A few men were standing next to a tall tree, and one of them, whose sight was unusually keen, saw an exquisite bird at the tip of the tree. Though he very much wanted to reach up there and catch it, he had no ladder. What did he do? He stood a couple of his friends on top of each others' shoulders, with himself uppermost, reached out, and caught the bird. The men underneath him, though they had helped him catch it, knew nothing of its surpassing beauty — but without them he could not have reached it. Indeed, if the man at the bottom had decided to walk away, they would all have fallen, and the man with the keen vision would not only fail in his aspiration, but would no doubt fall and break his neck.

"Now when I say *Shemoneh Esreh,* it so happens that all manner of hidden things are revealed to me, and my consuming desire is to ascend to the level which the *Zohar* calls 'the palace of the bird's nest' — the palace in the World Above which is the abode of the Messiah. But I cannot aspire to such a lofty height unless I first stand you, my disciples, on each others' shoulders. The entire feat is thus accomplished thanks to yourselves, when you are with me in my *beis midrash,* even though you may not be aware of it. Today, when you left, I fell; having nothing more to do in *Shemoneh Esreh,* I finished off."

A chassid once commented that in the light of this explanation one can understand the verse עִמְדוּ וְאֶשְׁמְעָה מַה יְצַוֶּה ה׳ לָכֶם (literally: "And Moshe said to them, Stand still, and I shall hear what God will command concerning you"). For the verse may be taken as well to suggest that Moshe requests his disciples: "Stand here next to me, and then, by virtue of your merits, I shall be able to hear what God will command."

◆§ *Desiring Mastery vs. Mastering Desire*

הִתְאַוּוּ תַּאֲוָה
They fell a-lusting (11:4)

By no stretch of the imagination could Rabbi Enzil of Staria be termed a sympathizer of Chassidism. Once he tossed the following gibe in the direction of Reb Yehudah Zvi of Rozla: "It seems to me that to be a chassidic rebbe is just a desire like all other desires ... "

The chassidic rebbe was quick with his retort: "You are right — except that one cannot fulfill this desire before one has learned to master all one's other desires.

◆§ *Charity Begins at Home*

הֶאָנֹכִי הָרִיתִי אֵת כָּל הָעָם הַזֶּה
Did I conceive all this People? (11:12)

The son of a certain chassid came to visit Reb Yehudah Aryeh Leib of Ger, the author of *Sfas Emes,* with the complaint that his father gave him no financial support whatever. At his next visit the father was duly asked for an explanation, and he answered that he had no money.

"We read," said the tzaddik, "that Moshe Rabbeinu says to the Almighty: מֵאַיִן לִי בָּשָׂר — 'Whence should I have meat to give all this People?' But in the same breath he has just said הֶאָנֹכִי הָרִיתִי אֵת כָּל הָעָם הַזֶּה אִם אָנֹכִי יְלִדְתִּיהוּ — 'Did I conceive all this People? Did I beget them?' Now this is difficult to understand. For if the speaker wishes to argue that he has no meat, then surely it is immaterial whether he did beget the hungry People, or did not beget them. Either way, will he not still be without meat?

"But this passage proves that if a person says 'I conceived him' and 'I begat him,' then the claim of 'I have not' is insufficient. One is obliged to take pains and find ways and means to support one's son!"

◆§ *It's Only Me*

וְהָאִישׁ מֹשֶׁה עָנָו מְאֹד
And the man Moshe was very humble (12:3)

Hearing that the chassidic book *Noam Elimelech* was written by a disciple of Reb Dov Ber of Mezritch, a certain prominent *misnaged* chose to give unmistakable expression to his sentiments toward "the Sect" by depositing it under the bench he sat on. Nevertheless, when he was once visited by Reb Shneur Zalman of Liadi, he asked his guest to describe for him the character of its author, Reb Elimelech of Lyzhansk.

"Rabbi," said the guest, "even if you were to put the author himself under your bench, he would not say a word."

❀ ❀ ❀

Reb Elimelech once said that he was without a doubt assured of a place in the World to Come. For when his time came to go up to the World Above and he would be asked if he had studied Torah to the best of his ability, he would answer "No"; if he had served God fully through worship, he would say "No"; if he had done his quota of mitzvos and good deeds, he would say "No". Then they would say: "If so, then you are telling us the truth — and in that case you deserve to be rewarded in the World to Come."

❀ ❀ ❀

"Do you know," he would ask, "why people are always coming to me with all kinds of requests, whether for a cure for their children, or for a livelihood for themselves, or whatever? It is because through my sins I have brought suffering into the world. That is why they cry out to me: 'Melech, give us a livelihood! Melech, give us children! It's all your fault that we are lacking these things, so it's up to you to make good what you've spoiled!"

◆§ *Camouflage*

In his youth, Reb Menachem Mendel of Vitebsk studied under Reb Dov Ber, the Maggid of Mezritch. By the time he was ten years old his mastery of the legal intricacies of the Talmud amazed all who saw him, and the Maggid was very fond of him. One *Shabbos* morning he was standing at the door of his study, holding it open for a moment, and as he looked out he saw his young pupil walking up and down the adjoining room in the highest of spirits.

"Mendel!" he called. "How many pages of *Gemara* have you studied today?"

"Six," answered the prodigy.

The Maggid spoke on as if he were thinking aloud: "Let us see. If after six pages of *Gemara* one is so excited that one's hat slips like that over one ear, how many pages does it take for a hat to topple off altogether? ..."

Weeping in remorse, the boy ran to the rebbe's room, knocked on the door, and said: "Rebbe, advise me what to do, for it is true that my studies have made me a little conceited."

"Have no fear," the Maggid reassured him. "Let us travel, you and I, to the Baal Shem Tov, and he will teach us both the path in which we should walk."

They set out on a Tuesday for Mezhibuzh, and arrived on Friday, in good time before *Shabbos*. The Maggid went straight to the Baal Shem Tov to receive his greeting of *Shalom*, while his pupil tarried until he had washed and tidied himself — and indeed he maintained this habit into adulthood, being meticulous about his outward appearance at all times. The Baal Shem Tov, as always, was ready to receive the *Shabbos* with its lyrical prayers of welcome some hours before sunset, but though he stood in his place in the *beis midrash*, he waited some two hours until the boy arrived.

He did not greet him, though, until *Shabbos* had passed. After marking the conclusion of the Day of Rest by the recitation of *Havdalah* he sat down with his pipe, called for young Mendel, and told him a story. But this was no ordinary story, for every episode in it contained a hint of the events which befell its young listener from the moment of his birth until the time of his death many years later in *Eretz Yisrael.* The boy did not listen alone, for both the Maggid and Reb Yaakov Yosef of Polonnoye stood with him. One of them later said that he had understood the whole story while the other confessed that he had understood only half — and the traditions among elder chassidim are divided as to which of these statements is to be attributed to which of these venerable disciples of the Baal Shem Tov. The boy, at any rate, said that he understood that part of the story which related to his life until that day.

The Baal Shem Tov later commented to the Maggid that his pupil appeared to be truthfully humble. And, in fact, to the end of his days Reb Menachem Mendel was to sign הַשָּׁפָל בֶּאֱמֶת — "he who is in fact lowly."

When he reached adulthood, he said that he now comprehended the whole of that story. It happened once while he was still in Vitebsk that he became so ill that he utterly lost the faculty of speech. The wailing of the chassidim, who were fearful that they were about to lose their rebbe, aroused him, and he said: "Have no fear! From the story that the Baal Shem Tov told me I know that one day I am still going to be in *Eretz Yisrael.*"

And so it was. He recovered, and set out for the Holy Land. Passing through Polonnoye, he took up lodgings in an inn, lit up his pipe, removed his *gartl* — the belt which is worn by chassidim for prayer and as an expression of reverence on certain other occasions — and went off to pay his respects to the celebrated tzaddik who lived there, Reb Yaakov Yosef. When the local chassidim saw with what a free and easy air he seemed to be making this awesome visit, they felt it to be their duty to warn him: "Rebbe, we think you ought to know in your own interest that Reb Yaakov Yosef is likely to express his displeasure when he sees such a lack of deference!"

The visitor ignored their advice, and when he spoke to Reb Yaakov Yosef he was received warmly, and was asked whether he understood the story that he had heard from the mouth of the Baal Shem Tov. When he answered that he did, the next question was: "And which part of the story are you up to now?"

Reb Menachem Mendel sighed: "I have already used up more than half of the story."

"And do you know," asked his host, "that there is a hint in the story that you would be visiting me?"

"I do," replied Reb Menachem Mendel, "and that is why I passed through Polonnoye, so that I should have the honor of calling on you."

At length, after a free and cordial exchange of ideas, Reb Yaakov Yosef walked his younger guest to his lodgings.

The local chassidim were curious, so finally some of the elder disciples of Reb Yaakov Yosef broached the question: "What kind of a man is this who dared to pay a visit to you, rebbe, without his *gartl,* and with a long pipe in his mouth, and with silver-threaded shoelaces in his shoes?"

"Come and hear a parable," said the tzaddik. "Once upon a time there was a king who owned a priceless gem, but he lived in constant fear lest thieves discover his best hiding places. What, then, did he do? He hid it in the toilet, for he knew that it would occur to no one to expect to find a treasure *there.* And so it is with Reb Mendel. He is most lowly in his own eyes, and is afraid that whatever visible expression he gives his humility may be misinterpreted in this world of falsehood, thereby nourishing the evil in the cosmos instead of the good. And that is why he has chosen to conceal his humility in a place of filth, namely — pride!"

◆§ *A Vision Earned*

בַּחֲלוֹם אֲדַבֶּר בּוֹ
In a dream do I speak to him (12:6)

Reb Eliezer of Dzikov, the son of Reb Naftali of Ropshitz, dreamed once that he was being shown to the Garden of Eden. He was taken up a luminous hill and found himself in a splendid courtyard, wherein stood a palace built of scintillating jewels. Asking who was the man looking out of the window of the house, he was told that this was Reb Elimelech of Lyzhansk, and to him all of this opulence belonged, though he was master of much besides. Reb Eliezer gazed upon his face, the face of an angel, and experienced a rare moment of spiritual bliss.

Early in the morning he went off to tell his father of his wondrous dream, but Reb Naftali was loath to believe him — until he described the features of the face that he had seen.

"My son," he said, "it is true that it is my rebbe Reb Elimelech that you have described. But a man has to have reached a very lofty level before he is able to see Reb Elimelech."

"What does 'level' mean if not serving God through prayer and the study of Torah?" countered his son. "Then what *do* I do?"

"True again, my son," said Reb Naftali, "that you have reached a certain level. Still, in order to see Reb Elimelech one has to climb even higher. Could it be, for example,that you did someone a great favor, and because of that you were granted this beautiful gift?"

Reb Eliezer recalled that a few weeks earlier he had encountered one of the grandsons of Reb Elimelech making his rounds to collect alms, and he was sorely in need of a warm garment. Reb Eliezer had then taken off his own fine fleece coat and had given it: a dual gift — for while it gave the body warmth, it gave the man esteem.

"Now," exclaimed his father, "it is clear that you did in fact see Reb Elimelech, and that you deserved to see what you saw! For Reb Elimelech asked the Almighty that his descendants should be reduced to begging, so that they should remain righteous, and he retains a liking for anyone who helps them without indignity."

◆§ *Leaving it to His Discretion*

בְּכָל בֵּיתִי נֶאֱמָן הוּא
For he is trusted in My house (12:7)

Reb Nachum of Stefanesti, the son of Reb Yisrael of Ruzhin, once said of his brother, Reb David Moshe of Chortkov: "As soon as he opens his Book of *Psalms* and starts reading *Tehillim,* the Almighty says to him, 'David Moshe, my son! I am now entrusting the whole world into your hands; do with it as you will.' Now if that were to happen to me, then I would most certainly know what to do with the world. But my brother is such a faithful servant that he returns it to the Almighty exactly as he was given it ..."

◆§ To Give Each Man His Due

וּמַדּוּעַ לֹא יְרֵאתֶם לְדַבֵּר בְּעַבְדִּי בְמֹשֶׁה
Why then were you not afraid to speak against my servant Moshe? (12:8)

Rabbi Aryeh Leib Heller, the author of *Ketzos HaChoshen,* was an opponent of Chassidism, and it so happened that a great number of chassidim of Reb Yaakov Yitzchak of Lublin lived in his hometown, Staria. If the truth were to be told, there was no great love lost between the two sides, and the chassidim did not show him the respect that is due to a *mara de'asra,* the local rabbinic authority. The rabbi, for his part, was in the habit of reproving these nonconformist townsfolk for their chassidic customs, which he held to contravene the dictates of the Code of Jewish Law. He felt that it was improper that his rulings should be ignored, and eventually pronounced a ban of temporary excommunication on them, which was to last thirty days. Obedient to this *shamta,* the bulk of the local population promptly severed all contact with them. The chassidim put their heads together, and decided to set out to Lublin, there to spend the few weeks in the heartwarming company of their rebbe, until with the passage of time they would find themselves a little less unwelcome in their own hometown.

Now the custom in Lublin was that the *shammes* would bring the rebbe — who is known as the Chozeh, or Seer, of Lublin — a list of all the recent arrivals who were waiting to be greeted by him; the rebbe would then indicate who was to be invited to enter his study for a private *yechidus.* When the group from Staria arrived, the Chozeh told the *shammes* that they would have to wait to receive their greeting for two weeks and so-and-so many days — exactly as long as it would take for the *shamta* to expire ...

When the time finally passed, they came together to speak to the Chozeh, who said: "We read in the Torah that the Almighty rebukes Aharon and Miriam with the question, 'Why then were you not afraid to speak against my servant Moshe?' Since these words appear to be repetitious, Rashi comments: *'Against My servant —*

even if he were not Moshe; *against Moshe* — even if he were not My servant.' Now the first half of this comment is understandable. But such a Moshe who is not 'My servant' — why should one stand in awe of *him?*

"And the answer is as follows. The House of Israel is made up of two categories of people: those whose main concern is to be expert and punctilious as regards every word in the Code of Jewish Law, and those whose first love is to cleave to God in devoted *dveikus,* serving him not only in prayer, but also — as is explained at length in *Duties of the Heart* — in the manner of their walking and sitting, lying down and rising, their eating and their drinking. This, then, is what Rashi means. One is commanded to stand in awe of Moshe — the great legalistic scholar — even if he is not 'My servant' in the sense of having unceasing communion with God; likewise in awe of 'My servant' — who delves rather into the mysteries of the Torah, in order to draw closer to his Maker — even though he may not be a Moshe in his mastery of the legalistic side of the Torah. Both are to be held in awe.

"And if this be the case, consider now the *rav* of your town, who is a veritable pillar of the revealed Law. *Why were you not afraid to speak against him?"*

סדר שלח

Sidra Sh'lach

◆§ *Unfinished Symphony*

שְׁלַח לְךָ אֲנָשִׁים וְיָתֻרוּ
Send men to spy out (13:2)

Reb Yaakov Yitzchak (the Yid HaKadosh) of Pshischah once fell violently ill while on a visit to his rebbe, Reb Yaakov Yitzchak (the Chozeh) of Lublin. His son hurried to the Chozeh to ask him to intercede in heaven on his father's behalf, and received the following answer.

"In connection with the twelve spies whom Moshe Rabbeinu sent to the Land of Canaan, it is written: 'Send men to spy out.' Now it sometimes happens that the Heavenly Court sees that a certain Jew has completed the tasks which were divinely allocated for him during his stay in This World, that he has elevated whatever it was his duty to elevate. In such a case, the Almighty *sends* him willing disciples, men who are eager to *spy out* the way in which they should go. When a person is thus given a fresh task, he is enabled thereby to continue living in This World."

And so indeed it was. The Yid HaKadosh was immediately restored to health, and from that time on he became the spiritual mentor of thousands of his fellows.

☙ *The Wondrous Ways of Heaven (i)*

וַיָּבֹא עַד חֶבְרוֹן
And he came to Hebron (13:22)

And he came to Hebron: Caleb went there in order to pray at the graves of the Patriarchs *(Rashi).*

An upright young merchant once set out from his home in Vilkomir to buy up stocks of tobacco in Niezhin. Though not a chassid himself, he was on very friendly terms with a celebrated chassid by the name of Reb Yaakov Kaidaner, so before he left he called on Reb Yaakov, who said: "My friend! Even though you are not one of our chassidic brotherhood, I would still ask you to visit the grave of a renowned tzaddik who is buried in Niezhin, Reb Dov Ber of Lubavitch, the son of Reb Shneur Zalman of Liadi."

The young man gave his promise, was bidden farewell, and set out for a journey that was to take six months, for in those days there was not yet any railway train that could clatter its way all the distance from Vilkomir in Lithuania to Niezhin in White Russia. While he was far away trying to do business, his wife became so desperately ill that the doctors despaired of her life. One evening she lost consciousness, and though three expert physicians sat by her bedside all night, there was nothing they could do to help her. Then at ten in the morning her illness loosened its hold on her, she began to regain her strength, and within a month, without the aid of doctors or medicaments, she was strong and robust. Her friends were amazed, but not nearly so much as were her doctors.

When her husband finally came home, he barely

managed to put his nose inside the door when he ran off in agitation to the home of his friend Reb Yaakov, without so much as stopping to take off his overcoat.

"Now I ask you," said Reb Yaakov, "is this the way to do things? After you have been away from home for over half a year you don't even stay there a little while to gladden the hearts of your wife and little ones, but off you run to say hello to me?! There must be something behind your behavior, something remarkable."

"And indeed," affirmed the other, "something remarkable did bring me to you, something of a marvel. You see, my business dealings out there fell through, and I not only lost everything I owned, but as well got myself deep into debt through all kinds of unfortunate circumstances that befell me on the way. To make things worse, throughout all that time I was in a state of fear: I seemed to imagine that my wife was desperately ill. When I arrived in Niezhin I recalled my promise to you, and went to the local *mikveh* to immerse myself in preparation for my visit to the holy resting place of the tzaddik. Though all the way there my warm clothes had sufficed to keep out the bitter cold, as soon as I came close to where he lay I was overcome by an awesome fear, the like of which I have never experienced. My hair stood on end, and despite my warm clothes I trembled in a feverish cold. It even occurred to me to flee from that fearful place, but then I thought: 'No evil is going to befall me on account of the tzaddik who lies here. Why should I flee from the presence of the tzaddik?' So I began instead to read the quotations from the *Zohar*, and the chapters from *Psalms*, and other passages from *Maavar Yabok*, which are inscribed there on a tablet, on the wall of the enclosure which is built around the grave. And while I read, I wept rivers of tears. Then I wrote out two notes which expressed my special requests — one *kvitl* bearing a prayer for the welfare of my family and myself, and the other especially for my wife, for my heart was uneasy. The moment I put those two *pidyonos* on the grave, I was overcome with a most exquisite joy, the like of which I had never known before. It was just as I imagine the flavor of the Garden of Eden to be. It took me two full hours to tear myself away from that bliss, and to depart from there with a heart full of gladness and peace.

"That joy accompanied me all the way home, and when I arrived, I was told the whole story of what my wife had been through, including the events of that long, long night that ended only at ten in the morning. I asked what date this had been. Sure enough, it was the very day on which, at ten o'clock in the morning, I had placed the *pidyonos* on the resting place of the tzaddik. You cannot be surprised, therefore, that when I heard all of this, I did not even take off my greatcoat, but ran as fast as I could to tell you, my friend, of the wondrous ways of heaven.

"I have only one thing to add. If your rebbes are so alive and luminous *after* they have departed from This World, then they must be even greater and even holier in their lifetime!"

"Not so," answered Reb Yaakov. "For our Sages have taught: 'Tzaddikim are greater in their death than in their life.' "

◆§ *The Wondrous Ways of Heaven (ii)*

Reb Moshe Teitelbaum of Ujhely, the author of *Yismach Moshe,* saw that his nine-year-old son was so ill that he was in mortal danger. He prayed to heaven for mercy, and sent a number of righteous men to Lyzhansk to do likewise at the resting place of Reb Elimelech. He instructed them that when they arrived at the entrance to the cemetery they should say: "We hereby promise to give a copper coin to charity for the benefit of the soul which will go and inform the soul of Reb Elimelech that we have come to his resting place to pray to the Almighty." Then, he went on to explain, "All the souls that are then in the vicinity will hasten to pass on the message to the tzaddik, for it is not at all times that a man's soul is to be found near the place of his burial; and the souls of the departed are always eager to 'earn' the coin which is given in the World Below for the greater elevation of their souls. You are then to approach his grave, where you will pray for my son. And mark well what time it is that you pray there."

The chassidim of course followed their rebbe's instructions exactly.

Meanwhile, back in Ujhely, the little boy suddenly sat up out of his feverish stupor and said: "Father! With God's help I'm going to be well now! For just this moment I was visited by a venerable old man" — and the description he gave exactly matched the appearance of Reb Elimelech — "and he blessed me, and promised me that I would get better!"

His father looked at his watch, and saw there — as it transpired some days later when his chassidim returned — exactly the same time that they had seen on their watches that day in far-off Lyzhansk.

☙ *To be Cruel to be Kind*

וַיֹּצִיאוּ דִּבַּת הָאָרֶץ *And they spread an evil report of the Land (13:32)*

From the example of the spies sent by Moshe Rabbeinu we may observe how great is the power of slander *(Talmud, Tractate Arachin).*

Before he became renowned as a tzaddik, Reb Yisrael of Koznitz was a tutor in a well-to-do household. As Pessach drew near, and it was time for him to go home, his employer approached him with a suggestion.

"I would advise you," he said, "to come with me to Chenshin for the *Shabbos* before the festival, and there we will be able to hear the discourse which will be given in honor of *Shabbos HaGadol* by the rabbi there. They say he is quite a scholar. Besides, the rabbi's *mechutan* will be there, and you will be able to ride back to your hometown in his carriage, instead of having to plod all the way on foot."

Reb Yisrael thanked him for his suggestion, and on the eve of *Shabbos HaGadol* they called on the rabbi of Chenshin to pay their respects, as too did all the worthies of the town. The householder mentioned to the rabbi that his *melamed* was outstanding in both scholarship and piety. But when the host took one look at the *melamed* — a man of unprepossessing presence, short of stature, though with a pleasant face and kindly eyes — he disdained him. When he had nevertheless given his hand in greeting, he asked the newcomer where he came from.

 Reb Yisrael answered that he came from Apta, and his employer whispered to the rabbi that his *melamed's* father was Reb Shabsi the bookbinder.

The rabbi could not restrain the offensive jest that immediately sprang to his mind, and at the expense of his guest's self-respect he allowed himself to pun on the similarity between קֹרַח (Korach, the rebel who was swallowed up by the earth) and כּוֹרֵךְ (*korech,* which means "bookbinder").

"In that case," he said expansively, "we are related! For I am Levi, and the descendants of Korach are Levites, too. And didn't you say this fellow's father is a *korech?"*

The *melamed's* face dropped, and he left.

Now the time-honored custom in learned Torah circles is that when a scholar advances a legal hypothesis before an academic audience, any listener who finds a fallacy in his reasoning is allowed to interject and challenge him. The next day, then, the *melamed* went along to the *beis midrash* to hear the same rabbi's discourse. But every novel deduction that he proposed, the young visitor refuted. Whenever the rabbi attempted to reconstruct his thesis, the stranger rebutted him again — until the rabbi lost his dispassionate objectivity, took offense, and left in a huff. It was clear that he held his congregants to be at fault for allowing this young upstart to show up his failings in public. And Reb Yisrael, seeing the vengeful way the wind was blowing, promptly left the *beis midrash,* and hid.

On *Motzaei Shabbos,* though, when the Day of Rest had passed, he called on the rabbi alone in order to make the peace — but the rabbi refused to forgive him. At this point the future Maggid of Koznitz was forced to reveal to him that he had acted as he had during the discourse for the rabbi's own good. For when he had offended him and insulted him the day before, the Heavenly Court had sentenced him to death, and only through the efforts of the Maggid had the Court agreed to avert the decree — by substituting the punishment of being shamed in public.

◆§ Some are More Equal

A God-fearing young scholar from Apta, the son of an honest workman, was conscripted to serve in the ranks of the brutal battalions of those times. On Friday afternoon, when Reb Avraham Yehoshua Heschel (the Ohev Yisrael) was resting on a seat just outside the local bathhouse before returning home, he turned to the prominent citizens who were sitting around him, and appealed to their finer feelings: perhaps they could find a way to ransom this young man from the violent fate that awaited him?

They were all convinced readily enough — until one of their number spoke up: "I sure don't know why you, rebbe, should exert yourself so much to ransom this young fellow, what's-his-name's son. After all, if what's-his-name's son is missing from our town, won't our town be a town any more?"

And that comment was enough to cool off the enthusiasm of the little group.

The tzaddik was taken aback. He rose and re-entered the bathhouse, while the speaker headed for home. On his way there, however, he was gored by an ox, and was carried home in a critical state. When his family heard from bystanders that it seemed that he had offended the rebbe, they hastened to appease him, and met him as he came out of the bathhouse.

The Ohev Yisrael assured them: "I did not punish him, God forbid, nor did I pray that he be punished — especially since I have been in the bathhouse all this time, and as you know one may not say a single word of prayer in there. To tell you the truth, though, when he made his comment — 'If what's-his-name's son is missing from our town, won't our town be a town any more?' — the thought occurred to me: 'If *this* citizen is missing from our town, won't our town be a town any more?' I made every effort to prevent that thought from occupying my mind, but I had no choice in the matter. It was heaven's will that it be there."

And a short time later, as a result of his wounds, that citizen was in fact missing from the town.

◆§ A Venomous Tongue

It once happened that the sons of Reb Yaakov Yitzchak (the Yid HaKadosh) of Pshischah were afraid to leave Lvov, because they had no passports. One night a certain rich merchant introduced himself to them and put himself at their service — he invited them to his home for *Shabbos* and offered to conduct them without fear or hindrance to wherever they needed to go. And, in the course of their conversation, he recounted an incident that involved their father many years earlier.

"I was once a tutor in a household not far from Lublin," he began. "During one of my visits there to see Reb Yaakov Yitzchak, the Chozeh of Lublin, I encountered another visitor, Reb Kissele by name, who said all kinds of slanderous things to the Chozeh about your father. And how did I come to hear this *lashan hara?* Well, they were closeted together in a room, but I hid behind a wardrobe in order to overhear the conversation. I was so overwrought by what I heard there that I couldn't restrain myself. I bounded out from my hiding place, grasped the *tefillin* of the Chozeh which were then on the table (for he was wearing the *tefillin* of Rabbeinu Tam at the time), and I said: 'I hereby swear, as I hold this sacred object in my hand, that every word this man is saying is an unspeakable lie!'

"Reb Kissele left the room in a hurry, and the Chozeh thanked me for my rude interruption. Then he went on: 'For the last forty years Satan has been guarding Reb Kissele from even thinking an improper thought, so that his credibility should be such that I should now be prepared to believe what he said about the Yid HaKadosh!'

"Now your father saw all of this through Divine Inspiration, and in a few minutes the word spread that he had arrived. I ran ahead and told him the whole story, and he gave me his blessing for success. And indeed, from that day on I am a rich man, for God prospers whatever enterprise I put my hand to.

"And now tonight your father appeared to me in a dream and told me that you were here in my town,and that you were in a fix. Do come to my home for *Shabbos*,

I beg you; all your needs I will take care of, with God's help, and then I will see you safely on your way."

◆§ Rose-Colored Spectacles

טוֹבָה הָאָרֶץ מְאֹד מְאֹד

The Land is very very good (14:7)

Year by year Reb Shmuel Abba of Zichlin would send many thousands of rubles to *Eretz Yisrael* for the paupers there, and in addition, a separate sum every three months for a family for which he retained a particular affection — the children of Reb Moshe of Lelov.

One of his chassidim once returned from the Holy Land with a letter for his rebbe written by Rabbi Meir Auerbach, the author of *Imrei Binah,* who had formerly been head of the rabbinical court in Kalisz, and was now a prominent *rav* in Jerusalem. In the letter this sage expressed surprise that money should be sent especially for a family that did not seem to invest their time in holy pursuits.

The tzaddik of Zichlin read the letter and said: "It will all become clear to Rabbi Meir in due course ... "

Some time later a wealthy chassid called Reb Leib Koshmirk made the voyage to *Eretz Yisrael.* When he visited Rabbi Meir, he was asked to call in again in order to take a letter to his rebbe on his return home. When he duly came again, Rabbi Meir told him that this letter was an expression of regret and apology for his earlier remarks.

Reb Leib was curious: "If I may ask, rabbi, what did you think then, and what makes you now think otherwise?"

The scholar explained: "A few weeks after I had written my first letter, an old man appeared to me in a dream and rebuked me. 'How dare you,' he demanded, 'write slanderous comments to a tzaddik about the holy children of Reb Moshe of Lelov?' So I protested in my dream: 'But I see various faults in them!' He answered: 'That is only because you are lacking in humility. Ifyou manage one day to acquire that attribute, you will find all kinds of positive qualities in them. For after the other spies had slandered the Holy Land, Yehoshua and Caleb insisted: טוֹבָה הָאָרֶץ מְאֹד מְאֹד. Literally, this means *The Land is very, very good.* But at the same time that verse reminds one of a Mishnah which says מְאֹד מְאֹד הֱוֵי שְׁפַל רוּחַ — *Be very, very lowly of spirit.* You see, when a person reaches the level of humility, the מְאֹד מְאֹד, of which the Mishnah speaks, then he sees only מְאֹד מְאֹד טוֹבָה הָאָרֶץ — he sees only that the Land is very, very good, and sees no evil there, God forbid!'

"I awoke from my dream," concluded Rabbi Meir Auerbach, "and recalled the letter I had written to the tzaddik of Zichlin. I then worked steadily on myself for a long time with the aim of becoming more and more humble — and now, in the very same children of Reb Moshe of Lelov, I can see all kinds of positive and attractive qualities."

◈§ *How to Spell the Name of God*

וַיֹּאמֶר ה׳ סָלַחְתִּי כִּדְבָרֶיךָ
And God said: I have forgiven according to your word (14:20)

The Yid HaKadosh of Pshischah once related the following episode from his childhood.

"When I was a little boy, still being taught the *aleph-beis* by my *melamed,* I learned a lesson to last a lifetime: that when two people sit together over a glass of vodka, and each of them is willing to play down his ego for the sake of his friend, and neither of them considers himself higher than the other — then the Almighty forgives them all their sins.

"You see, one day I asked my *melamed:* 'What is one dot?' And he answered: 'The letter *yud.*' I asked again: 'And what about two dots?' So he said: 'Two *yuds* spell out the holy Name of God.'

"Some days later I saw a colon in a book, and asked him whether this too spelled the Name of God. So he answered: 'There is an easy way to tell. If you see these two *yuds* on a level, neither trying to raise itself up over its comrade, then you have the holy Name of God. But if you have the same two dots on *top* of each other, that is definitely no holy Name.'

"From that I gathered that two Jews who meet over a glass, neither of them considering himself superior to the other, together constitute the Name of God. For the word for glass, כּוֹס, is made up of the initial letters of וַיֹּאמֶר סָלַחְתִּי כִּדְבָרֶךָ — 'And He said: I have forgiven according to your word.' But the second word of the verse is still

שלח

missing — the Name of God. However, when these two Jews meet over their glass of vodka in the way we've been talking about, then *they* make up the Name of God, as we said before. And now we have the verse in full: וַיֹּאמֶר ה׳ סָלַחְתִּי כִּדְבָרֶךָ — 'And God said: I have forgiven according to your word.'

"You see, then, how it is that when two Jews meet the way they should, the Almighty forgives them all their sins!"

◆§ *A Perceptive Eye*

רֵאשִׁית עֲרִסֹתֵכֶם *The first of your dough (15:20)*

Reb Meirke of Mir, one of the chassidim of Reb Mordechai of Lechovitch, once interrupted a journey in order to enter an inn to say his prayers. While he was there a whole caravan of wagons arrived, full of itinerant paupers with their wives and little waifs. Reb Meirke saw one man in their midst, of old and venerable appearance, whose face bespoke a rare purity of mind. As he watched him closely, the inkeeper's wife placed bread and other food on the table, and while the other poor folk all grabbed their slices to allay their hunger, that old pauper walked deliberately over to the water basins, and examined a dipper carefully to see if it was suitable for *netilas yadayim*. Before washing his hands, however, he took up the slice of bread over which he was due in a moment to say the blessing *HaMotzi* — but he immediately laid it down, took instead some other bread that was there, and sat down to eat.

The paupers all left the inn soon after, and this old man left with them. But throughout his prayers and his evening meal, Reb Meir could not stop thinking about that aged beggar. *Why did he not eat that slice of bread?*

He had to find out. He approached the landlady and asked: "Excuse me, but when did you bake that bread?"

"Why yesterday or the day before," she replied.

"And do you recall," he continued, "whether you remembered at the time to separate the tithe of *challah* from the dough?"

"Woe is me!" exclaimed the woman. "I forgot to take off the tithe!"

It was now clear to Reb Meirke that this old man was

 divinely inspired. He immediately harnessed his horses and made all haste to catch up to that ragged crew, whom he found soon enough — though his man was nowhere to be seen.

"Where is that old man who was with you?" he asked.

"Why should you ask after that crazy old fellow?" they answered. "He tagged on to us a few weeks ago, and he travels wherever we travel, and sleeps wherever we sleep — but he behaves as if he was out of his mind. Look, sometimes he leaves us for a while and stands alone for some time among the bushes in the forest. And once, in midwinter, when he saw a lake frozen over, he broke the ice and went for a dip in that freezing cold water."

When Reb Meirke now followed the direction in which they pointed, he came upon this strange man standing under a tree, entranced in his thoughts, his face burning like a brand.

"Rebbe, bless me!" he exclaimed.

The pauper asked him for a copper coin, and then gave his blessing.

When in due course Reb Meirke again visited Lechovitch to see his rebbe, Reb Mordechai, and told him the whole story, the tzaddik said: "How fortunate you are! For the man who gave you his blessing was none other than the saintly Reb Leib Sarahs!"

❀ ❀ ❀

This same Reb Meirke once lost his way while traveling alone through a forest. As evening fell he spotted a house with a stable next to it, and on entering the house found no one at home but a woman who was busy cooking.

"Is there room here to lodge for the night?" he asked.

"Most certainly," she said.

But when the owners of the house came home later at night, he saw at once that they were a gang of murderers. Nor was he at all reassured to overhear the women telling them: "We have a very worthwhile guest ... "

There was no chance to escape; every door and every window was locked. He therefore found himself in a quiet corner, and as he recited *Vidui,* wept over his confession with the honest tears of a man who is nearing his end. When they had finished their rude meal, they pounced on him from all sides and bound him hand and foot, ready for the slaughter.

"Open up, there!" a raucous voice snarled at the window.

The murderers were so alarmed by the insistent battering on the shutters that they were afraid to oblige. But the cold was bitter outside. The impatient callers broke down the door, and a noisy crowd of sturdy Russian merchants, who had also lost their way, burst their way in. In a flash they gathered what was going on before their eyes. A couple of them unbound the poor victim, while the others seized the murderers and trussed them up. At daybreak they lifted them on to their wagons and drove off to the nearest town, where they handed them over to the local gendarmerie.

"You wont't believe this," they said to Reb Meirke, "but we often take this road, and know it well. In fact we have never lost our way around these parts. But today for some funny reason we somehow got mixed up and strayed from the highway, until we landed here. It is clearly the finger of God, so that we should be able to save you from death."

When Reb Meirke next visited Reb Mordechai of Lechovitch, no sooner had he appeared in the doorway than his rebbe said: "It's all because of you that I couldn't sleep that night. But thanks to the fact that you once gave a coin to Reb Leib Sarahs, and received his blessing, those merchants lost their way and arrived out there just in time to save you."

◆§ *Memory and Piety*

לְמַעַן תִּזְכְּרוּ
In order that you may remember (15:40)

A scholarly chassid once came to Kotsk and complained to Reb Menachem Mendel of weakness of memory in his studies.

"Why, the Torah itself gives us a *sgulah* to improve the memory," said the tzaddik. And he went on to quote excerpts from two adjacent verses in the *Shema,* omitting the words that follow them in order to make his point. "It is written ... וְלֹא תָתוּרוּ אַחֲרֵי לְבַבְכֶם וְאַחֲרֵי עֵינֵיכֶם

לְמַעַן תִּזְכְּרוּ! — 'You shall not stray after your hearts and after your eyes ... *in order that you may remember!"*

◆§ *Memory and Modesty*

It was an ordinary weekday, but Reb Yitzchak Meir of Ger — then still living in Warsaw — had invited all of his closest chassidim to a festive meal, and he sat radiant at the head of the long table in his *Shabbos* garb. When asked for an explanation, he said: "In my childhood I once visited Reb Yisrael, the Maggid of Koznitz. There were all kinds of learned folk there, and he asked whether anyone present could clarify a certain problematic commentary by *Tosafos* on the Talmudic tractate *Bava Metzia.* No one was able to answer. I jumped up and said: 'This passage means so-and-so.' The Maggid gave me a gentle slap on the cheek and said: 'When no one else knows the answer, one doesn't jump forward and give it!' I immediately forgot the explanation I had just given, and was never able to recall it — *until today.* And that is why I am celebrating."

◆§ *An Unforgettable Memory*

The sons of Reb Menachem Mendel of Lubavitch, who is known as the Tzemach Tzedek, were once sitting with a group of chassidim, exchanging reminiscences of their father. Reb Shmuel, later his successor in Lubavitch, recounted the following, for example: "A certain scholar and I were once wrestling with a complex Talmudic problem when my father, who had been sitting in the adjoining room, joined us, and explained it so beautifully that we thought he had just been working on it himself. When he had completed his exposition he mentioned that it was thirty-five years since he had last thought over this problem."

Another son, Reb Yehudah Leib, later rebbe in Kopust, rejoined: "Why, do you folk think that the marvel is that he remembered what he had thought thirty-five years earlier? Not at all! The marvel is that he remembered that in the course of those thirty-five years this thought had not occupied his mind. From this we see that all his thoughts of thirty-five years were preserved in his memory to the point that he was able to say what he had thought and what he had not thought in the course of that period."

סדר קרח
Sidra Korach

◆§ *An Unintentional Compliment*

ומדוע תתנשאו
Why do you raise yourselves up? (16:3)

The chassid who served as the *shammes* of Reb Yitzchak of Vorki once recalled that when he had accompanied the rebbe on one of his many missions to Warsaw for the public good, they had returned in the evening only to find their hotel door besmirched from top to bottom with all manner of insults and abuse against the rebbe. From sheer embarrassment the *shammes* did not know which way to look, but the rebbe reassured him: "Do not allow this to dampen your spirits. For I learned a lesson on this subject from the *Ilui* ['genius' — so was Reb Yitzchak in the habit of referring to his teacher, Reb Avraham Moshe, the son of Reb Simchah Bunem of Pshischah]. My teacher used to point out that those who foment controversy always slander that very attribute of character about which their victim is most vigilant. In support of this observation he used to cite the case of Korach, whose complaint to Moshe Rabbeinu was: 'Why do you raise yourselves up over the congregation of God?' — as if he were arrogant — whereas the Torah itself testifies that 'The man Moshe was very humble, more so than all the men on the face of the earth."

◆§ *A Painful Paradox*

Though he was emphatically anything but a chassid, a certain sage was so bothered by his problem that he decided to pose it to Reb Yaakov Yitzchak, the Chozeh of Lublin.

"Why, rebbe," he asked, "should so many thousands flock to you from all sides? What can they see here? And why don't they come to me? For am I not a greater scholar than yourself?"

"To tell you the truth," confided the Chozeh placidly, "I am quite as amazed as you are. For I know my true worth. Who am I, what am I, that people should come to me in search of ways to approach their Maker? And why, in fact, should they not go to visit yourself, whom I know to be a scholar of unquestioned repute, a veritable Mount Sinai in the knowledge of Torah?

"But perhaps here lies the catch. Because I am surprised that people come to me, that is *why* they come to me; and because you are surprised that they do not come to you, that is why, rabbi, they do not come to you ... "

◆§ *I Cannot Tell a Lie*

During the time that Reb Yaakov Yitzchak (the Chozeh) was rebbe in Lublin, the city's rabbinical seat was occupied by Rabbi Azriel Horovitz, whose logical acumen was so invincible that he was nicknamed "the iron-headed." He made it his business to constantly bother the Chozeh with all kinds of questions, but especially with the charge that though he himself knew that he was not really a rebbe, he nevertheless continued to draw a large following after him and to teach them his ways.

"But what can I do about it," argued the Chozeh, "if they all make the journey here of their own accord?"

"Simple," said the rabbi. "Next *Shabbos* announce to your followers that you are not a rebbe, and then they will leave you alone and stop coming to you."

Sure enough, the tzaddik faithfully took his advice. The very next *Shabbos* he stood up meekly before his congregation, and told them in plain, quiet words that he was really a man of very poor worth indeed. The effect, though, was not as expected. His chassidim were so moved by the genuine self-effacement of their rebbe that they made every attempt to emulate his humility, and cleaved to him more ardently than ever.

When the Chozeh next met the *rav*, he told him that

he had followed his advice, but to no avail.

The *rav* now had an alternative suggestion: "Your chassidim love humility and spurn arrogance. Tell your followers, therefore, that you are a true tzaddik. Then they will be *sure* to go home and leave you in peace."

"I may not be a rebbe," returned the Chozeh, "but neither am I a liar. How, then will I be able to get up and say that I am a true tzaddik?"

◆§ A Searching Question

וַיִּשְׁמַע מֹשֶׁה וַיִּפֹּל עַל פָּנָיו
And Moshe heard and he fell on his face (16:4)

A *misnaged* once came to Reb Shneur Zalman of Liadi and expressed his antagonism to the chassidic movement by confronting him with allegations of pride — for did he not have an attendant at his door, and so forth? The tzaddik rested his head on his arms, just as one does during the penitential *Tachanun* prayer, and after an interval of silence replied: "The expression the Torah uses for the leaders of the People is רָאשֵׁי אַלְפֵי יִשְׂרָאֵל — 'the heads of the thousands of *Yisrael*' — from which we see that our leaders are known as 'heads'. Now even though the head and body are joined to each other, nevertheless they are clothed separately, and differently. Why so? Because the head must be distinct from the body, just as the heads of any generation must be separate from the people."

The questioner found the answer satisfactory, and went on his way. But the rebbe's son, later to be renowned as Reb Dov Ber of Lubavitch, was left with a different question: "In order to give that answer there was no need to rest your head in your arms. Why did you not give him his answer immediately?"

Replied his father: "In the episode of Korach, first we read 'Why, then, do you raise yourselves up over the People of God,' then we read 'And Moshe heard, and he fell on his face.' Only later did Moshe give his answer — that in the morning God would make the matter clear. The same question could be asked there. Why did Moshe first fall on his face, before giving his answer? But Moshe Rabbeinu suspected for a moment that perhaps this question was really being asked of him from Above, while Korach was no more than a messenger. If this were so, and he were to give an answer at once, then some other questioner would no doubt be summoned from Above to pose the same query afresh. He therefore fell on his face first, in order to meditate a while as to whether there really was any fragment of pride in himself. After he had found that this was not the case — as the Torah itself avers: 'The man Moshe was very humble' — he knew now that this was no divine messenger confronting him, but simply quarrelsome Korach. Only then could he go ahead and give his answer.

"And a similar thing happened here today ... '

◆§ *In Defense of the Living*

וַיַּעֲמֹד בֵּין הַמֵּתִים וּבֵין הַחַיִּים
And he stood between the dead and the living (17:13)

An epidemic had broken out in Vloshchov, and a respectful delegation of householders came to ask Reb Shlomo of Radomsk to return with them to his hometown to pray for its stricken residents. He was greeted on his approach by the venerable sages of the town, headed by the local *rav*, and behind them the whole eager populace, men, women and children, all decked out in their *Shabbos* best, with music and dancing and firebrands.

"How great is the *ruach hakodesh* of the Yid HaKadosh of Pshischah!" exlaimed Reb Shlomo as he saw the sight before him. "For I recall that when he once visited this town — I was then a little boy — all the townsfolk came out to greet him with due pomp. My father, Reb Hirschele, who was the respected lay head of the community, traveled with the Yid HaKadosh in his carriage, and sat me on his lap. When the tzaddik saw me there next to him, he tweaked my cheek in a grandfatherly way, and said: '*Nu, nu* ... When you come here, you'll be honored more!"

The next day the tzaddik instructed all the townsfolk to walk with him around the edge of the local cemetery, and then he began as follows: "Concerning Aharon the High Priest we read, 'And he stood between the dead and the living, and the plague was stayed.' Now reason dictates that there should be only living people, not dead — for what use does the Almighty have from the dead? Even if they are righteous and dwell in the Garden of

Eden, what benefit does he have from them as they sit there, basking in the soothing warmth of Paradise? But living people thank, and pray, and praise, and bless! Besides, they drink *LeChaim* now and again! [And here Reb Shlomo indulged in a fanciful play on the similarity between לְחַיִּים — the toast *To Life!* that accompanies a convivial sip of vodka, and לְחָיַיִם — the jowls of the sacrificial animal offered as a reminder of *prayer,* which is breathed and mouthed by the worshiper.] When Pinchas prayed to God that he remove the plague, he pointed out to the Almighty these two advantages of the living over the dead: first, that they pray; and secondly, that they say *LeChaim.* And so we find, indeed, that 'he stood [in prayer] between the dead and the living *(hachaim).*' And through the strength of this argument the plague was indeed banished.

"Now, you good folk," concluded Reb Shlomo, "would you please learn from Pinchas, and bring a drop of vodka here, so that we can all say *LeChaim?*"

A few of the townsfolk hurried home to bring some spirits and refreshments, and right where they were, just outside the cemetery walls, they drank *LeChaim,* and in loud and happy voices wished each other *To Life!*

From there they went home with happy hearts, and the epidemic vanished from their town.

⬥§ *A Sense of Perspective*

וַיִּקְחוּ אִישׁ מַטֵּהוּ *And each man took his staff (17:24)*

From time to time Reb Yaakov of Moglenitz would visit Reb Yisrael of Ruzhin. Once, on a *Shabbos* on which the weekly Portion of *Korach* is read, he came to see him at Sadigora, where he was then living. From the day he had come to settle in Sadigora, Reb Yisrael was in the habit of isolating himself in his study for *Seudah Shlishis,* the mystical Third Meal which is held at sunset. On this *Shabbos,* therefore, the tzaddik of Moglenitz arranged to have his own *Seudah Shlishis* at his lodgings, where a number of chassidim foregathered to join him at his modest table.

On that occasion he taught as follows: "We read in the Torah this morning that the Almighty told the princes of the Tribes that they should each place their staffs in the Tabernacle, and among them the staff of Aharon, in order that the people might see for themselves whom God had chosen for the office of High Priest. The Torah goes on to say that the staff of Aharon blossomed, 'and they saw, and each man took his staff.' Now the question is: Why does the Torah tell us that they each took their staffs? Aharon, of course, had to take his staff, in order that the rebellious Levites should see what God had made clear. But to whom does it matter whether the other heads of the Tribes took their staffs or not?

"But the Torah here teaches us how great was their humility — that they each hastened to show those around them that their staffs had not blossomed, as if to say: 'Look! God chose not me, but Aharon.'"

Those sitting around the table of the quietly-spoken rebbe understood the relevance of his message.

◆§ *Higher Hurdles Ahead*

הַאִם תַּמְנוּ לִגְוֹעַ
Are we to perish utterly? (17:28)

Are we to perish utterly? Have we reached the level of utter perfection (תְּמִימוּת) that a person must reach during his lifetime so that he should be ready to pass away *(Tiferes Shlomo)*?

When Reb Avraham of Sochatchov was a little boy he once fell dangerously ill, and his father, Reb Ze'ev Nachum of Biala, set out at once to Kotsk to ask Reb Menachem Mendel to intercede in heaven on his behalf. When he arrived there, he began to tell the tzaddik of the intense desire and assiduity with which his brilliant son studied Torah.

"You call *that* studying?" the tzaddik said, half to himself.

The father was alarmed. Why should the rebbe seek to utter such a negative appraisal of his son in the hearing of the Heavenly Court? And why especially now, when the child stood in mortal danger?

By the time he arrived home he found his son on his cheerful way to recovery. But when he asked his father exactly what the tzaddik had said when he had asked for his blessing, the father was at a loss for an answer. Then when the boy begged him repeatedly, he could only say: "Believe me, my son, I too do not understand what he said."

Finally, when he had persuaded his father to repeat the words of the tzaddik, the prodigy said: "What is difficult to understand in that? For what he said is exactly parallel to what we find in the Talmud Yerushalmi. We learn there that when Rabbi Tarfon was ill, his mother said to the Sages who came to visit him: 'Pray for my son Tarfon, who honors me even more than one is obliged to do.' And when they asked her: 'Why, what does he do?' — she told them that one *Shabbos,* when she was about to return to her house after strolling in the courtyard, he had gone out and put the palms of his hands under her feet, moving them step by step so that she could walk on them, until she reached her bed. The Sages then retorted: 'Even if he does that a thousand times a thousand, he still will not have reached one half of the respect which the Torah commands children to show their parents.'

"Now, father," concluded the young boy, "surely we should ask the same question here. Could it possibly be that the Sages wanted to play down Rabbi Tarfon's merits in the eyes of heaven at the very moment that he stood in need of mercy? Is it not likelier that they were apprehensive lest his task on earth had thus reached its fulfillment? If so, he would now have nothing to do in This World. And just as they wanted to remind the Heavenly Court that there were even higher levels at which that mitzvah could be fulfilled, in order that he should live on, so too with the rebbe of Kotsk. When you told him how well I study, he was fearful lest I had already completed my life's work. So he too wanted to make it clear that there were many challenges still waiting for me in This World, in the field of Torah study."

Amazed at his son's perception, the father repeated his explanation to Reb Menachem Mendel when he was next in Kotsk.

"Now, now!" said the tzaddik. "Do you mean to say that he already guesses at what I have in mind?"

◆§ My Brothers Do I Seek

כִּי לֹא יִטֹּשׁ ה׳ אֶת עַמּוֹ
For God will not abandon His People (Haftarah)

Before making the long voyage to *Eretz Yisrael*, Reb Wolff Kitzis called on the Baal Shem Tov to receive his farewell blessings. As they parted, the tzaddik told him: "Reb Wolff! Be careful with your words, and know what to answer!"

The chassid (who is also known by his Hebrew name, Reb Ze'ev) set out, and on the way his ship dropped anchor near an island in order to have its provisions replenished. While the crew was thus occupied, he found himself a quiet spot on the island where he could commune alone with his Maker. But so rapt was he in his holy thoughts that he quite forgot about his ship, and when he came out of his inspired trance he found that it was already quite out of sight. He was in very serious trouble. As he turned around he stumbled upon a path and followed it, until he reached a house, where an old man greeted him, and asked: "Reb Wolff, why are you so worried?"

"How should I not worry," he said, "when my ship has gone, and I am left alone?"

"Be composed, Reb Wolff," the old man reassured him. "Stay with me for *Shabbos*, and then next week you can travel from here with one of the ships that pass by. We have a *minyan* here for prayer, and a *mikveh* for immersion."

When the time came for him to board ship, the old man turned to him: "Reb Wolff, I forgot to ask you something. How are the Jews making out where you come from?"

The chassid was preoccupied with his imminent departure, so he replied briefly: "The good God does not abandon them."

And he boarded ship, and sailed on his way.

When he had time to think things over, the old man's question came to mind. He could not forgive himself, and tormented himself with accusations: "What did I answer him? Did the Baal Shem Tov not tell me that I should know what to answer? Why, then did I not tell the old man how wretched is the plight of our persecuted brothers?"

So overcome was he with remorse that he decided to change his direction at the first opportunity, and to speak with the Baal Shem Tov.

As soon as he walked into the familiar room, the tzaddik greeted him and said: "Day after day Avraham Avinu presents himself before the Almighty and says, 'Master of the Universe! My children — *where are they?*' and the Almighty assures the Patriarch: 'I do not forsake them. And look,' he adds, 'here you see Reb Wolff on his way to *Eretz Yisrael.* Now there is a fine Jew. Ask *him* how they are faring!'"

The Baal Shem Tov concluded: "Now if you had told Avraham Avinu how intense is the suffering of the Children of Israel throughout this long exile, then the Messianic Redeemer would have come! But you did not heed my warning ... "

סדר חקת
Sidra Chukas

◆§ *Of Books and Bookmen*

זאת הַתּוֹרָה אָדָם
This is the Torah: a man (19:14)

This is the Torah: a man ... : A man is a living Scroll of the Torah *(Traditional).*

One *Shabbos* in the year 1840 Reb Yitzchak of Vorki was visiting Lublin, where a circumcision was to take place in the very *beis midrash* in which Reb Yaakov Yitzchak, the Chozeh, had taught and inspired thousands until his passing some twenty-five years earlier. The table around which all the local dignitaries were ranged was the same table at which the Chozeh used to sit, and it was expected that the tzaddik of Vorki would now occupy the seat of honor, on its east side.

Reb Yitzchak declined, though, saying: "When our rebbe was alive, I never stepped forward more than half the length of the *beis midrash* out of sheer awe."

But as soon as he took up a place on the west side of the table, scores of chassidim jostled their way eagerly towards him.

Reb Yitzchak turned to them and remarked gently: "Every Jew, you know, is likened to a holy book; that is why you mustn't lean on him or push him around ... '

"But isn't one allowed to stack one holy book on top of another?" countered Reb Getzel, the grandson of the celebrated Rabbi Zvi Hirsch Ashkenazi.

Replied Reb Yitzchak: "Yes — but every Jew should consider himself as not being a holy book."

This remark was overheard by the *rav* of Lublin, Rabbi Meshullam Zalman Ashkenazi, who later commented: "If I had come only to hear that remark, that would have been sufficient."

One way and another the table talk continued on the subject of books, and on the *mitzvah* involved in making Torah works available for public use. And when the *rav* of Lublin left the gathering, he wrote a will that bequeathed his entire scholarly library to the *beis midrash* for the continued edification of his townsmen after his passing.

☙ *A Crumb of Comfort*

זאת הַתּוֹרָה אָדָם כִּי יָמוּת בְּאֹהֶל
This is the Torah: a man who dies in a tent (19:14)

This is the Torah: a man who dies in a tent ... : The Torah truly becomes the possession only of him who gives his very life in the effort of its study (Talmud, Tractate Berachos).

Reb Yitzchak Aizik of Komarna recalled that his father, Reb Alexander Sender of Komarna, was so utterly entrenched in his studies that he would sometimes forget to eat or drink for four or five days at a time. Though he lived in grinding poverty, he never seemed to notice the fact.

"Once," recounted his son, "when I was a boy, I hadn't had a slice of bread to eat for almost two days. On the second day, in order to allay my suffering, my father taught me a Mishnah from the Tractate *Nedarim,* and then introduced it to me afresh with all its mystical meanings, according to the Kabbalah of the ARI*zal.* By then I was very weak, and close to fainting. So my father said: 'Go along to the woman next door; she will give you something to eat.'

"I was surprised to hear this, for I knew that she would not give me food without payment. But I trusted in his every word, and stood at her door. There was an old gentile sitting there, and as soon as he saw me he said: 'My son! Would you like some vodka? How about some bread?'

"And he gave me as much as I needed. All the bystanders looked on in wonderment, but I was so hungry that I didn't take time off to pay close attention to anything in particular. But — because I am such a worthless sinner — I later understood from my father's words that I had been allowed to see Eliyahu the Prophet only in this garbled guise."

⟨§ *A Five-Wheeled Carriage*

בַּמְסִלָּה נַעֲלֶה
We will go up by the highway (20:19)

Reb Aizik of Safrin was the father of five celebrated sons: Reb Zvi Hirsch of Zhidachov, who was the teacher of all his younger brothers; Reb Moshe of Sambor; Reb Alexander Sender of Komarna; Reb Beirish of Zhidachov; and Reb Lipa of Sambor.

Their father never occupied a rabbinical position; he earned an ample livelihood by the toil of his hands, and was a great philanthropist. His oldest son used to quote a Talmudic metaphor when referring to himself and his less famous father: "I am like vinegar the son of wine" — and was fond of repeating some of the ways in which his father's character excelled. His father, he affirmed, never spoke of another man; every single meal in his home was graced with learned table talk — his sons took daily turns at preparing a scholarly discourse to be delivered at the table; and he always made a point of eating together with his servants out of sheer love for his fellow Jews.

When he was already well advanced in years, he once woke up in the middle of the night, and uttered a long, deep sigh.

"Why do you sigh?" asked Hinda, his pious *rebbitzin.*

"And why should I not sigh?" he countered. "We are now well on the way to old age — and how will we go up to the World Above?"

"Don't worry," she said, "for בַּמְסִלָּה נַעֲלֶה!" [Literally, "We will go up by the highway" — but her meaning was: "We will go up (נַעֲלֶה) by virtue of our sons, whose initials make up the word בַּמְסִלָּה — namely: בֵּירִישׁ, מֹשֶׁה, סֶנְדֶר, לִיפָּא, הִירְשׁ."]

◈§ *An Envoy to the World Above*

וַיִּרְאוּ כָּל הָעֵדָה כִּי גָוַע אַהֲרֹן
And all the congregation saw that Aharon had passed away (20:29)

And all the congregation saw that Aharon had passed away: On a hint from the Almighty, the angels raised aloft the coffin of Aharon, and it floated in the heavens *(Yalkut).*

It was in Mezhibuzh, on the night of the fifth of Nissan, 1829, that Reb Avraham Yehoshua Heschel, the Ohev Yisrael of Apta, departed This World. On the very same night, in the holy city of Tiberias, people heard a knocking on the windows of Kollel Vohlin. The beadle inside, alone, was the one who held the keys to the gates of the cemetery. The voice from outside said: "Go outside, go outside, and follow the bier of the *rav* of Apta!"

He ventured outside and was chilled by terror, for the bier was being followed by a grim retinue of a myriad human forms from the Other World. One of these followers intimated to him that this was the funeral procession of the tzaddik of Apta; he had died in Mezhibuzh, and angels from Above had borne his coffin here for entombment in the soil of the Holy Land.

The beadle repeated his story in the morning. People refused to believe him, until on the suggestion of an elderly sage they went together to the cemetery, where they found a newly-covered grave.

Letters from Apta later confirmed that the tzaddik had indeed passed away on that very day. Before his passing he had cried out to heaven in bitter protest over the length of the exile. Why was the Messiah tarrying so long? And in his heartache he had wept and said: "Before Reb Levi Yitzchak of Berditchev left This World he promised that he would not rest, nor allow the tzaddikim in the World of Truth to rest, until their insistent pleas would bring about the Messianic Redemption. But when he arrived there, the saintly souls in the Garden of Eden found spiritual delight in his company, and ascended with him to the palaces of supernal bliss — until he forgot his own promise. But I will not forget!"*

❀ ❀ ❀

When Reb Chaim Eleazar of Munkatsch visited the holy sites in *Eretz Yisrael* in 1930, he asked about among the oldest citizens of Tiberias as to whether any of them knew where the *rav* of Apta was buried. They led him to a certain stone slab in the old cemetery which their hoary elders, who were now in the World of Truth, had shown them — the place where the Ohev Yisrael had been brought to rest.

◆§ *Antics with Skeptics*

וַיְדַבֵּר הָעָם בֵּאלֹקִים וּבְמֹשֶׁה
And the people spoke against God and against Moshe (21:5)

If one entertains doubts regarding his rebbe, it is as if he entertained doubts regarding the Divine Presence, as it is written: "And the People spoke against God and against Moshe" *(Talmud, Tractate Sanhedrin).*

Reb Moshe of Kobrin was once visiting Reissin, in Belorussia, where he lodged in the *shtibl* of the local chassidim. At the festive evening meal which was arranged in his honor, all the leaders and citizens of the community listened respectfully to the learned discourse which he delivered — except for one chassid at the end of the table, who kept up a whispered conversation with his neighbor.

* When it was granted me some years ago to leave the Vale of Tears which is known as the USSR on my way to settle in *Eretz Yisrael,* and I had to visit Moscow in order to arrange the formalities, my fellow chassidim there arranged a farewell gathering. On that occasion, on the eve of my departure, they told me the above story, and then added the following words: "We do not have to tell you, rabbi, that here in this wretched exile we live a life of torment and anguish. We are supported only by the hope that our Father will one day deliver us too out of this dungeon, and bring us to the Holy Land. But all our friends from here who were fortunate enough to go there, and who promised that from the moment they arrived they would never rest until they found some way of getting us out of here, — when they arrived, the same happened to them as happened to Reb Levi Yitzchak of Berditchev in the World Above: they savored the spiritual delights of the palaces of bliss, and forgot us completely. But on you, our friend, we rely. You will not forget us!"

By reason of my imperfections, no doubt, the hope they placed in me bore no fruit. They probably assumed that I too spent my years in the Holy Land disporting myself in the quest of spiritual or other delights ... My heart bleeds for them.

S.Y.Z.

"Sh!" said his companion. "It's not right to talk during a *tish.*"

The talker said nothing, but he thought to himself: "Why, he's not *my* rebbe!"

Suddenly, in the middle of his discourse, Reb Moshe said: "כָּל הַמְהַרְהֵר אַחַר רַבּוֹ ... — If one entertains doubts regarding his rebbe, it is as if he entertained doubts regarding the Divine Presence!"

None of those present knew whom the rebbe was referring to. As to the talker, he thought: "Could he really mean me? Why, my rebbe is someone else!"

Reb Moshe spoke again, this time playing on the similarity between אַחַר ("regarding") and אַחֵר, ("someone else"): "כָּל הַמְהַרְהֵר: אַחֵר רַבּוֹ ... — If someone thinks his rebbe is אַחֵר, someone else, it is as if he entertained doubts regarding the Divine Presence!"

This time the talker felt that Reb Moshe must really mean himself — but then he found solace in the thought that perhaps after all the rebbe had someone else in mind, for he did not know him at all.

Reb Moshe now spoke a third time: "כָּל הַמְהַרְהֵר: אַחֵר רַבּוֹ ... — If someone thinks that the rebbe is really thinking of אַחֵר, of someone else, it is as if he entertained doubts regarding the Divine Presence!"

The chassid — at last — got the message.

❦ ❦ ❦

This story has also been handed down among chassidim in an alternative version.

Two chassidim had occasion to pass through Vilednick in the course of a business trip, so one suggested to the other: "Since we are already here, let us drop by and see Reb Yisrael Dov of Vilednick, the famous wonder-worker."

His friend reacted with a contemptuous grunt. Nevertheless, when *Shabbos* came they both went along to *Seudah Shlishis* — just out of curiosity, let us say. The little hall was so packed that these two merchants found themselves jostled into a spot right behind the chair of the rebbe, where, of course, he was unable to see them.

In the midst of his exposition of some other learned topic, this tzaddik, too, interrupted himself by quoting the above Talmudic teaching — once, twice, three times, as before — except that he then quoted it a *fourth* time: "... כָּל הַמְהַרְהֵר אַחַר רַבּוֹ — If one entertains doubts מֵאֲחוֹרֵי רַבּוֹ, while standing *behind* (מֵאֲחוֹרֵי) his rebbe, it is as if he entertained doubts regarding the Divine Presence!"

סדר בלק
Sidra Balak

◆§ A Visual Restriction (i)

לֹא הִבִּיט אָוֶן בְּיַעֲקֹב
He sees no iniquity in Yaakov (23:21)

Reb Yisrael of Ruzhin recounted that Reb Zusya of Hanipoli was once present in the home of his rebbe, the Maggid of Mezritch, when a man entered and proceeded to recite his list of requests. With the penetrating perception which accompanies the divine gift of *ruach hakodesh,* Reb Zusya saw that this man's sins were grave indeed. He was indignant. How dare the man stand so fearless and unpenitent before the holy Reb Dov Ber of Mezritch!

"A man who has committed such-and-such!" he exclaimed. "Is such a man not ashamed to stand there before the tzaddik without at least a glimmer of *teshuvah?"*

After the man had left Reb Zusya expressed his profound regret at having spoken thus in the presence of his rebbe, whereupon the Maggid gave him his blessing that from that day on he would never see evil in a fellow Jew — only good.

◆§ A Visual Restriction (ii)

At a gathering on the festival of Simchas Torah, Reb Yosef Yitzchak of Lubavitch recalled a childhood dialogue with his father, Reb Shalom Ber of Lubavitch.

"When I was four years old," he said, "I asked my father: 'Why is man created with two eyes, but only one mouth and one nose?'

"'Do you know your *aleph-beis?*' he asked.

"When I answered that I did, he asked again: 'And what is the difference between the letter שׁ *(shin)* and the letter שׂ *(sin)*?'

"'Why, the שׁ has the dot on the right, and the שׂ has the dot on the left,' I answered.

"'And that is why you have two eyes,' my father explained. 'There are things that one should look at with the right eye, and there are things that one should look at with the left eye. A fellow Jew one should always look at with one's right eye, and a candy and a toy — with one's left eye.'

"And it was from that time," concluded Reb Yosef Yitzchak, "that it became a principle deeply rooted in my heart — that one must look at any Jew, whoever he may be, and in whatever spiritual state he may be, with a kindly eye."

⇜§ *Evil Be to Him who Evil Thinks*

כִּי לֹא נַחַשׁ בְּיַעֲקֹב
For there is no sorcery in Yaakov (23:23)

In a town near Liadi there lived a promising young scholar whose father-in-law supported him for a few years after his marriage so that he would be able to advance his Torah studies. After some time, however, the fluctuations of business were such that the young man had to go out and try his own hand at merchandising in order to provide for himself. So it was that once, on the way back from a fair where he had bought up a good deal of merchandise, he passed through a forest near Liadi. It was a day or two before Shavuos, and as he recalled how it had always been his custom to spend the Festival of the Giving of the Torah in the company of his rebbe, Reb Zalman of Liadi, he was so overcome with nostalgia that he decided to leave the wagon with its costly load in the forest and to make his way on foot to Liadi.

He arrived in *shul* just in time for the afternoon prayers, and when the rebbe saw him he commented to his son: "This young man may well be called a chassid of *mesirus nefesh*, a man of self-sacrifice."

The son was surprised to hear this, for his father had not exchanged a word with the young stranger. He later went to speak with the visiting chassid himself, until he eventually understood where lay his self-sacrifice.

When the visitor went to speak to the rebbe after the festival, he was assured: "You will find the wagon and the merchandise untouched, with God's help."

And when the chassid told the rebbe that his business took his mind away from his study and his devotions, the rebbe said: "I would suggest that you find yourself some inn with a tavern in a village. That kind of livelihood will not bother you unduly. Your wife will be able to help out in the business, and you will be left with time for study and prayer."

As the chassid reached his wagon in the forest soon after, untouched as expected, a certain nobleman passed by, and asked him how he had left a loaded wagon unattended.

The chassid laughed heartily. "Good sir," he said, "this wagon of mine has been standing unguarded for three whole days!"

The nobleman was so amazed to hear the young man's story that he said: "Young man, I see that you are straight and honest: I would like to make you a business proposition. In my village there stands a fine inn. You could make a decent living out of it, and I am willing to lease it to you."

"But I haven't got a penny to my name," protested the young man. "I haven't even got what it takes to buy fodder for the horses, let alone vodka, beer, or whatever."

"Very well, then," said the other, "I shall lay out all that is needed now, and in the course of time you will repay me."

It was a deal. The chassid went home, sold his stock, and took over the inn as arranged — despite the friendly warnings of his new Jewish neighbors, who told him that even though one could make a living out of the inn, the people next door were a malevolent old Russian couple who wielded the mysterious threats of the black arts. No Jew living in that inn had ever survived one whole year.

"I'm not afraid of witches," he answered them, "for my rebbe told me that I would make a living out of this place. Now tell me: would my rebbe direct me to a living from which I would die, God forbid?!"

Within a few months his little business had done so well that he was able to return his entire debt to the nobleman. A little while later, however, he began to feel weak. An ominous malady seemed to be taking hold of him. He was barely able to walk. Suspecting the dread influence of the sorcerer next door, he hastened to make the journey to his rebbe, and arrived at Liadi on the eve of the *Shabbos* on which the weekly Portion of *Balak* was to be read. On Friday evening he could not muster the strength to go to synagogue, but in the morning, with great effort, he managed to walk to the *shul* where his rebbe was wont to pray.

Reb Shneur Zalman of Liadi was accustomed to reading the Torah himself, and when it was time for a fifth congregant to be honored by being called up to the public reading, he asked that this young visitor be so honored. The other worshipers were somewhat surprised, for the rebbe never gave instructions as to who should be called forward to the reading; besides, he could not have seen the stranger coming in, because he had arrived when the prayers were already under way. At any rate, the stranger made his way forward to where the Torah Scroll was being read, and the rebbe proceeded to intone the next passage with especial intensity, which came to a climax in the verse: "For there is no sorcery in Yaakov, nor any divination among Israel." He threw his head back, his face burned like a brand and his eyes blazed — for such was his way when his soul ascended to a higher realm — and while still in a state of *dveikus,* read the same words again and again.

After *Shabbos* the young man felt his health returning, but before leaving Liadi he went to tell the rebbe his whole story.

"Do not worry," the rebbe reassured him. "With God's help you will be well, *for there is no sorcery in Yaakov*" — and again the rebbe repeated the *pasuk* several times with the same impassioned intensity as before.

On his way home the young man felt hale and hearty, and as he approached the outskirts of his village a few of the Jewish villagers ran up to him excitedly: "Have you heard what happened right next door to your inn? That malicious old peasant died suddenly, and so did his wife!"

"When?" he asked.

"On *Shabbos* morning," they said.

"I sensed it in Liadi," he said, "when I was called up to the reading of the Torah."

◆§ *When He Wills It*

אֶרְאֶנּוּ וְלֹא עַתָּה
I see it, but not now (24:17)

Soon after the passing of Reb Shneur Zalman of Liadi, his grandson Reb Menachem Mendel of Lubavitch happened to be in a certain town for a wedding. There he overheard a few chassidim in the adjoining room lamenting the state the world was now left in: God alone knew when the Messiah would finally come.

He opened the door and said: "But that is what the gentile prophet Bilam said concerning the Messianic Redemption — 'I see it, but not now; I behold it, but it is not near.' We Jews, though, should hope and look forward to the coming of the *Mashiach* every day! And in this connection I heard from my grandfather that his teacher, the Maggid of Mezritch, had the ability to cause even a day-old child to experience the loftiest levels of the awe of God; *his* rebbe, the Baal Shem Tov, could have fired even an inanimate object with the same. Why did they not do this, and thereby — since the whole of creation would then be fired by an awareness of the Divine Presence — cause the *Mashiach* to come at once? The answer is that God did not yet will it. And if the arrival of the *Mashiach* depends on the Divine Will, then how is the situation altered by the passing of our rebbe, my grandfather? When the propitious time comes, and God so wills it, the *Mashiach* will surely appear."

◆§ *Incognito (i)*

וְהַצְנֵעַ לֶכֶת עִם אֱלֹקֶיךָ
And to walk humbly with your God (Haftarah)

After having consulted one physician after another to no avail, the father of an eleven-year-old boy who had lost the power of speech came to visit Reb Shneur Zalman of Liadi.

"Make the journey to Metz, in Germany," advised the rebbe, "take up lodgings in the house of a certain timber merchant who lives near the hill at the entrance to the city, and wait there until the Almighty sends a cure for your son."

"And what am I to do there in Metz?" asked the man.

"Don't do anything," answered the rebbe. "Just stroll about the market places and the streets, until salvation comes."

Now the poor fellow could not afford anything approaching the costs of traveling to Germany, but as soon as his fellow chassidim heard what the rebbe had said, they collected amongst themselves all that was needed and sent him off with his son, perfectly confident that the rebbe's words would be fulfilled.

After an arduous journey the chassid finally arrived in Metz, and discovered soon enough that there was in fact a hill near the approach to the city, next to which there lived a Jewish timber merchant. He was well received by his host, and then spent day after day walking about the streets and the market places with his unfortunate son — but his long journey seemed to be quite pointless. Nor only to himself, for one day his host said: "Excuse my asking, but what business brought you here? For you have been here quite some time now, and you do not appear to be occupied with anything."

When he was told the whole story, he was amazed: How did the rebbe know of his existence from such a great distance? And what connection could there possibly be between a cure for the boy and — himself? But an idea crossed his mind.

"Listen here, my friend," he said. "It seems to me that the person your rebbe had in mind was my son-in-law. Let me tell you *my* story.

"A certain youth used to sit in our local synagogue all day, studying Torah. I felt sorry for him, and invited him to be my regular guest. He agreed, but after some time he said: 'I have one request of you. I don't want to eat unearned bread, and you could probably do with a watchman for your timber yard. Why don't you build me a little cabin out there, and I'll look after your yard for you.'

"And that is exactly what we did.

"Once, though, I woke up in the middle of the night.

What do I see through the window? — A huge fire raging in my timber yard, right where I built the cabin for this watchman of mine! In my imagination I could already see it racing through my stacks of timber, and I felt angry at the young man who was no doubt sleeping soundly, quite unaware of what was going on around him. I ran out to wake him up, and to put out the fire. But what fire? When I got there I was astonished to see that there was no fire at all. And when I told my wife of this odd illusion she only laughed and said: 'You only saw it in your dreams!'

"A few days later, though, I again saw the same thing in the middle of the night — and in the same place. But this time I made a point of waking up my wife, so that she should see the thing with her own eyes.

"'Run out there and put it out!' she screamed.

"But again I arrived there breathless only to find that there was no fire to put out. We talked over this weird occurrence, and came to the conclusion that this was no ordinary young man. We decided not to breathe a word of it to a soul, as if we knew nothing and had seen nothing.

"Some time later I asked this young man whether he would like to become my son-in-law. He agreed, but on one condition: that I would build a house at the other end of town for himself and his wife — though I was never to visit them there on any account. He promised that they would come to visit us in our home, and said the he would support himself and my daughter by baking bread, a craft at which he was expert. But the condition was an absolute one. I accepted it, and we both did as we had undertaken to do. They visit us from time to time, and my daughter says she is very happy with her young husband.

"It would seem, then," concluded the timber merchant, "that the man your rebbe had in mind is this hidden tzaddik, my son-in-law."

The guest heard him out, and decided to pay a visit to this unusual baker, whom he addressed as follows: "The rebbe of Liadi sent me to you so that you should cure my son here of his dumbness."

"So he has found me here too?" said the young man,

stupefied. "Tell him that I am now going to move to some place where he will not find me any more!"

He blessed the boy, nevertheless. His prayer was heard, and the child was healed.

◆§ *Incognito (ii)*

The waiting room of Reb Simchah Bunem of Pshischah was once occupied by the venerable inner circle of elder chassidim, whose hushed deliberations were interrupted by the entry of a young man dressed in the modern garb of a "Deitsch'l" (for this was the nickname given to assimilationists and *Maskilim).* His request: to be allowed to speak with the tzaddik. Now this was a most unusual phenomenon. People like this did not normally believe in tzaddikim nor mix with chassidim. There was no doubt about it: this stranger was here only to pester their rebbe with vexatious questions. They therefore made him unwelcome.

The man only answered meekly: "So what can I do? I'll have to go somewhere else" — and he went on his way.

His quiet answer, though, affected them, and they decided to tell the rebbe of his visit. The tzaddik trembled to hear their report, and expressed his displeasure at the fact that they had allowed him to leave. He even ordered them to go out at once in search of the stranger, and to bring him back.

They caught up with him on the highway and explained themselves, but when he had returned with them they were flabbergasted to hear the question he put to the rebbe: "Two *shidduchim* have been proposed to me. One match is with a beauty, though she is not of noble birth; the other is of distinguished ancestry, but is not a beauty. Which should I choose?"

Surprised as the chassidim were that this should be the question he had brought to the rebbe, they were far more surprised to see with what earnest deliberation the rebbe weighed his question before answering: "Beauty! That really is beauty!"

As soon as the stranger left, the tzaddik turned to his

chassidim: "This 'Deitsch'l' asked me whether he should study the Kabbalah according to the school of Rabbi Moshe Cordovero or according to the teachings of Rabbi Yitzchak Luria, the Ari*zal;* I told him that he should follow the teachings of the Ari*zal.*"

◆§ *Incognito (iii)*

Though he was the son of the celebrated tzaddik Reb Yitzchak of Vorki, young Menachem Mendel always managed to give the impression — to a superficial observer — that he was merely a mischievous lad who enjoyed strolling in the open fields. Few men indeed knew that this was no more than a mask. So it was that when his father passed away, and the chassidim installed him as their rebbe, dissident whispers could be heard from various quarters.

Once, for example, a famous sage called on Reb Beirish of Biala, who was one of the first chassidim to cleave to the new young rebbe, while he was visiting Warsaw.

"Does the Talmud not teach us," he queried, "that לֹא יָגַעְתִּי וּמָצָאתִי אַל תַּאֲמִין? 'If someone tells you, *I have not toiled, but I have found — do not believe him!*' Let's face it: we have never seen Reb Menachem Mendel exerting himself in the study of Torah or in divine service generally. Why believe in him?"

"You don't even know what that Talmudic quotation means," replied Reb Beirish, "and you dare to speak thus about a tzaddik from whom tens of thousands of our brethren draw inspiration! It is time you understood the meaning of this phrase *Do not believe him.* Why, is this question a matter of *belief?* Not at all! All you have to do is to open up the scholarly literature with him and you will be able to see for yourself whether he has *found* or not. What the Talmud is teaching us here is something else altogether: 'If someone tells you, *I have not toiled* — do not believe him!' Our rebbe has toiled well and truly toiled — but has kept his exertions hidden modestly from sight."

◈ Incognito (iv)

Reb Betzalel of Ozoritch, a chassid of Reb Menachem Mendel of Lubavitch, once lodged at the home of a certain Jewish villager whom he had encountered in the course of his travels. His host told him that he employed a youth to shepherd his flocks all day long. At night he would come home and lie down to rest in his favorite nook high up on the huge stone fireplace, and early in the morning he would go out to the fields. True enough, he was a trustworthy young man, but his host said that he had never once seen him washing his hands before a meal or saying the words of a blessing.

Approaching the fireplace, Reb Betzalel found the shepherd eating beans.

He asked him gently: "Why do you not wash your hands and say a *berachah* as one should?"

"What difference does it make to you?" the young man answered.

Since his further questions all received the same response, Reb Betzalel left the fireplace disappointed.

When he had occasion to be passing through that region a year later, his host said: "Let me tell you something remarkable about that young man whom you met a year ago. One day I decided to go out to see for myself just what that young man did out there in the fields, to see whether he was looking after my flocks, at least. I found myself a hiding place under a bush, where he could not possibly see me. And as I listened, I heard him reading the words of the Book of *Psalms*, one melodious phrase after another, in a measured voice that gradually rose in holy ecstasy. This was clearly not the ordinary peasant that I had imagined him to be. I revealed nothing of what I had seen to anyone, but from the greater respect that I now showed him, he must have sensed that I had discovered what manner of man he was.

"Then one Friday night soon after, ten gentiles burst into my house to take this young man off for military service. They said that they were acting on orders issued by the conscription authorities in the neighboring town. I begged them to give him a reprieve at least until the end of our Day of Rest. You see, I thought that I would then be able to speak to the leading Jewish citizens of that town, and tell them about this young man, and perhaps induce them to make efforts to have him released. But those ten *goyim* took absolutely no notice of my entreaties, and took him away.

"Distressed at my failure to save him I waited impatiently for *Shabbos* to pass, and then, as soon as I had recited *Havdalah*, I set out for that town to see what I could perhaps still do for him. But when I spoke of this case to the regional conscription authorities there, it turned out that they didn't know what I was talking about. They had never sent anyone to my village, and they had never heard of this young man!"

Reb Betzalel wept on hearing this story, and said: "How gross and unspiritual are our eyes, that we sensed nothing and knew nothing!"

◆§ *Incognito (v)*

Reb Yechezkel Halevi, the son-in-law of Reb Yisrael of Koznitz, repeated the following story which he had heard while visiting his uncle, who was a scholarly *rav* in a certain town in Hungary.

"Many years ago," recalled this uncle, "two men came to me and testified that they had seen one of the common villagers in the district — he held the franchise on the sale of milk from the local squire — committing a certain vulgar sin. I immediately gave out word that all the peasants in the villages in my district should come to town for *Shabbos* in order to hear a *derashah* from me. My sermon was of course full of moral exhortation, with particular reference to the heinous nature of the sin in question, though of course I did not mention the man's name. So earnestly were those good people aroused to true feelings of penitence, that they were even brought to tears — except, that is, for that peasant, whose face I watched intently as I spoke. It was clear that my *derashah* had made absolutely no impression on him: he remained utterly unmoved.

"I couldn't contain myself. 'Villain that you are!' I thundered out at him. 'At least you owe us a word of thanks! It's because of you that I made all this fuss, because people have testified thus and thus about you!'

"'It wasn't me that committed the sin,' the villager answered quietly.

"I tried again, but received the same reply.

"'Very well,' said I to the assembled villagers. 'You had better all go back to your lodgings and eat your *Shabbos* meal, for today is the holy Day of Rest, and tomorrow I will somehow find a way of punishing this fellow.'

"That night, though, my father appeared to me in a dream and said: 'My son! What have you done? For today you shamed publicly one of the hidden tzaddikim of our generation, one of those who fulfill the teaching of the Prophet Michah, to walk humbly with God. Go out at once and beg his forgiveness — but beware not to reveal his identity.'

"Now when I woke up I told myself: 'Dreams are neither one way nor the other.' Nevertheless, just to be sure, I decided not to go ahead with the punishment that I had contemplated giving that man. But then the next night the same dream appeared again, and once more on the third night. So first thing the next morning I hired a wagon and headed for his village. I found his wife, but when I asked her where her husband was, she told me that he had just left the house.

"After waiting all day I went home, and tried again the next day — but with no better results. I kept on trying, once a week, week after week, then once a month, for months on end — but every time his wife tells me that he has just left the house. For ten long years I have been calling at his house, but it has not yet been granted me to meet that tzaddik; and I am not allowed to mention his name publicly, by order of my late father. It seems to me that he is hiding from me because he senses through Divine Inspiration that I want to beg his forgiveness, and once that has happened he knows that the Heavenly Court will want to punish me. But so long as he does not forgive me, he knows what torments of self-incrimination I undergo — and he knows that this spiritual anguish suffices to ward off the severer punishment which would otherwise be my just desserts."

סדר פינחס
Sidra Pinchas

◆§ Shall Your Land be My Land?

לָאֵלֶּה תֵּחָלֵק הָאָרֶץ
For these shall the Land be divided (26:53)

Evening fell while the Baal Shem Tov was on a journey with a few of his disciples, so they stopped to spend the night in a village inn. The little building soon echoed to the revelry of a wedding party, but the Baal Shem Tov and his companions spent the night quietly in their room. In the morning, when the families of the bride and groom were standing outside, ready to make the journey home, the Baal Shem Tov was also there, for he too was preparing to leave. While they were waiting for their wagons a little bird chirped away on a tree, right in front of the bride and groom.

"Do you know what the bird is saying?" said the Baal Shem Tov to his chassidim. "It is saying לָאֵלֶּה תֵּחָלֵק הָאָרֶץ: 'For these shall the Land be divided.'"

They did not understand his meaning, of course, but neither did they ask him to explain himself.

Decades later, after this couple had lived a good life together and had raised children and grandchildren, the husband decided that come what may, he was going to spend his old age in *Eretz Yisrael*. Since his wife refused to leave her children, and they could find no way out of their dilemma, they brought their case before a rabbinical court. The *beis din* ruled that the wife would receive a bill of divorce: she was not allowed to prevent him from going, nor could he force her to join him. After their monetary matters had been settled according to the court's ruling, the husband departed for *Eretz Yisrael*, and the wife remained with her children.

Word of this incident spread far and wide, until it reached the disciples who had accompanied the Baal Shem Tov to that village inn.

"So this was what the rebbe meant," they said in wonderment. "לָאֵלֶּה תֵּחָלֵק הָאָרֶץ: Between these shall the Land divide!"

◆§ Soul vs. Soul

וַתִּקְרַבְנָה בְּנוֹת צְלָפְחָד
And the daughters of Tzlafchad drew near (27:1)

The passage concerning inheritance should rightly have been written through Moshe Rabbeinu. It was the daughters of Tzlafchad, however, who were thus privileged, for merits are brought about through the meritorious *(Talmud, Tractate Bava Basra).*

Reb Yisrael of Ruzhin once went for a stroll with one of his elder chassidim who was a grandson of Rabbi Yechezkel Landau, celebrated both as the illustrious author of *Noda BiYehudah,* a classic work of halachic responsa, and as a determined opponent of Chassidism. Said Reb Yisrael: "Since you are a grandson of the *rav* of Prague, let me tell you what I heard from Reb Avraham Yehoshua Heschel of Apta, who in turn heard it from Reb Yechiel Michel of Zlotchov, at the time that the tzaddik of Zlotchov was suffering from the antagonism of your grandfather.

"And this is what Reb Yechiel Michel said: 'I harbor him no grudge, for God commanded him to oppose the chassidim. You see, when the Heavenly Court decided that it was time for the soul of the Baal Shem Tov to descend to This World, the voices of all kinds of prosecuting angels spoke up, arguing that if this were to be allowed the Messianic Redemption would be brought about before its time. But at that moment whole choirs of kindlier voices chimed in, so it was decided that the soul of the Baal Shem Tov would indeed be sent down to This World — but at the same time another lofty soul would be dispatched down here, to dwell in a man who would also be a leader of his generation, but an antagonist to the teachings of the Baal Shem Tov and his disciples. That man was your grandfather, the sage of Prague.

"It thus works out that it was Reb Yechezkel Landau who caused the soul of the Baal Shem Tov to come down here; without him this would not have taken place. For, as our Sages say: Merits are brought about through the meritorious.'"

◈ Leadership (i)

יִפְקֹד ה׳... אִישׁ עַל הָעֵדָה
Let God... appoint a man over the congregation (27:16)

The Baal Shem Tov passed away on the festival of Shavuos in the year 1760. The mantle of leadership was immediately assumed by his son, Reb Zvi, who was accepted by all the chassidim of the day as his father's rightful successor.

On the same festival exactly one year later, in the presence of all the disciples who were seated around his table, he rose, turned to Reb Dov Ber, the Maggid of Mezritch, and said: "This night my father appeared to me, and told me that the Divine Presence, together with all the hosts of heaven, has now passed over and now rests upon you."

With that he removed the white gown which had been his, and placed it around the shoulders of Reb Dov Ber. The Maggid did not decline, but agreed to occupy the seat of leadership.

❀ ❀ ❀

When Reb Shalom Ber of Lubavitch recounted this incident he added: "Reb Zvi was renowned for his self-effacement. But still, what greatness of spirit does a man need in order to do what he did! For we find examples in the Talmud of sages who did not want to be thrust into positions of greatness — but once they were already there ... "

◈ Leadership (ii)

A group of chassidim from Reissin once came to Reb Dov Ber of Mezritch with a problem. On the one hand it was such a long way to Mezritch that they were unable to visit him for spiritual guidance as often as they would wish; on the other, they did not want to remain without a rebbe for long periods of time.

The rebbe gave them one of his cloaks, together with a black silk belt and a staff, and said: "Take these things and give them to a man by the name of Mendele who lives in Vitebsk. Whenever you find it difficult to come here, you will be able to draw inspiration in your divine service from him."

Off the chassidim all went to Vitebsk in search of a man called Reb Mendele. The tzaddik whom we know as Reb Menachem Mendel of Vitebsk was not yet renowned, so most of the townsfolk whom they asked simply answered: "There isn't any Reb Mendele of that kind around here!"

In the course of their investigations, however, they encountered a woman who asked: "Gentlemen, whom do you seek?"

"We are looking for Reb Mendele," they said.

"There is no Mendele around here of the kind who is called rebbe," she said, "but there *are* plenty of people called Mendele — my son-in-law, for example."

Surmising that this was perhaps the man whom they were seeking, they entered her house, met her son-in-law, and handed him the articles that they had received from the hand of the Maggid of Mezritch. Reb Menachem Mendel garbed himself in the cloak, wrapped the *gartl* around his waist, and took the staff in his hand. And from that moment the chassidim did not recognize him: he was a man transformed, and they stood before him in awe.

◆§ *Leadership (iii)*

After the passing of Reb Dov Ber of Lubavitch, the son of Reb Shneur Zalman of Liadi, the chassidim all decided at once to appoint as his successor his son-in-law, Reb Menachem Mendel, better known by the name of one of his works as the Tzemach Tzedek. Reb Menachem Mendel, who was also the son of Reb Shneur Zalman's daughter, was unwilling to accept the appointment. His first argument was that in point of seniority the next rebbe should rightly be his uncle, Reb Chaim Avraham, the son of Reb Shneur Zalman of Liadi, and he sent the chassidim to speak to him.

Reb Chaim Avraham told the delegation that came to him: "Go and tell him that he should stop deluding people. Everyone knows that he is fully suited to the position of rebbe, to support and lead the People of God. I will soon follow you and back your words."

Soon after they had returned to speak again with Reb Menachem Mendel they were joined by Reb Chaim Avraham, and as he entered, his nephew rose as a mark of deference.

"Please keep your seat," requested the visitor. "I am the uncle, but you are the rebbe."

"But how can I be a rebbe," argued Reb Menachem Mendel, addressing himself to the group at large, "when a rebbe must be familiar with the secrets of the Torah?"

One of the chassidim answered: "In enumerating the gifts which mastery of the Torah bestows upon its devotees, the Mishnah in Tractate *Avos* first says וְנוֹתֶנֶת לוֹ מַלְכוּת — 'it grants him kingship' — and only *thereafter* says וּמְגַלִּין לוֹ רָזֵי תוֹרָה: 'the secrets of the Torah are revealed to him.'"

Reb Menachem Mendel spoke again: "If I should have been rebbe, I would have heard some hint of this from my grandfather, Reb Shneur Zalman."

"Rebbe, you have most certainly heard," the chassidim insisted, "And one of the hints was the dream you had not long ago."

For Reb Menachem Mendel had cried out in his sleep while ill, about a week before the passing of his grandfather, the author of *Tanya.* When Reb Shneur Zalman had asked him why he had cried out, he had answered: "I dreamed that a Torah Scroll fell to the ground. No man could pick it up. I ran towards it as fast as I could, raised it up, and returned it to its place."

"That is right," his grandfather had answered. "You raised it up."

And everyone had understood the meaning of his words.

In due course, at any rate, in response to the earnest entreaties of large numbers of chassidim, Reb Menachem Mendel undertook to lead the multitudes of followers of the school of *Chabad.* It was then that he began to light them along the path in which they were to progress in the service of God, and to spread his teachings far and wide in both the revealed and the hidden sides of the Torah — a task which he was to maintain, unwearied, for some thirty-eight years.

◆§ Leadership (iv)

The chassidim were perplexed. Their rebbe, Reb Yaakov Yitzchak of Pshischah, better known as the Yid HaKadosh ("the holy Jew"), had passed away, and they did not know where to turn in search of a successor.

At length they consulted one of the giants in their midst, Reb Simchah Bunem, who answered them with a parable: "A shepherd once fell to the ground, and was soon fast asleep. At midnight he awoke, and saw that the moon was shining, and the air was cool, and there was clear drinking water before him. As for his sheep, there was not one missing, and they were all pasturing contentedly. His heart surged with gratitude and joy, and he cried out: 'O my beloved God! How can I thank You for all your kindness to me? If You entrust me with Your sheep, I will guard them like the apple of my eye!'"

Reb Simchah Bunem concluded: "If such a shepherd could be found, he should be our rebbe."

They listened to his parable, and every single man present savored the same thought: he himself, Reb Simchach Bunem, should be their rebbe.

Now one of those present was Reb Abba'le of Neustadt, who had been the mentor of the departed rebbe, the Yid HaKadosh, in the study of the mysteries of the Kabbalah, and in fact many had earlier assumed that he would be his successor. Reb Abba'le sensed what thought was passing through the minds of those around him, and shared it, too. He thereupon stood up from his place of honor and seated Reb Simchah Bunem there in his stead.

◆§ The Altar and the Table

אֶת קָרְבָּנִי לַחְמִי לְאִשַּׁי
My sacrifice, the bread of My burnt offerings (28:2)

Scholars and sages, the rich and the poor, used to come in their hundreds and thousands to hear Torah teachings from the mouth of Reb Avraham, the Maggid of Trisk, and whether it was *Shabbos* or a festival or an ordinary weekday, he always made a point of providing for them all at his massive table. After each festival, of course, when the greatest multitudes of chassidim had just returned to their homes, he always found himself to be deep in debt. A group of elder chassidim of his inner circle approached him therefore with a suggestion: since the cost of providing meals for all of his chassidim got him so seriously into debt that he was forced to dispatch an emissary to collect contributions from them to cover his losses, would it not be better to dispense with the meals and to be spared the necessity of collecting?

Understanding his silence to imply consent, the same delegation came to speak to him again in order to determine the new arrangements. This time, however, he answered: "Our Sages teach us that so long as the *Beis HaMikdash* stood on the Temple Mount in Jerusalem, the altar conferred atonement on the House of Israel; after the Destruction of the Temple, a man's table grants him that atonement. Now in connection with the daily sacrifice on the altar we read אֶת קָרְבָּנִי לַחְמִי לְאִשַּׁי: 'My sacrifice, the bread of My burnt offerings.' And that is what I say, too: אֶת קָרְבָּנִי — *my* sacrifice is — לַחְמִי לְאִישַׁי: my bread which I give to my people [for here, instead of reading לְאִשַּׁי: "my burnt offerings," he punningly substituted לְאִישַׁי: "my people"]. And just as the burnt offerings on the altar gave rise to a רֵיחַ נִיחֹחַ, a savor pleasing to God, so too the bread I provide for my chassidim brings atonement for me, and for them too."

And the custom in Trisk continued as before.

סדר מטות
Sidra Matos

◆§ Words have Weight

או הִשָּׁבַע שְׁבֻעָה
Or swear an oath (30:3)

Or swear an oath...he shall not break his word: He shall not treat his words recklessly *(Rashi).*

Money and merchandise he had in plenty. Only one thing was lacking — children, and he tirelessly plied his rebbe with his request for this blessing. Every time he asked, though, his entreaty was deferred by the rebbe, Reb Aryeh Leib of Shpola, until one day the chassid decided that he would give him no rest, and plead with him with such clamorous urgency that the tzaddik would be forced to give him a blessing which heaven would fulfill. The chassid arrived at a moment when the tzaddik was contemplating secrets of higher worlds, so when he opened with his barrage of pleas, the tzaddik said: "Please leave me for the moment, for I am now involved in a matter concerning the welfare of the House of Israel at large; this is not a propitious time for me to undertake the request of an individual."

"Ah!" thought the chassid. "If this is indeed a propitious hour, and that is why he is occupied with the needs of all of Israel, then I am not going to budge from here until he grants me my request!"

And he simply pestered the tzaddik without interruption so that he was utterly unable to concentrate. The Shpoler Zeide first implored him to give him some peace, and later warned him that he would live to regret his insistence — but to no avail, until in a moment of anger he said: "I swear that you will never have children!"

The chassid was terror-stricken. "My soul-root does not belong *here*," he concluded, and, taking his leave from the rebbe, he left Shpola with a heavy heart.

Some time later his business interests brought him to Korets. One day, his transactions over, he retired to the *beis midrash* in which Reb Pinchas of Korets used to study and pray. Now although Reb Pinchas was as yet unknown as a tzaddik, this chassid had any eye for these things; he perceived that he was a man with a lofty soul, and surmised that he was probably inspired as well by *ruach hakodesh*. He interested himself in his material situation, and was told by neighbors that Reb Pinchas was quite penniless. To make things more acute, the month of Nissan was already underway, and the festival of Pessach with its extra household expenses was just around the corner. On top of that, as the guest heard from some of the townsmen, what bothered Reb Pinchas most was that he would be losing precious time from his Torah studies through the preparations which had to be made at home for the approaching festival.

"This could be my lucky hour," thought the visiting chassid.

He went straight to the home of Reb Pinchas, and asked his wife whether she had whatever was needed for Pessach. When she told him that she did not have so much as a single copper coin, he took out his wallet and gave her enough money to enable her to buy the flour which was scrupulously guarded against contact with moisture; to pay the baker who made the *matzos*; and to buy fish and meat and all manner of dishes in honor of the forthcoming *Yom Tov*. He then went out himself and bought a table and benches, and a bed as well, and asked her to arrange everything in the most generous style possible, for he wanted to be their guest for Pessach. He asked her besides to keep these preparations from her husband's attention until Pessach eve. To this she agreed, and day by day he would call at her home to see whether there was anything lacking.

Reb Pinchas, for his part, was somewhat surprised that his wife was not bothering him with requests for money to cover the expenses of the festival. He did not raise the subject, however, and continued with his studies in the *beis midrash* as before, night and day.

Before sunset on the eve of the festival, when the tzaddik was already at prayers, the chassid paid one last visit to his house to give it his finishing touches. When the tzaddik came home and opened the door of his humble dwelling, he was greeted by a table decked with all manner of dishes and delicacies, and a room lit up on all sides by tall white candles. He was overjoyed, and asked his wife where all this festive joy had come from.

"Our guest who stands here before you — he prepared it all," she said.

The tzaddik greeted his guest warmly, but asked him no questions, for they sat down at once to the *Seder* service, which Reb Pinchas conducted with joy and with fervor. Later on in the evening, in the course of the meal, he turned to his guest: "What brings you here? Do you have a request?"

The chassid finally told him all that had passed between himself and the Shpoler Zeide, begged him to undo the oath that he had heard, and asked him to give his blessing that his wife would bear a child.

Reb Pinchas thereupon said: "If any good deed I have

 ever done carries any weight in heaven, I swear to you that this year your wife will bear a son."

And his blessing was fulfilled within the year.

❀ ❀ ❀

When Reb Yisrael of Ruzhin recounted this story he added: "At that moment, when Reb Pinchas of Korets made his oath, the entire Heavenly Court was thrown into upheaval: whose oath would give way to whose? And the verdict was that the oath of him who had never made an oath in his life before, even a truthful one, was to prevail. The records were searched, and the Heavenly Court accordingly honored the oath of Reb Pinchas."

But the tzaddik of Ruzhin had one further comment: "From this episode we see how one should not be obstinate in the face of the decree of a tzaddik. For the grandson of that chassid, who came into the world through the oath of Reb Pinchas, grew up to be a treacherous enemy of Israel who slandered his own grandchildren — the saintly brothers from Slavita — to the barbarous authorities."

◆§ *A Blissful Anger*

וַיִּקְצֹף מֹשֶׁה
And Moshe was angry (31:14)

Reb Baruch of Mezhibuzh had a distinctive manner of teaching: he would impose his authority on his disciples with a heavy hand, and would gruffly rebuke all those who came to hear him teach. He was fond of quoting, as a kind of proof-text for his unique style, the verse which speaks of the gentiles whom Avraham and Sarah taught a belief in One God: וְאֶת הַנֶּפֶשׁ אֲשֶׁר עָשׂוּ בְחָרָן. Literally, this means "The souls which they made in Charan," but Reb Baruch would read the place-name not as חָרָן but as חָרוֹן, which means "anger," as if to say: the Patriarchs accomplished their holy task by the exercise of anger...

In 1811 Reb Baruch — whose name means "blessed" — breathed his last, and by his bedside his chassidim found a volume of the holy Zohar. It was open at the passage which says: "There are two kinds of anger. There is one kind of anger which is blessed both in the World Above and in the World Below. Its name is Baruch..."

◆§ Keeping One's Head מטות

Reb Mordechai of Neshchiz of course already owned at least one *tallis katan* — the four-cornered garment, worn like a tunic and with a hole for the head, that carries the fringed *tzitzis* at its corners. But he yearned to have a *tallis katan* that came from *Eretz Yisrael.* After all kinds of strenuous efforts, therefore, his chassidim finally managed to grant him his wish, and to bring a suitable length of white lambswool cloth all the way from the Holy Land. One of his disciples asked for the privilege of cutting it to size and sewing its hems. In his enthusiasm, however, he made a false fold and discovered to his horror that while cutting a hole for the head he had made another gaping hole right in the front of the garment! What would the rebbe say? After waiting for this cherished object for so long, and after all the exertion that had gone into acquiring it, it was now irreparably ruined.

When the rebbe next saw him, and asked him whether the garment was ready, he stammered out his story in the utmost consternation.

"My good man, why are you afraid?" said the rebbe. "Don't you realize that a *tallis katan* really needs two big holes? One, as usual, to *put* one's head through; and the other — to test whether Mordechai will *lose* his head..."

◆§ A Soft Answer

After the death of the first wife of Reb Yaakov Yitzchak (the Chozeh) of Lublin, he summoned Reb Yaakov Yitzchak (the Yid HaKadosh) of Pshischah, and told him that he was responsible: he had made her liable to punishment at the hands of heaven by causing her to speak evil of him to her husband, the Chozeh. (Her remarks were evidently in sympathy with the grudge that was borne by many of the disciples of the Chozeh against the Yid HaKadosh, because he had cultivated a following of chassidim of his own during the lifetime of the Chozeh, their rebbe.)

"God forbid!" said the Yid HaKadosh. "I know nothing of it."

"Then what did you do at the time [that chassidim started following you]?" demanded the Chozeh.

"I read *Psalms*," said the Yid HaKadosh.

"And is that nothing in your eyes?" the Chozeh persisted.

"Well, what could I have done?" asked the Yid HaKadosh.

"At least you should have been angry," said the Chozeh.

"Rebbe," said the Yid HaKadosh, "please look into my heart and see whether I am able to be angry."

The Chozeh leaned forward, looked into the deepest recesses of his heart, and said: "True! The Yid is incapable of becoming angry!"

◆§ *Near Now, Nearer Hereafter*

וּמִקְנֶה רַב *An abundance of cattle (32:1)*

A chassid by the name of Reb Peretz of Pshischah very much wanted to make the journey to *Eretz Yisrael*, but when he came to ask his rebbe for permission, the Yid HaKadosh withheld it. A few days later Reb Peretz fell ill, and his rebbe, who had come to visit him, asked him whether he still wanted to go to the Holy Land.

Reb Peretz answered: "We read in the Torah וּמִקְנֶה רַב הָיָה לִבְנֵי רְאוּבֵן וְלִבְנֵי גָד — the men of the Tribes of Reuven and Gad had an abundance of cattle. Now why does the Torah tell us this? Is this a compliment worthy of such tzaddikim as they were? Their argument, rather, was that they had מִקְנֶה רַב [to be read as if to mean קִנְיָן בְּרַבָּם]: they had acquired a share in their *rav*, Moshe Rabbeinu. And since he was to be buried on the east side of the Jordan, they wanted to be allocated their tracts of land there, for they did not want to part with him. And we see that their argument was accepted. So it is with me. I can see that my rebbe will soon be leaving This World, and that is why I no longer desire to leave for *Eretz Yisrael*. I want to remain together with my rebbe, for I have acquired a share in him."

And indeed, in the course of that illness Reb Peretz departed for another world, where he was joined very soon after by his rebbe.

☙ Early Inklings

בְּטֶרֶם אֶצָּרְךָ בַבֶּטֶן יְדַעְתִּיךָ
Before I formed you in the womb I knew you (Haftarah)

When Reb Baruch of Mezhibuzh, the grandson of the Baal Shem Tov, was a little boy, his *melamed* at school introduced him for the first time to the study of *Gemara*. Perceiving that the first page of the text was numbered ב, the second letter of the alphabet, the child asked: "And where is page א, the first page?"

The *melamed* duly explained that page א was the title page, which bore the name of the tractate.

"Then I will start with the first page," announced the young pupil. "Here it says בָּבָא קַמָּא. Do you see? The name of this tractate makes up the initials of six words: בָּרוּךְ בֶּן אָדִיל, קָדוֹשׁ מִבֶּטֶן אִמּוֹ — Baruch the son of Adel, holy from the womb of his mother."

סדר מסעי
sidra mas'ei

☙ Reprieve

וְנָס שָׁמָּה רֹצֵחַ מַכֵּה נֶפֶשׁ בִּשְׁגָגָה
That the person who kills unawares may flee there (35:11)

In a village near Zanz there lived a God-fearing Jew who owned a tavern and an inn. One day a wayfarer came by, dressed in rags and tatters; the innkeeper gave him a square meal, and after the Grace after Meals offered him money. Since the visitor declined the offer the host assumed that it was less than he expected to receive, so he prepared to increase the amount, but the pauper said: "Please do not insist that I accept a donation from you, for I am quite a rich man."

The innkeeper was so stupefied to hear this statement that he asked the stranger to explain why he wandered about in this state. And this is the story he was told.

"I live in the city of Pest, near which I own several villages, fields and vineyards. Once a large sum of money was stolen from me, and I did not know who the thief was. We had a maid — an orphan — and since we suspected that this was her doing we took her along to the local authorities. The police there beat her in order to induce her to confess, but she insisted she had stolen nothing, and they sent her home to us. The harsh treatment that she had endured left its mark. For some days she languished in bed, and then died. Two weeks later the thief was found. I was stricken by terror: I had suspected an innocent person, and through my doing this orphan had met her death!

"I set out to speak to Reb Meir of Premishlan, hoping that he would teach me some way of repenting, and atoning for my sin.

" 'Choose one of these three,' he said. 'Either you die, though you will be granted a place in the World to Come; or you will be ill and bedridden for three years, while the suffering you undergo will cleanse you of your sins; or for three years you will wander about as a vagabond, as the law prescribes for an unwitting manslaughterer.'

"I couldn't bring myself to agree to any one of these three alternatives, and returned home. For several days I suffered headaches, but mentioned this to no man. Pain gradually spread over my whole body, I was confined to my bed, and the doctor who was summoned by my family almost despaired of my life. 'The rebbe,' I told myself, 'has evidently chosen death as my means of expiation without waiting for my consent.' I immediately sent off a telegram to Premishlan, accompanied by a *pidyon* contribution for charity, asking him to pray that I be restored to health and promising that I would then call on him and accept upon myself whatever he would tell me to do. And that is exactly what happened. He prayed on my behalf, I recovered, and as soon as I was strong enough I set out for Premishlan.

"When I went in to speak to him he said: 'You still have ample time to die; and you have already been ill; so choose the exile of a vagabond.'

"As soon as I expressed my willingness to proceed with my punishment, he said: 'Let me teach you now how one goes about *praven galus*, living the life of an exile. First of all, leave everything you have with you at the moment — clothes, money — with me, and leave my house wearing some tattered old garment. Do not spend any day in the place where you found lodging for the night. If you are hungry, ask no man for money or for food, but if people offer you something out of compassion, you may accept it. Throughout the three years you are not to visit your home. This alone I will permit you to to do: at the end of a year you may visit your hometown and stand outside the city limits, while you send a messenger to your wife to bring you the account books of your business. If you see that your business is running at a loss, I allow you to return to your home — but I promise you that your business will not flounder. Throughout these three years you are not to ride in a wagon, but to make your way from place to place only on foot. And when the three years have elapsed you are to come to me. I will return all your possessions to you, and teach you how to conduct your life thereafter so that you will be able to set your soul aright.'

"I took my leave of the tzaddik, and took to the road, exactly as he instructed me to do — a trek of two years so far. Now I heard very recently that Reb Meir had passed away, and since he told me to come to speak with him when three years had elapsed, I didn't know what to do. But then I heard that in Zanz, not too far from here, there lives a tzaddik called Reb Chaim. In fact I'm heading in that direction now, in the hope that he will guide me. And that is why I will not accept your donation, thank-you, because at the moment I am not setting out on another leg of my trek as an exile: I am on my way to visit Reb Chaim of Zanz."

The innkeeper was so curious to know what the end of the story would be that he set out to Zanz with his ragged guest. The vagabond did not even manage to put his question to Reb Chaim, when the tzaddik said: "Return to your home, traveling by way of Premishlan. Find the grave of Reb Meir, and tell him that the *rav* of Zanz says that two years are enough for you, for you observed them with the true self-sacrifice of *mesirus nefesh.*"

ספר דברים
Deuteronomy

סדר דברים
Sidra Devarim

☙ Jesting in Earnest

וַחֲצֵרֹת וְדִי זָהָב
And Chatzeros and Di-Zahav (1:1)

It was a sad story that this penniless chassid brought to his rebbe, Reb Shlomo of Radomsk: his daughter was of marriageable age, and he did not know where to begin to find all the money needed for a dowry and a wedding. All this was written out in the *kvitl* which he handed the rebbe.

The tzaddik read it through, and exclaimed: "What is this I read here about your being 'a poor man'?! You had better leave my house at once, for our Sages teach us that 'a pauper is accounted as if dead,' and I am a *kohen*, one of the priestly family, who may not be defiled by such contact!'

The man ran out from sheer fright, but the tzaddik called after him: "Come now, come now! This must surely be a case of a *mes mitzvah,* a dead body which can be attended to by no one else, in which case a *kohen* is allowed to defile himself."

Those present laughed at the seeming jest, and the tzaddik addressed himself once more to the poor fellow: "You are worrying about marrying off your daughter. Tell me: do you have bread to eat?"

"To tell the truth," stammered the pauper, "I haven't."

"But you do say the *HaMotzi* benediction over bread every day, don't you? So where do you get the bread for that?"

"Most of it comes from my wife; she works, and earns a little."

'What a fine business!" cried the rebbe. "His wife supports him! Shouldn't we be warned by the example of Adam, whose wife gave him something to eat? ... And this fellow says that his wife supports him! Tell me: in what way does your wife earn her income?"

"She goes to all the courtyards [in Hebrew: חֲצֵרוֹת] of the squires in the area, sells vegetables and whatever, and earns a little from that," the pauper replied."

"If so," said the tzaddik, "we have a verse in the Torah which lists place-names, and there it says וַחֲצֵרֹת וְדִי זָהָב: that if she goes to חֲצֵרוֹת, she will no doubt encounter דִי זָהָב [literally, "ample gold"]. Go home in peace, my good man, and the Almighty will help you, and your wife will prosper with דִי זָהָב."

But when he came home and his wife asked him what he had brought back from the rebbe, he did not know what to answer.

After some time his wife came home with a package, and said: "Look here. Today I found this thing lying about in the mud."

They opened it, and found three hundred rubles — quite a sum in those days. Half of it they set aside for their daughter's dowry and the wedding expenses, and with the rest the happy man set up a little business in which he prospered for the rest of his life.

❧ ❧ ❧

After the passing of Reb Shlomo of Radomsk, this chassid came to visit his son and successor as rebbe, Reb Avraham Yissachar, and told him the above episode.

"My father," said the tzaddik, "was a remarkable man. Every expression of his supernatural powers and his *ruach hakodesh* he managed to clothe in jests and witticisms, so that no one should detect that there was anything extraordinary afoot."

◆ *Not Far from the Tree*

יֹסֵף עֲלֵיכֶם כָּכֶם
May He increase you...as you are (1:11)

Seated at his *tish* one *Shabbos*, Reb Yaakov Yitzchak (the Chozeh) of Lublin began rebuking himself in such merciless terms that his disciples could bear it no longer, and one by one they slipped out of the room.

Perceiving this, he changed his tone and said: "May God grant you all sons no worse than myself!"

Relieved, the chassidim returned to their places around the table.

On this incident Reb Leibl Eger of Lublin commented:

"We find a similar situation with Moshe Rabbeinu. When he began to rebuke the Children of Israel — as Rashi explains on the opening verses of the Book of *Devarim* — he no doubt perceived that they had fallen into melancholy. He therefore changed his tone suddenly and said: "יֹסֵף עֲלֵיכֶם כָּכֶם אֶלֶף פְּעָמִים" — 'May God increase you a thousand times *as you are*'; that is to says, 'For all that, may Israel be blessed with many more people *like yourselves!*' And then their hearts too were cheered."

◆§ The Summons

לֹא תַכִּירוּ פָנִים בַּמִּשְׁפָּט
You shall not respect persons in judgment (1:17)

When Reb Aryeh Leib, the Shpoler Zeide, had been rebbe for three years, a fearful famine descended on the region. The tzaddik, who had always found ways of providing for the needy and the widows and the orphans like a devoted father, now could find no rest, for he had no way of allaying the suffering of the thousands of paupers on all sides. So great was his anguish that for weeks on end he could bring himself to partake of nothing more than bread and tea.

As the famine extended over the furthest provinces of Russia, rebbes from the starving communities wrote to Shpola, begging Reb Aryeh Leib to clamor On High to have the decree rescinded — for was he not a tzaddik who was accustomed to working wonders? The Shpoler Zeide thereupon dispatched letters to ten of the mightiest tzaddikim of the day — Reb Zusya of Hanipoli, Reb Yaakov Shimshon of Shipitovka, Reb Ze'ev of Zhitomir, and others — asking that they come at once to Shpola.

When they arrived he sat them around his long table and addressed them in the following words: "My masters, I am taking the Almighty to a lawsuit. You are to be the judges. It is true that according to the law of the Torah the plaintiff is obliged to take his suit to the place where the defendant is to be found, but since 'there is no place devoid of His presence,' and since, more particularly, 'wherever ten are assembled the Divine Presence rests,' we shall conduct the court case here."

That holy congregation then prayed in unison — their supplications would melt a stone — and the Shpoler

 Zeide instructed his beadle to announce: "By order of the assemblage here foregathered, I do hereby proclaim that Reb Aryeh Leib the son of Rachel summonses the Almighty to a lawsuit, to be duly conducted in this room in three days' time!"

Those three days they spent in fasting and prayer, and no man was permitted to interrupt them in their devotions. On the fourth day, when their morning prayers had come to an end and they were still enwrapped in their *talleisim* and adorned by their *tefillin*, the Shpoler Zeide solemnly signalled his *shammes* to announce that the court case was now to begin.

"In the name of all the women and children of the Jews of Russia," opened the tzaddik, "I hereby state my claim against the defendant. Why does the Almighty not provide them with food, decreeing instead that they perish (God forbid) by famine? Does the Torah itself not say: כִּי לִי בְנֵי יִשְׂרָאֵל עֲבָדִים עֲבָדַי הֵם — 'For unto Me are the Children of Israel bondmen: they are *My* bondmen'? And do we not further have His promise, delivered to us by the Prophet Yechezkel, that even if His children should want to walk in the ways of the nations of the earth, this will never come about? It follows, then, that the Children of Israel are the Almighty's servants for all eternity, in which case at worst they should belong to the category of Jewish bondmen. And does not the law as set out in the *Mechilta* and the Talmud oblige the master to provide for the wife and children of his bondman? How, then, can the Almighty disregard his own Torah so blatantly, God forbid?

"Now I know well that some prosecuting angel will argue in the Almighty's defense that these servants do not serve their Master as perfectly as they should. To this I have two answers. Firstly, where is it written that if a bondman is somewhat lazy his wife and children are to be deprived of their daily bread? Secondly, if these bondmen are slack in their service, their Master has no one to blame but Himself. For who else loaded each bondman with an Evil Inclination which tries its best to dampen their enthusiasm and loyalty? I am even willing to swear that if not for this Evil Inclination which the Master Himself imposed on them, they would render the most faithful service imaginable!"

His case stated, the Shpoler Zeide resumed his seat, and the bench of ten venerable judges consulted their volumes of Torah law. After some moments they rose to their feet, and declared their unanimous verdict: "This court finds that justice lies on the side of Reb Aryeh Leib the son of Rachel. The Almighty is accordingly obliged by whatever means are possible to provide for the women and children of His People. And may the Heavenly Court concur with the verdict of this court in the World Below."

So they declared three times. The Shpoler Zeide then asked to have vodka and refreshments served. They drank *LeChaim* and ate together with happy hearts, and when evening fell they all went their separate ways.

Five days later the government announced that they would soon bring thousands of tons of wheat and other grain from Siberia, where it was abundant and inexpensive; the roads had been impassable, but now a new route had been hit upon. Whatever grain was already available suddenly dropped in price, for all the dealers were eager to dispose of their stock before the new consignments arrived. A month later the new grain was available, and for the whole of that year there was bread in plenty for the humblest purse.

A Man of Principle

אִם תֹּאבוּ וּשְׁמַעְתֶּם... וְאִם תְּמָאֲנוּ וּמְרִיתֶם...
If you are willing and obedient..., but if you refuse and rebel (Haftarah)

Late last century the Russian Imperial Government decreed that none of the rebbes of the Twerski family, who belonged to the chassidic dynasty of Chernobyl, were to leave the bounds of the various towns in which they lived. Reb Mordechai Dov of Hornisteipl was one of those compelled to sign their assent to this decree, for he too was a scion of this dynasty.

One day Reb Mordechai Dov found himself faced with a dilemma. His son, Reb Baruch David, was soon to be married in Homil. How could he attend? But then again, how could he not attend? ... He quickly disguised himself as a merchant, and smuggled himself out of town.

On the way he encountered a chassid who gazed at his

face very intently, and then said: "*Shalom* to you, rebbe!"

"You're a fool yourself!" retorted the rebbe.

But nothing would help. By the time he arrived at the *chuppah* under which the bridal couple were soon to be led for the wedding ceremony, thousands of people from all the towns and villages around had converged on Homil, if not to receive his greeting of *Shalom* then at least to catch a glimpse of the unassuming nobility which rested on his features. But for the rebbe this was a grim prospect: who could know where the Evil Eye of the authorities might be lurking? He asked that a wagon be prepared so the he would be able to leave immediately after the ceremony. Someone secured the services of the first wagon-driver who happened to pass by, and the rebbe hastened away.

As they passed through a forest on their way, the wagon-driver suddenly called the horses to a halt, and turned to his lone passenger: "I would like you to know that I am a professional robber. What I ask of you is that you give me your blessing that I should succeed in my work. If you don't, I will kill you on the spot."

The tzaddik was not alarmed, and answered calmly: "Here, let me tell you something. You know, a very similar thing once happened to Reb Zusya of Hanipoli. He was traveling out on some highway when he met a gang of robbers. They too asked him to bless their work with success, and threatened to kill him if he would not oblige. So Reb Zusya said: 'A wealthy squire is soon going to come past your way. You won't have to kill him, because he is going to die anyway while he is quite near you. This *paritz* will leave a considerable sum of money behind him. Now if you satisfy yourselves with that amount, and become penitent, and abandon your present careers completely, then I promise you that you will prosper in all your ways. But if (God forbid) you persist in your evil ways, then you will most certainly fall into the hands of the authorities, and the day will come when you will be led in fetters before the very door of my house.' And that is exactly what happened. Some of that gang repented, and followed the straight road, and did well; others continued to rob and murder until they were eventually caught, and they were in fact led in chains past the cottage of Reb Zusya in Hanipoli.

"Now as far as I am concerned," concluded Reb Mordechai Dov to his wagon-driver, "I don't promise you any fat squire. But this much I can tell you: that if you decided to abandon your crooked ways and follow the straight road, good for you. If you don't, then you will certainly come to a bitter end. I have warned you!

"And now, if you want to kill me — kill me."

But the wagon-driver accompanied him home in peace.

סדר ואתחנן
sidra vaeschanan

Prompt and Impromptu

וָאֶתְחַנַּן אֶל ה׳ בָּעֵת הַהִוא לֵאמֹר
And I pleaded with God at that time, saying (3:23)

In their younger years Reb Beirish of Alisk and, to a lesser extent, Reb Uri of Strelisk had both been close disciples of Reb Mordechai of Neschiz. With time, as the true stature of the Saraph ("the fiery angel") of Strelisk became apparent, his former friend came to regard him as his rebbe. So it was that Reb Beirish once hastened to spend *Shabbos* in a certain town because he heard that Reb Uri would be there.

At the *Shabbos* table, Reb Uri turned to his chassid: "*Rav* of Alisk! Could you perhaps honor us with a Torah thought, a *dvar* Torah, but without any preparation?"

Reb Beirish answered at once: "It is written, וָאֶתְחַנַּן אֶל ה׳ בָּעֵת הַהִוא לֵאמֹר — 'And I pleaded with God at that time, saying.' You see, in order to be able to *say* something *at that time*, unprepared, one has to *plead with God* ..."

Seeing is Believing

וְיָדַעְתָּ הַיּוֹם
And you shall know this day (4:39)

Returning home from his first visit to Reb Shmelke of Nikolsburg, Reb Levi Yitzchak of Berditchev was challenged by his father-in-law: "And what did you learn there?"

"I learned that there is a Creator of the universe," was the answer.

The father-in-law called for the maid and asked her: "Do *you* know that there is a Creator of the universe?"

"Why, of course!" she answered.

Returned Reb Levi Yitzchak: "She says; I know."

Each Servant has his Style

וְיָדַעְתָּ הַיּוֹם וַהֲשֵׁבֹתָ אֶל לְבָבֶךָ
And you shall know this day, and consider it in your heart (4:39)

Two towering figures had come to Lubavitch at the same time to stay for a few weeks and to hear the teachings of Reb Menachem Mendel, who is known as the Tzemach Tzedek: one was Reb Yitzchak Aizik of Homil, the author of *Chanah Ariel,* and the other was Reb Hillel of Paritsh, the author of *Pelach HaRimon.* According to the custom among chassidim, these two elder disciples used to repeat the many discourses on ethics and *Chabad* philosophy that the rebbe had delivered publicly, as a means of refreshing the memory. Following the instructions of his father, whom he was later to succeed as rebbe, Reb Shmuel of Lubavitch was one of those who used to listen attentively to these repetitions.

On one occasion the Tzemach Tzedek asked his son to repeat one of these discourses as he had heard it from the mouth of these two chassidim, for he wanted to know how they went about their task. When Reb Shmeul had completed his piece, his father said: "Reb Aizik is a *maskil,* and Reb Hillel is an *oved.*" [Among Lubavitcher chassidim these two words have special meanings of their own, quite distinct from their usual connotations. In *Chabad* circles a *maskil* is one whose chief aim is the intellectual comprehension of the teachings of Chassidism on subjects such as the relationship of the Creator to the cosmos; the prime goal of the *oved* is self-refinement — in thought, word, and deed.]

"What is the difference between a *maskil* and an *oved?*" asked Reb Shmuel. "For is not a *maskil* also an *oved*, and an *oved* also a *maskil?*"

The rebbe gave no answer. A week later, however, he delivered a learned discourse especially for his sons and for these two elder chassidim. That night, some two or three hours after midnight, he called for his son and told him to go and see for himself what these two chassidim were doing ... He was not to disturb them by entering their lodgings, but was simply to take a peek through the window.

Accompanied by an attendant, Reb Shmuel went off to find where Reb Aizik was staying. He saw him plunged in thought, his head thrown back, his eyes closed, his face ablaze, and in his hand — a pipe.

From there Reb Shmuel proceeded to the lodgings of Reb Hillel. There he sat, crouched forward, looking even smaller and leaner than he looked at any time, a finger in his mouth — a sign of profound concentration, his face pale, and apparently worried.

The Tzemach Tzedek listened to his son's report of what he had seen, and said: "They are both meditating on yesterday's discourse. Reb Aizik is contemplating the mysteries of the supernal Crown *(Keser Elyon)* which were elaborated there; Reb Hillel is reflecting on the subject of self-effacing obedience *(kabbalas ol)* which was discussed there, and is applying it to himself."

❦ ❦ ❦

Reb Shmuel was succeeded in turn by his son, Reb Shalom Ber of Lubavitch, who repeated this story, and added: "The difference between a *maskil* and an *oved* is that for the first, his starting point is intellectuality, and from this he labors to find himself tasks in the *avodah* of self-refinement that are in harmony with what he has studied. The *oved* starts with his tasks of *avodah*, and only then seeks the teaching that explains their place in academic terms."

Silent Partner

שָׁמוֹר אֶת יוֹם הַשַּׁבָּת
Observe the Sabbath day (5:12)

A certain shopkeeper complained to Reb Yisrael Yitzchak of Alexander, the author of *Yismach Yisrael*, that his shop did not provide him with a livelihood. The tzaddik gathered that the shop was open seven days a week, and made a proposal: "If you agree to accept me as a partner in your business to the extent of fifteen percent, though without any investment on my part, then I will promise you a proper income."

The shopkeeper agreed at once and they drew up a legal partnership contract. But the rebbe still had something to add.

"Since I now own one seventh of the business," he said, "the share I am choosing as mine is *Shabbos*. The profits of that day are to be mine, while the profits of the other six days are to be yours. You will therefore close the shop on *Shabbos*, for that is my day. And now, my good man, go along — and prosper!"

And the merchandising policy of the shop's new joint management quickly showed tangible results.

Bad Examples

Reb Meir Yechiel of Ostrov used to fast a great deal. "A person is obliged," he would say, "to change his very nature and to accustom his digestive system not to demand its needs. When a perfect tzaddik eats and drinks," he would add, "by this very activity he comes closer to God. But I, not being a tzaddik, must as far as possible abstain from food." And in fact he reached a point where he fasted even on *Shabbos*.

It once happened that he summoned to his study a Jew who had desecrated the Day of Rest publicly, and rebuked him for his shamelessness.

"But rebbe," retorted the sinner, "you also desecrate *Shabbos!*"

"I — what?" asked the startled tzaddik.

"Rebbe," explained the other, "you fast on *Shabbos* – surely a mark of disrespect for the Holy Day!"

"You are right, my son," conceded the tzaddik. "But still, my desecration of *Shabbos* is not quite the same as your desecration of *Shabbos*. You see, from your example people will learn; from my example, that is not so likely..."

❧ *A Share in a Mitzvah*

כַּבֵּד אֶת אָבִיךָ וְאֶת אִמֶּךָ
Honor your father and your mother (5:16)

Reb Yaakov Yitzchak of Pshischah, who is known as the Yid HaKadosh ("the holy Jew"), used to conduct a daily Talmud class for a group of his disciples, one of whom was a local youth who had lost his father. During one such class the tzaddik encountered an extremely problematic text, and was soon plunged deep in thought in an attempt to untangle it. The youth knew from experience that when this kind of thing happened, the rebbe could be depended on to be so carried away in his concentration that he would have time to slip out to his mother's house and take some light refreshment, for he was feeling somewhat faint.

Having eaten, he quickly rose to return to the house of his rebbe – but then he heard his mother calling after him, to climb up to the attic in order to bring down a bundle of fodder. At first he continued on his hurried way, for he was afraid that the rebbe had perhaps resumed his exposition by now. But then he thought again: "Isn't actual performance the ultimate goal of my study? If, then, the mitzvah of honoring my mother has presented itself, how can I not fulfill it?"

He ran back home to do the little chore that his mother had asked of him and then hastened off to the house of the rebbe. Exactly as he opened the door the Yid HaKadosh sat up alert, then stood up in his place and asked the youth: "What mitzvah did you perform now?"

The youth recounted the events of the previous few minutes, and then the tzaddik explained himself: "When you came in, young man, I saw that you were accompanied by the soul of Abbaye, the Talmudic sage – and I immediately had my answer. You see, the Talmud tells us that Abbaye was orphaned as an infant. Indeed, his very name — אַבַּיֵי — is made of the initials of the words from the Prophet Hoshea: אֲשֶׁר בְּךָ יְרֻחַם יָתוֹם — *'for in You the orphan finds mercy.'* Since he knew no father nor mother of his own, it is Abbaye's custom to accompany anyone who fulfills this mitzvah of honoring his father and his mother, in order that he too should have a share in the mitzvah. And once he was already here, and found me grappling with that text in which his arguments figure, he gave me the answer..."

◈§ *Spoonfeeding a Penitent*

וְלֹא תִגְנֹב
You shall not steal (5:17)

Reb Baruch of Mezhibuzh, who was accustomed to speaking harshly of Reb Levi Yitzchak of Berditchev, once made an announcement at his Friday night table: "If anyone here is willing to speak evil of the *rav* of Berditchev, I hereby promise that he will be rewarded by receiving a portion in the World to Come."

Now there was one young man present who wanted to step forward at once and oblige, but the elder chassidim who stood near him dissuaded him.

"God forbid that you should do such a thing," they said. "Our rebbe has no doubt some profound intention in saying what he did; his words are not to be taken at face value!"

The next day, at the *Shabbos* midday meal, the same offer was repeated, and again no chassid present dared say a bad word about Reb Levi Yitzchak — except for the same young man, who again seemed intent on earning his reward effortlessly. His friends once more appealed to him to hold his peace, and he heeded them, because he was certain that he would be given one more chance to do what he wanted, at the late afternoon meal of *Seudah Shlishis.* This opportunity in fact came, and as soon as Reb Baruch repeated his strange announcement, this impetuous young man broke loose from the entreaties of his friends, and burst his way forward towards the rebbe.

Seeing his efforts at pressing his way through the

crowd, Reb Baruch called to him: "Come near, my son, come near, and tell me what you know of the *rav* of Berditchev."

"I once traveled to Berditchev for a fair," said the young man, "and it occurred to me that this would present me with a fine opportunity to drop in to his *shul* to watch him at his prayers, for I had been told that this was a wonderful sight. So I took off time that morning in the middle of my business affairs and found my way to his synagogue. When I arrived there and heard the sound of his ecstatic prayers I did not dare to walk in; I just remained standing at the entrance. But when he reached the passage... יוֹצֵר מְשָׁרְתִים וַאֲשֶׁר מְשָׁרְתָיו — 'He creates ministering angels who stand in the heights of the universe' — the tzaddik suddenly burst across towards me in a passion of anger, and in the middle of his prayers, when one is least allowed to interrupt oneself by speaking, and demanded of me: 'What will the Angel Michael say? What will the Angel Gavriel say?' And he ran back to his place.

"Now whichever way you look at it," concluded the young man, "this episode sounds crazy. How was he allowed to speak in the middle of the morning prayers? And on top of that to be angry? And what do those strange words about the angels mean? And what did he want altogether?"

Reb Baruch of Mezhibuzh heard the young man out to the end of his story, and then addressed him in the hearing of that entire assemblage: "You should know that Reb Levi Yitzchak is an advocate for all of Israel in the Heavenly Court, speaking up in defense of his fellow Jews even when they have sinned. When in the course of their morning prayers Jews in This World reach the passage that speaks of the ministering angels who stand in the heights of the universe, that is the moment at which Michael and Gavriel and all their hosts speak in defense of the House of Israel, seeking to have them acquitted of the charges that have been laid against them. And when the *rav* of Berditchev reaches that passage, he joins them in their noble endeavors and reinforces their arguments. Now when he suddenly saw you standing there before him, besmirched with the sin that you had committed that very morning in your inn — for did you not pocket a silver spoon that caught your fancy at breakfast? — he was enraged, because he could find no mitigating circumstances to submit to the Court in your favor. You were not pressed into theft by hunger or dire need: you are a rich man, lacking nothing. Why then did you steal that silver spoon? *This* was what made the tzaddik ask in desperation: 'What will the Angel Michael say? What will the Angel Gavriel say?' "

The young man was shaken to his very foundations. His entire being surged with shame and regret for his conduct. He begged his rebbe to guide him to repentance, but Reb Baruch declined: only the tzaddik of Berditchev could teach him how to atone for his sin, and only by following his instructions would his repentance be found acceptable in the Court in the World Above.

The young man complied, and in the fullness of time found peace for his soul.

◈§ *What is Thine is Thine*

Reb Zelig of Shrintzk happened to be in the house of his rebbe, Reb Shmuel of Karov, who was taking a nap, when a certain wealthy chassid came in with a gift which he had intended to present to the rebbe: a fine set of tableware to be used on festive occasions. He had bought two sets, one for himself and one for the rebbe, and he left them both on the table so that the rebbe could make his choice between them. Now in fact when he had bought them he had already made up his mind which he wanted for himself and which he would give the rebbe. Later though, thinking it over, he had decided to leave the matter to the rebbe's choice, and he left a message with Reb Zelig to that effect.

Reb Shmuel woke up, received the message from Reb Zelig, and chose the set which the wealthy chassid had in fact intended to give him. Perceiving that Reb Zelig was most impressed by his choice, the tzaddik assured him: "Do not assume for one moment that this was a divinely-inspired feat of *ruach hakodesh*. Nothing of the sort! But there is a story that I would like to tell you involving myself and my brother, who is a *rav* of standing and — a *misnaged.* My brother once invited me to the marriage of his son with the daughter of some magnate, and when I arrived, my brother began to show me all the magnificent clothes which his *mechutan* had prepared for his daughter, the bride. Among these was a splendid gown, embroidered from head to foot in gold and studded with precious stones. Now as soon as my brother stepped forward with this thing in his hand so that I should see it more clearly, I shrank from it and could not approach him; it smelt, I told him. Seeing how he laughed aloud and scoffed at my reaction, I asked that his *mechutan* be requested to join us. When he came I began asking question after question, in an endeavor to establish exactly how he had come by this resplendent garment. It transpired that he had received it as a gift from a prominent gentile nobleman; more precisely, as a token of appreciation — for the twelve thousand gold rubles which this *mechutan* had caused him to earn at the expense of some other Jew.

"My brother was awestruck — but that does not mean that I was making use of the supernatural gifts of *ruach hakodesh.* It simply means that if a man is uncompromisingly meticulous about the boundary between his own property and that of his fellow, then whatever object has proceeded in the subtlest degree from theft *becomes revolting in his eyes* — though he may not know the reason — to the point that he cannot even step near it."

◆§ *O God, Israel Hears! (i)*

שְׁמַע יִשְׂרָאֵל
Hear, O Israel (6:4)

Reb Zusya of Hanipoli once came to Nikolsburg and asked Reb Shmelke to teach him.

"Very well," said Reb Shmelke. "If you teach me the esoteric works of the Kabbalah, then I will teach you the revealed aspects of the Torah — the Talmud and the legal codes."

Seeing that his visitor was agreeable to this arrangement, Reb Shmelke asked him what text he would like to start with. Reb Zusya's reply, true to his custom, was in the ego-effacing third person: "Zusya is a great ignoramus and simply has to be taught *Mishnayos,* with every word explained to him in Yiddish."

Reb Shmelke thereupon turned to the first Mishnah of the Talmud, in Tractate *Berachos,* which opens with the question as to when in the evening one is obliged to read the passage *Shema Yisrael,* the Jew's daily profession of faith. Intending, as requested, to translate the text word for word, he began: "מֵאֵימָתַי — *From when,* קוֹרִין אֶת שְׁמַע — *does one read the Shema ...* "

Reb Zusya fell to the floor in a paroxysm of terror.

"And what makes you think that מֵאֵימָתַי means *From when ...?*" he asked, still trembling. "Perhaps it means *Out of dread does one read the Shema!*" [The word אֵימָה means dread, or awe.]

"Perhaps," suggested Reb Shmelke, "you had best learn by yourself, the way *you* understand."

❧ *O God, Israel Hears! (ii)*

Reb Yosef Yitzchak of Lubavitch, who passed away in New York in 1950, once delineated the personality of a certain ordinary chassid — not a figure of towering stature, just one of the chassidim of the rebbe's grandfather, Reb Shmuel of Lubavitch.

This Reb Pessach lived in Homil. He was no Torah scholar, nor for that matter was he schooled in worldly matters, but he made a comfortable living by buying various kinds of merchandise in Homil and selling it to the shopkeepers in the hamlets round about.

Just before Rosh HaShanah in the year 1866 he joined a group of chassidim which was led by a chassid of renown by the name of Reb Mordechai Yoel, and they journeyed together from Homil to Lubavitch in order to spend the Days of Awe at the court of their rebbe, Reb Shmuel. When his turn came for *yechidus* — his first private interview with the newly-inducted rebbe — he handed him a *kvitl* in which he had written, amongst various personal details, the manner in which he made his livelihood.

The tzaddik blessed him and said: "You can always fulfill the words of the prophet, שְׂאוּ מָרוֹם עֵינֵיכֶם — 'Raise your eyes heavenward.'" And then he added: "*Shema* is *Yisrael.*"

Reb Pessach went straight from the rebbe's study to find Reb Mordechai Yoel, who would no doubt be able to explain what the tzaddik meant.

"Every synagogue," began Reb Mordechai Yoel, "is built with large windows: not only in order to admit light, but also to enable people to look out at the sky. For the heavens, we read, are reminiscent of the Throne of Glory, and looking skyward inspires a man with the awe of heaven. And this is what the rebbe told you. Since you spend much of your time on the road, and see the sky not only when you are seated in *shul,* you are thus able at all times to fulfill the instruction of the Prophet Yeshayahu: שְׂאוּ מָרוֹם עֵינֵיכֶם וּרְאוּ מִי בָרָא אֵלֶּה — 'Raise your eyes heavenward, and behold Who created these.' Now the word שְׁמַע is made up of the initial letters of the first three words of this verse, and when a person says the *Shema* with every fiber of his being, he is elevated thereby to the level of *Yisrael.* For as you may know, the name *Yaakov* denotes a Jew when he is at the stage where his service of God is that of a servant, motivated by awe; the name *Yisrael* is reserved for him who serves like a son, for the Jew who has reached the stage where his service is prompted as well by his love of the Creator. And that is what the rebbe meant when he said *'Shema* is *Yisrael':* through making the *Shema* a living experience, one can become worthy of being called a *Yisrael."*

Reb Yosef Yitzchak of Lubavitch continued his account of Reb Pessach with the following reminiscence of his own childhood: "Twenty-five years later, in 1891, when Reb Pessach paid a visit to Lubavitch for the Rosh HaShanah season — as he did every two or three years — he told me in detail all about that first *yechidus* in 1866, and added: 'When Reb Mordechai Yoel explained me what the rebbe Reb Shmuel had told me, I felt my soul lighting up, and from then on I yearned to understand the Torah. My neighbor, a chassid whom we knew as Hirschel the Watchmaker, taught me every so often, so that within a few years I was able to study a few lines for myself out of *Tanya, Likkutei Torah,* and various other classic texts. The rebbe's words put me on my feet!'

"The pleasure and the liveliness with which Reb Pessach recalled this experience were striking," recounted Reb Yosef Yitzchak.

As the years rolled by Reb Pessach became a rich man and he moved to Lodz, where he dealt in manufactured goods. Then in 1928, when he was about ninety years of age, he again repeated to Reb Yosef Yitzchak what he had heard from the mouth of the rebbe's grandfather, Reb Shmuel — and still with the same excitement and delight, as if this encounter had happened the day before. This time he concluded his recollection as follows: "From the time I first set out to try my own fortune on the road, I have always sought lodgings with large windows, and I always take a seat near a window, so that I will always be able to fulfill those words: שְׂאוּ מָרוֹם עֵינֵיכֶם — 'Raise your eyes heavenward.' Sixty-two years have now passed since I was privileged to hear from the rebbe, your grandfather, that *Shema* is *Yisrael.* Throughout all those years, whenever I say *Shema Yisrael,* at whatever point in the prayers — whether it be in the obligatory daily reading, or while the Torah Scroll is being brought out of the Holy Ark, or during the responses of *Kedushah,* or in the additions to the penitential *Tachanun* prayer on Monday and Thursday mornings, or during the climax of Yom Kippur at the conclusion of the *Ne'ilah* service — I always recall that *Shema* is *Yisrael.*

"One request I have yet to the Almighty: When the time comes for me to return Him the soul which He has entrusted in my keeping, and I am to breathe *Shema Yisrael* for the very last time, I pray that He grant me a clear mind, so that then too I will be able to recall those words the rebbe told me — *Shema* is *Yisrael!*"

"Such," observed Reb Yosef Yitzchak, "was one of the ordinary chassidim of my grandfather, Reb Shmuel."

The Password

וְאָהַבְתָּ אֵת ה׳ *And you shall love the Lord* *(6:5)*

"I hear that you have a *segulah* for a great variety of needs, and that these spiritual remedies and talismans that you dispense actually bring results," said a certain non-chassidic *rav* to Reb Avraham of Stretyn.

"In fact I would like you to give me a *segulah* for being God-fearing."

"I am afraid that for the fear of heaven I do not have a *segulah,*" replied the tzaddik, "but for the love of heaven I do."

"That's fine with me," said the visitor, "for is not the love of heaven a loftier thing than the fear of heaven? Let me have such a *segulah,* please."

"A great *segulah* for the love of heaven," said the tzaddik, "is the love of one's fellow Jew. Whoever has attained this can readily arrive at the love of heaven."

◆§ *Equal Time*

בְּכָל לְבָבְךָ
With all your heart (6:5)

With all your heart: Love Him with both your Good and your Evil Inclinations *(Mishnah, Tractate Berachos).*

The day before Reb Yisrael of Ruzhin arrived at the age of *bar-mitzvah* he was called to his father, Reb Shalom Shachna Friedmann, who asked him: "Do you know, my son, that tomorrow an important guest is coming to you, and that you should prepare yourself to receive him well so that he will agree to stay with you always? Receive him cordially, as befits a guest of such standing."

"I know full well, father," was the reply, "that tomorrow the Good Inclination will come to me; I made my preparations for his arrival a long time ago, when the Evil Inclination wanted to join me. This is what I told the Evil Inclination: 'You and the Good Inclination are partners in the heart of each man, and it is not proper that one partner should arrive before the other. I would ask you therefore to wait until the Good Inclination comes, and then you can come along too.'

"And in that way," concluded the boy, "I prepared to receive them both together!"

◆§ *In the Eye of the Beholder*

וּבְכָל מְאֹדֶךָ
And with all your might (6:5)

A man is obliged to utter a blessing on hearing evil tidings just as he does on hearing good tidings, as it is written: וּבְכָל מְאֹדֶךָ ... — "and with all your might," teaching us that we are obliged to thank Him בְּכָל מִדָּה וּמִדָּה — *"for whatever measure He metes out to us" (Mishnah, Tractate Berachos).*

Reb Shmelke of Nikolsburg asked his rebbe, Reb Dov Ber of Mezritch: "How is it possible to fulfill the injunction of our Sages, that 'A man is obliged to utter a blessing on hearing evil tidings just as he does on hearing good tidings'?"

"Go along to the *beis midrash,"* advised the Maggid of Mezritch, "and there you will find my disciple Reb Zusya of Hanipoli. He will explain the Mishnah to you."

Now throughout all his life Reb Zusya lived in utter poverty. When he was now told what brought Reb Shmelke to him he said: "I am most surprised that our rebbe should have sent you with this question to me, of all people. A question like this should surely be put to a man who at some time has experienced something evil, God forbid. *I* can't be of any help to you: nothing evil has ever befallen *me,* even for a moment. Thank God, I have had only good things happening to me from the day I was born until today. How could *I* know anything about how to accept evil joyfully?"

Reb Shmelke had his answer. This obligation — to bless God on hearing evil tidings just as one does on hearing good tidings — was now clear. All a man has to do is to rejoice in his lot to the point that he is not even aware of harsh experiences.

☙ *Yea, though I Walk ...*

And with all your might: וּבְכָל מְאֹדֶךָ — teaching us that we are obliged to thank Him בְּכָל מִדָּה וּמִדָּה — "for whatever measure he metes out to us" *(Mishnah),* whether it be a measure of benevolence, and whether it be a measure of suffering *(Rashi).*

A certain chassid once visited Reb Menachem Mendel of Lubavitch, who showed him frequent marks of friendly encouragement. The rebbe's son, Reb Shmuel, noticed this and was curious to know what manner of man this visitor was. The *gabbai* of the rebbe could not enlighten him, for he of course did not accompany the chassid when he entered the rebbe's study for *yechidus*. None of the other chassidim could add much: he was no one of particular repute, they said — just an ordinary chassid. Reb Shmuel then asked the man himself where he came from and was told he came from Paritsh, but through talking to him he could not discern any indication of unusual spiritual stature. He decided at length that he would ask his father, the rebbe.

"It would be hard to find a man who has undergone such suffering and abject poverty," said Reb Menachem Mendel, "but he accepts it all with faith and equanimity. And this is what our Sages mean when they say לְקַבּוּלֵי בְּשִׂמְחָה, that suffering is to be accepted joyfully — for joy does not necessarily mean rollicking and dancing. Another thing. This man is an accomplished Talmud scholar and well versed in the philosophy of Chassidism, but you will not detect in him any sign of holy aloofness. People treat him lightly and to him this simply does not matter. A man like him," concluded the rebbe, "deserves to be granted heaven's blessings of the visible and revealed kind."

For three years thereafter the visitor was not seen in Lubavitch — but when he next came he was accompanied by a *minyan* of ten chassidim whom he had brought at his own expense. The rebbe's blessing had been fulfilled, and he was now a man of means.

☙ *Bending the Twig*

וְשִׁנַּנְתָּם לְבָנֶיךָ *And you shall teach them diligently to your children (6:7)*

One day when Reb Yosef Yitzchak Schneersohn of Lubavitch was a child of seven he was given a watermelon by his grandmother, the widow of Reb Shmuel of Lubavitch. He gave a piece to a little friend, but as soon as they had sat down together on a bench in the courtyard to eat they were suddenly disturbed by a voice. It was the rebbe, Reb Shalom Ber, calling his son inside.

When he went in his father said: "It is true that you gave part of your watermelon to your friend — but you did not give it wholeheartedly."

The rebbe went on to explain the various levels that may be attained in the attribute of kindliness, as well as the nature of the opposite attribute, and the child wept in remorse to the point that he even felt unwell.

The boy's mother, seeing what was going on, asked her husband: "What do you want of the child?"

"Everything is in order," the rebbe reassured her. "This way he will have acquired a positive character trait."

Reb Yosef Yitzchak repeated this incident when he had already grown to be rebbe himself, and concluded with the words: "*That* is education!"

❀ ❀ ❀

At the *Seder* table, on the first night of the Pessach festival in 1943, Reb Yosef Yitzchak of Lubavitch recalled another childhood incident which had taken place fifty-three years earlier, when he was ten years old.

"In honor of Pessach 1890," he said, "I had been bought new clothes and new boots. The custom in Lubavitch was that after the *chametz* had been burnt in the morning of Pessach eve we would go off to immerse in the *mikveh,* and then, dressed in our best festive clothes, we would bake the *matzah* that was to be eaten at the *Seder* that evening. From that we would proceed to the other preparations that had to be made for the evening. One of my tasks was to remove the seals from the wine bottles, especially those on which letters were imprinted, and to ease out the stoppers, being careful not to let the corkscrew touch the wine inside. This job I did in my father's study, and as he watched my painstaking care not to soil my new clothes in any way, and especially my anxiety lest my new boots lose their shine, he said: 'Among the commentaries which Reb Shneur Zalman of Liadi wrote on the prayers in his edition of the *Siddur* we find a parable. A nobleman sits at the head of his sumptuous table which is laden with all manner of choice delicacies. His dog is busy under the table, gnawing bones. Could one picture this aristocrat forsaking his table and chair, and sitting under the table, gnawing bones?'

"This parable spoke to me so eloquently that I was ashamed to look at my new clothes. *That* is education!"

Words Worth Saying

וְדִבַּרְתָּ בָּם
And you shall speak of them (6:7)

And you shall speak of them: Of *them* shall you speak, and not of other things *(Talmud, Tractate Yoma).*

Reb Naftali of Ropshitz walked into his kitchen one morning before prayers, and complained to the womenfolk who were busy there: "And for all my efforts don't I deserve a little bit of milk?"

At that time Reb Asher, his son-in-law, had not yet learned to plumb the profundity of the rebbe's words, and it bothered him that his father-in-law should become so irritated over matters so paltry as food and drink.

"I'll have to rebuke him about this some day," he thought to himself.

Just at that moment a woman came along to the tzaddik and sobbed out her plaint: "Rebbe, I am a poor widow, and I haven't enough milk with which to nurse my twin babies!"

"Go back to your home, my good woman," he answered, "and the Almighty will help you."

Reb Asher in the meantime forgot to rebuke him because his mind was occupied with his studies, and besides, his father-in-law distracted his attention from the little incident.

A few weeks later Reb Naftali entered the kitchen with another angry complaint: "And I'm already given a bit of milk, it's all watery. Haven't I earned some good, *nourishing* milk?"

"This time," thought Reb Asher, "I will not keep silent. In fact I will rebuke him twice. A holy man like himself losing his temper over such trifles!"

Again his thoughts were interrupted by the bitter weeping of the same widow.

"Rebbe!" she cried to Reb Naftali. "Thank God I now have milk to given my little one — but it's like water, and the babies are as skinny as sticks! Won't you pray and ask the Almighty to bless me with good milk?"

"My good woman," said the tzaddik, "return home to your babies. God will help you and you will have *good* milk."

Reb Asher now began to follow the way in which the tzaddik worked, and from then on harbored no doubts as to his saintliness.

◆§ Early Warning System

From childhood it was a principle with Reb Shlomo Leib of Linchna – a disciple of both the Chozeh of Lublin and the Yid HaKadosh of Pshischah – to be scrupulously careful not to listen to idle talk; it goes without saying that he for his part never wasted a word.

As a youth he rented a room in a house which was also occupied by a tailor and various other people, and he always made a point of returning to his lodgings after the other boarders had retired for the night. It once happened that the *beis midrash* was closed early for some reason, so that the young scholar had no option but to return to his room. But as he approached the house he looked through the window and saw the tailor plying his needle as usual, surrounded by his apprentices, all of them bubbling their time away in empty-headed jests. In keeping with his principle he stood at a distance, but it was so bitterly cold that he had to try to keep himself warm by walking back and forth. Even this was not effective, and though he felt that it was almost going to cost him his life he still decided to remain outside until, weak and frozen, he lay down on the ground to rest. Had the hand of heaven not intervened he would have met his death soon after – but the lamp in the house suddenly went out, the tailor and his young helpers had to go to sleep, and the young Reb Shlomo Leib got up and entered the house.

"In order to avert a repetition of that incident," he later confessed, "from that time on I learned to give myself advance warning by developing the faculty of hearing even whispered conversations *while still at a distance.*"

◆§ Torah by Telex

וּכְתַבְתָּם
And you shall write them (6:9)

And you shall write them: With a perfect script [In the original: uksavtam – ksivah tamah] (Talmud, Tractate Shabbos).

ואתחנן

In the script used for writing Scrolls of the Torah, *tefillin* and *mezuzos*, there are subtle differences of usage between various schools of thought as to the precise shapes of certain letters.

Now when Reb Shneur Zalman of Liadi was a very young man he left Liozna, his birthplace, to study at the feet of Reb Dov Ber, the Maggid of Mezritch. One day the rebbe summoned his disciple and told him that the Heavenly Court was displeased with the lack of agreement regarding the script between those authorities whose legal decisions were based on the revealed aspects of the Torah — the *poskim*, and those scholars whose teachings were flavored as well by the mystical dimension of the Torah — the *mekubbalim*. He therefore charged the young scholar with the task of mastering both doctrines, with a view to proposing a mode of scribal writing which would answer to the minutest requirements of both schools of thought. The Maggid was pleased with his disciple's work when he saw it completed and thanked him for it, and revealed to him that at that moment a voice in the Heavenly Court had proclaimed that thus indeed should be the shapes of the letters.

The next day Reb Shneur Zalman came to the Maggid to receive his farewell blessings before setting out on a journey, in the course of which he passed through Hanipoli, the hometown of his friend, the tzaddik Reb Zusya. It was late at night, and since a light was to be seen in only one house, he directed his steps towards it in the hope that he would be able to spend the night there. It was the house of Reb David, the local scribe. Not wishing to disturb him while he was engaged in the holy task of writing a Scroll of the Torah, Reb Shneur Zalman slipped noiselessly in through the open door, peered over the shoulder of the scribe, and admired the deft discipline with which his goosequill sanctified the white parchment. But as he looked more closely he was stupefied: the letters being written under his very eyes were identical in every particular with those he had drafted only the day before as the original product of a wealth of scholarly toil! And it was clear that Reb David had not been in Mezritch when the letters had been shown to the Maggid.

After some time the scribe stood up from his work and was delighted to discover that he had such an honored guest. And when Reb Shneur Zalman asked him where he had learned to write his script in exactly this mode he answered: "I really know nothing about it. All I know is that today Reb Zusya told me that a voice in the World Above had proclaimed that this was how the letters should be written, since this style accords both with the *poskim* and the *mekubbalim*, and he gave me an exact copy of each letter."

Reb Shneur Zalman was overwhelmed by this new evidence of the sanctity of Reb Zusya. He called on him in the morning to pay his respects, and after they had refreshed each other's soul by sharing the sweet secrets of the Torah, he went on his way.

◆§ *Asleep, but Alert (i)*

וּכְתַבְתָּם עַל מְזֻזוֹת בֵּיתֶךָ
And you shall write them on the doorposts of your house (6:9)

When Reb Pinchas of Korets was still living in Ostrov, Reb Baruch of Mezhibuzh grew up and was educated in his house, and after his marriage he continued to visit his rebbe frequently. He was once taking a nap in his rebbe's room, when Reb Pinchas said to the people who were with him at the time: "If you stand around my disciple's bed, I will show you something novel."

With that he approached the doorpost of the bedroom, and with his hand covered the tiny parchment scroll — the *mezuzah* — which was affixed to it. Reb Baruch began at once to stir as if about to wake up, but the moment his rebbe removed his hand from the *mezuzah* he again fell soundly asleep.

After Reb Pinchas had repeated this a few times over, he said: "You have now seen a man of true holiness. Even when Reb Baruch is asleep his soul is not diverted from continuous cleaving to his Creator!"

◆§ *Asleep, but Alert (ii)*

Among the spiritual giants who gathered at Mezritch to pay their last respects to the departed Maggid, Reb Dov Ber, were the brothers Reb Elimelech of Lyzhansk and Reb Zusya of Hanipoli. After the burial was over the chassidim of the Maggid considered together the question of a successor, and after some deliberation a large number of those present agreed to appoint Reb Elimelech as their rebbe. He was duly inducted into office, and after they had all cried "Long live our rebbe, Reb Elimelech!" they set out together with him on the highway.

When night fell they stopped at an inn where Reb Elimelech, weary from the day's journey, slept soundly for several hours in the separate room which the chassidim had arranged for him. His new disciples were dismayed. Was it proper that the successor of the Maggid of Mezritch should sleep for hours on end? Some of them even had second thoughts as to their choice of rebbe, and went so far as to ask Reb Zusya, since he was his brother, to wake him up. Reb Zusya simply covered the *mezuzah* scroll on the doorpost with his hand, and Reb Elimelech awoke at once. The chassidim were amazed, and asked Reb Zusya to explain what they had seen. What connection was there between a *mezuzah* and — sleep?

"As we have all learned," said Reb Zusya, "every man is obliged to constantly keep before his mind's eye the four-letter Name of God, in fulfillment of the verse שִׁוִּיתִי ה' לְנֶגְדִּי תָמִיד — 'I have set God always before me.' When a man is asleep, however, and cannot fulfill this obligation, he must fall back on the Name of God that is inscribed on the outside of the *mezuzah*. Accordingly, when I covered that Name with my hand he could no longer sleep, and he had to wake up at once in order to resume his task of constantly setting God's Name before him."

The chassidim were overcome with relief and gratitude, and exclaimed: "Blessed be He Who did not leave us like a flock without a shepherd!"

☙ *Instant Returns, Instant Return*

וּמְשַׁלֵּם לְשֹׂנְאָיו אֶל פָּנָיו
And repays those that hate him to their face (7:10)

To their face: He repays them their due rewards in their lifetime, thereby depriving them of the spiritual rewards of the World to Come *(Rashi).*

Reb Menachem Mendel of Kotsk was on his way by foot to see his rebbe Reb Simchah Bunem of Pshischah, when he was overtaken by a magnificent carriage drawn by well-fed horses. When it slowed down and stopped, he recognized its owner as a childhood friend who in the course of the years had forsaken the path of the Torah. The tzaddik accepted his invitation to join him in the carriage, and in the course of their conversation on various moral questions he asked: "And where is your *This* World?"

"Why, don't you see?" smiled the rich man complacently. "I own all manner of good things in my house and in my fields, and do not lack even the luxuries of royalty."

"But all of these things are substitutes for what should have been your World to *Come*," the tzaddik corrected him. "My question was: Where is your *This* World?"

The materialist listened well. The words of the tzaddik found their way into his heart, and he became an earnest penitent.

◆§ *Instant Returns*

A freethinker once approached Reb Yitzchak Meir of Ger, the author of *Chiddushei HaRim*, and taxed him with a question: "In the *Shema* it says, 'Take care lest your heart be lured away, and you turn astray...for then God's wrath will flare up against you, and He will close the heavens so that there will be no rain...' — and so on. Now I observe the exact opposite to be true: the saintly folk have a hard life, while I, a freethinker, have everything I want!"

"Since you base your question on a verse in the *Shema*," said the tzaddik, "I assume that you have no doubt read that passage at least once in your life."

"That is so," said the freethinker.

"In that case," said the tzaddik, "in return for the mitzvah of a single reading of the *Shema* whatever you own is insufficient. You deserve more!"

☙ Of Cows and Cards ואתחנן

שְׂאוּ מָרוֹם עֵינֵיכֶם וּרְאוּ מִי בָרָא אֵלֶּה
Raise your eyes heavenward, and behold Who created these (Haftarah)

Reb Simchah Bunem of Pschischah was fond of saying that in three things he had been granted immediate success. Two of them he revealed.

He was once in the company of a group of "Deitschen" — the assimilationists and *maskilim* of the self-styled "Enlightenment" movement — who were drinking coffee with milk. He did not take milk, and when they made an issue of it, and insisted that he explain, he gave his reason, namely, the apprehension discussed in the Talmud — lest the milk provided by a gentile contain an admixture of milk from a forbidden animal. They ridiculed him from all sides: "The peasant woman from whom we buy our milk has fifteen perfectly kosher cows. Why worry about such unlikely admixtures?"

He breathed a silent prayer, asking heaven to vindicate the stand he had taken. Within a moment in walked the peasant woman and asked the little group: "Well, did you find the coffee unusually delicious today?"

"First class!" they chorused.

"And why do you ask only today?" asked the tzaddik.

"Why, because today I improved it with a touch of fresh pig's milk," she replied.

And from that day on the scoffers spoke of the words of the Sages with more respect.

The second episode involved the gifted son of one of the merchants with whom Reb Simchah Bunem used to do business before he became a rebbe. Seeing that his efforts at bringing this young man to an appreciation of Torah and chassidic thought were fruitless, the tzaddik decided to accompany him as a comrade in whatever activities he was engaged. Perhaps *that* would further his purpose. When the young man went to play cards, Reb Simchah Bunem went with him and even joined in the game.

In his own words: "Heaven is my witness that I had not the slightest notion of how to play cards — but I had the most extraordinary success, and won every time. At first I did not even know that I had won, but when I saw that no one else took the money that was on the table I assumed that it was mine, and took it. The young man longed to know by what clever secret I succeeded, because card-playing was more important to him than all the wealth and merchandising in the world. The more I deferred my answer the more curious he grew, until one day I took him for a stroll beyond the city limits, and he was certain that the precious secret would soon be his. But instead, I suddenly cried: שְׂאוּ מָרוֹם עֵינֵיכֶם וּרְאוּ מִי בָרָא אֵלֶּה — 'Raise your eyes heavenward, and behold Who created these!'

"The young man was of course taken by surprise. I told him the truth — that I knew absolutely nothing of card-playing, and that my extraordinary success had been granted me from Above only in order to enable me to bring him to an awareness of the Divine Presence. I went on to explain the vanity of such pastimes, and in response to words proceeding from the heart he became a penitent in all his ways."

סדר עקב
SIDRA EIKEV

◆§ *The Worth of a Worshiper*

וְהָיָה עֵקֶב תִּשְׁמְעוּן *If you listen...then as a result (7:12)*

During the height of the controversy that flared up in Vilna over the chassidic movement in the years 1796 to 1802, one of the mainstays of the *Chabad* school of Chassidism was Reb Baruch Mordechai, a disciple of the founder of the movement, Reb Shneur Zalman of Liadi. This scholar was the son-in-law of the last *av beis din* of Vilna, the celebrated Rabbi Shmuel, and despite his chassidic loyalties he was highly respected among the antagonists of the movement, the *misnagdim* of that city. In 1851 he made his home in Jerusalem, where after some time he passed away.

Late in 1801, while still a young man, Reb Baruch Mordechai was appointed *rav* of Bobruisk, where his repute as a Torah scholar spread throughout the nonchassidic communities of Shklov, Slutsk and Minsk.

When he left Vilna to take up his new position he was accompanied by dozens of families.

Among the chassidim of Vilna there was a scholar by the name of Reb Chaim Zelig who engaged in the study of chassidic thought. He earned his livelihood by hiring coachmen who drove his horse-drawn wagons from town to town with passengers and parcels, and one of his *shmeissers* — the Yiddish word for "wielders of the whip" — was a simple young man by the name of Reb Zalman Leib. He had grown up without a father and without education, until a *melamed* in the chassidic community gave him work as an assistant, his daily task being to bring the small children to and from school. Though he was a simple fellow he was upright and God-fearing, and taught himself with effort to read the basic sacred texts, so that he was able for example to read the weekly passage of the Torah twice over with its Aramaic translation, according to custom. Since, however, he could not understand the Hebrew texts that he read, he pored over their Yiddish translations, and derived pious inspiration from such folk classics as *Tzennah Urennah*. In the course of time he joined up with the brotherhood of chassidim in Vilna, praying with them and adopting their distinctive customs. His humble heart made him prone to tears, especially over his own ignorance of Torah, and when he poured out his soul to his Maker, the very sound of his prayers would arouse the tender emotions of those who stood around him — the more so since his voice had a tone of mellow pleasantness. The *misnagdim*, however, used to poke fun at him, and as he passed by they would jeer: "There goes our chassid, Reb Zalman Leib the *shmeisser!*"

When Reb Baruch Mordechai and his companions moved to Bobruisk, Reb Zalman Leib went with them, and taking the advice of the new *rav* he leased a vegetable field, from which he made a comfortable livelihood. He was happy in his new situation, and hired the services of a *melamed* who taught him Torah at a fixed hour every day.

Now it once happened that Rabbi Avigdor — the *rosh yeshivah* of Vilna, and the son of Rabbi Shmuel of the rabbinical court — was on a visit to Minsk. From the moment he had discovered his brother-in-law belonged to "the Sect" he had severed all relations with him, but when he saw how highly the *misnagdish* sages of Minsk spoke of him he sat down at once to write to Reb Baruch Mordechai, informing him that he intended to visit him in Bobruisk at a certain time. The dignitaries of the local council, presided over by the Seven Good Townsmen, decided at once to extend their expected guest the ultimate honor which was reserved for Torah luminaries — a deputation of venerable scholars would be sent in advance to greet him in a nearby township before he even arrived at Bobruisk. In addition they prepared a public welcome for him at one of the town's largest synagogues, at which he would deliver a learned Talmudic discourse.

On his arrival the guest was respectfully brought to the synagogue, but in order to enable him to rest a little from his journey he was first ushered into the antechamber. This tranquil nook was frequented by those devout worshipers who meditated at length over their prayers, according to the custom honored by the veteran chassidim of the *Chabad* school. From some corner behind him Rabbi Avigdor heard a voice in prayer so soulful that it tugged at his heartstrings. Knowing Bobruisk to be a town of chassidim, he asked his brother-in-law when he entered who this was who was still so enveloped in his morning devotions though it was now past noon.

"Why," answered Reb Baruch Mordechai, "that is Reb Zalman Leib the *shmeisser.*"

"And do you mean to say," scoffed the visiting pedant, "That Reb Zalman Leib the *shmeisser* is one of your lengthy worshipers? Why, he is only the *heel* of a worshiper!"

Reb Baruch Mordechai was silent. Soon after, Rabbi Avigdor delivered himself of a discourse that bristled with evidence of his impressive erudition. This he rounded off with eloquent words of *derush*, and he sat down a happy man. Just at that moment he caught sight of Reb Zalman Leib. He succumbed to temptation and repeated his jest aloud: "There goes the *heel* of a worshiper!"

עקב

Seeing this repetition as a deliberate public insult to chassidim and Chassidism, Reb Baruch Mordechai returned with a comment on the word "heel," the Hebrew word for which is עָקֵב *(akev)*.

"According to the Torah," he began, "the *akev* of a worshiper is something of importance, and brings about three things of benefit."

Accustomed to the quick mind of their *rav*, the scholars of Bobruisk now leaned forward to hear an astute reply.

He continued: "It is stated explicitly in the Mishnah that the *akev* of a worshiper teaches us three things."

This was an amazing statement, and Rabbi Avigdor and his companions waited skeptically to see whether he could substantiate it.

After a relaxed pause the speaker continued: "There is a Mishnah in the *Ethics of the Fathers* which quotes the Talmudic sage Akavya the son of Mahalalel as saying, 'Reflect upon three things and you will not come to sin. Know from where you came, and to where you are going, and before whom you are destined to give an accounting.' Now *Akavya ben Mahalalel* means 'the *akev* of him who is *mehalel E-l,*' the heel of him who praises God. And this *akev*, the *humblest* component of that worshiper, tells us: 'Reflect upon three things and you will not come to sin. *Know from where you came* — and you will not be arrogant; *and to where you are going* — and you will not be lustful; *and before whom you are destined to give an account* — and you will fear sin!' "

❀ ❀ ❀

During a visit to Chicago in 1942 Reb Yosef Yitzchak Schneersohn of Lubavitch told this story, and when it was repeated more widely, objections were raised from various quarters. Surely this *derush* was no more than lighthearted wordplay! For what real connection was there between Akavya ben Mahalalel and the heel of a worshiper?

The answer was given at the time by his son-in-law, the present Lubavitcher rebbe: "The small talk of a sage of the standing of Reb Baruch Mordechai of Bobruisk requires close study." And he substantiated the connection made by that chassid with detailed documentation from the Mishnah, the Midrash, the Torah commentary of *Baal HaTurim,* the writings of the ARI*zal,* and a commentary on *Proverbs* by the author of *Shnei Luchos HaBris.*

The "lighthearted wordplay" of a Torah giant requires very close study indeed!

◈§ *Hidden Earphones*

Among the guests who joined in the festive Purim meal of Reb Shalom Ber of Lubavitch during his visit to Minton in 1902 were a few who had been perhaps a little over-zealous in their fulfillment of the Talmudic injunction to drink wine on this joyous festival. In the course of their uninhibited conversation one of them said to his friend: "I hear you with my heel" — a Yiddish idiom signifying an utter lack of attention to what has just been said.

Overhearing this comment the rebbe said a few minutes later: "Even if this expression were used in a discussion on divine service it would indicate a sense of superiority in the speaker, and one would need to be wary of using it. If however it were to appear in any conversation — particularly to express scorn of another man — then it would bespeak arrogance and vulgarity, which are the exact reverse of the divine intention in sending down souls to dwell in This World."

The tzaddik went on to explain that the divine intention was that a man's heel should indeed attain the level of *listening,* and illustrated his point by recounting the following incident: "In Lubavitch there lived a chassid of Reb Dov Ber, who had heard from his father — one of the inner circle of chassidim of Reb Shneur Zalman of Liadi — that when Reb Menachem Mendel of Lubavitch was a little boy his grandfather examined him on the *Chumash* which he had recently begun to study. They came to the verse עֵקֶב אֲשֶׁר שָׁמַע אַבְרָהָם בְּקוֹלִי — 'Because *(eikev)* Avraham listened to My voice.' Asked to explain it, the child said: "Avraham heard God's command even with his heel!' [As if to say: So utterly permeated was his whole body with an awareness of the divine spark that animated it, that 'with his very *eikev (akev:* heel) Avraham listened to My voice'!] The grandfather, Reb Shneur Zalman of Liadi, was more than pleased with this answer, and said: 'In fact we find this very command in another verse — וְהָיָה עֵקֶב תִּשְׁמְעוּן [literally: 'And it shall come to pass that if you listen, then as a result ... ']. This verse tells us that we should strive to attain a level at which our *eikev (akev:* heel) should listen — that even our *heel* should hear God's command and hasten to fulfill it!' "

עקב

◈§ *Praise from a Stranger (i)*

בָּרוּךְ תִּהְיֶה מִכָּל הָעַמִּים *You shall be blessed more than all the nations (7:14)*

You shall be blessed more than all the nations (or, literally, '*by* all the nations'): Praise by her relatives does not make a woman feel praised — which is not the case with the praise that comes from her less loving co-wives *(Midrash).*

Suddenly, in the middle of leading his congregation in prayer, the Baal Shem Tov walked out to the street, bought a wagonful of firewood from a gentile whose livelihood this was, and asked him to deliver the goods to the *beis midrash,* where his chassidim were waiting for him, dumbfounded. He asked them to pay the gentile for the firewood, and to give him some vodka as well for his trouble in bringing it inside.

"Blessed be the God of the Jews Who has a People like this!" exclaimed the gentile in gratitude. "If one of *my* countrymen had bought this load from me he would have paid me nothing!"

Amazed that their rebbe should have interrupted his prayers for such paltry affairs, the chassidim asked the Baal Shem Tov respectfully for an explanation.

"The voice of a prosecuting angel was just heard in the Heavenly Court," he said, "alleging that certain Jewish villagers have acted dishonestly in their business dealings with the local gentiles. I had to silence that voice by having this gentile praise the Jews — and indeed that prosecuting attorney dropped his charges."

◆§ Praise from a Stranger (ii)

While Reb Shneur Zalman of Liadi was visiting a certain town a fire broke out in the house of one of the local citizens, and he asked to be taken there. When he arrived he stood leaning on his cane for a few moments, and the fire immediately died down.

Some of the soldiers who were encamped nearby had been trying to extinguish it, and when they reported to their officer what the tzaddik had done he ordered that he be brought to the barracks. After asking him to sit, the officer asked him whether he was the son or the grandson of the Baal Shem Tov.

"I am not his grandson in a bodily sense," replied Reb Shneur Zalman, "but I am his spiritual grandson — the disciple of his disciple."

"In that case," returned the officer, "I am no longer amazed at what you did today. Let me tell you a story about my father and the Baal Shem Tov.

"My father was a general, and once, while he was encamped with his troops in the town of Mezhibuzh, he almost went out of his mind with worry because no letter had arrived from his wife for so long. Seeing his extreme anxiety his friends advised him as follows. 'In this very town,' they said, 'lives the Baal Shem Tov, and he reveals things wondrously. Why don't you turn to him?'

"My father therefore sent a message to the holy man asking him to receive him for an interview. This request was denied. My father tried a second time — but again the Baal Shem Tov refused. This time my father sent him word that if he refused to see him he would issue a command forcing all the Jews of Mezhibuzh to billet his troops in their homes. Since this was just at the time when your festival of Passover was about to begin, this would mean that the soldiers would bring their leavened bread into the Jewish houses and wreak havoc with the preparations for your festival. Under the influence of that threat to his fellow Jews the Baal Shem Tov agreed that my father should come to visit him.

"When he arrived at his house together with his aide-de-camp they entered the first room, from which they could see through an open door into the room in which the holy man sat. He was reading a book, which my father was told was the *Zohar*. My father walked up to a mirror in the waiting room in order to tidy his hair before entering — but he was stupefied to see in the mirror a paved road which led to the town where his wife lived. He called his attendant to find out whether he too beheld this amazing sight, and as they stood together before the mirror they saw that the road led to the town itself, and within the town they saw the general's house. And as the door opened before their eyes they saw his wife sitting at her table writing a letter to her husband. Looking more closely they saw the letter itself, in which she explained that she had not written because she had recently given birth to a son; they were both well.

"My father was overwhelmed by this experience, and thanked the Baal Shem Tov from the bottom of his heart. After some time he received the letter which he had already seen at the time of its writing, and then recorded a chronicle of this whole episode in his diary.

"I who stand before you," concluded the officer, "am that infant, and here you may read for yourself my father's own diary."

◆§ *Praise from a Stranger (iii)*

A little before Rosh HaShanah in the year 1883 the Polish count Dravski — who had long ago earned fame as a poet and as a fighter in the battle for independence in 1831 — made the journey to Rimanov, there to pray at the resting place of the tzaddik Reb Menachem Mendel. All the nobility of the region gathered to pay their respects to him, and the eighty-year-old guest of honor explained the reason for his unusual pilgrimage.

"When I was a child of eight," he replied, "I became critically ill. My mother summoned the best physicians available, but none could help. Then one of her aristocratic friends found her weeping in despair over her only son, and told her that in Fristik — for that was where this holy man used to live — there was a rabbi who worked wonders. She had her horses harnessed at once, and by five in the morning the carriage with the two ladies had arrived at the rebbe's house. The household was already awake and active, for this was the time at which they used to bake bread for the needy. A servant informed the holy man of their arrival, and he sent back word that he would receive them at nine, after his morning prayers.

"At the appointed time the noblewoman told him of her friend's request, and he replied in perfect Polish: 'Is it because you think I am a sorcerer that you have come to me?'

"'No,' she replied, 'but your life-style is closer to God than that of most people, and that is why your prayer is heard more attentively.'

"'In that case,' said the rebbe, 'I shall pray for the child.'

"The two women left the room, but through the door, which they had left ajar, they saw him turning towards a corner and then praying with such fervor that beads of perspiration stood out on his face. After three hours of exertion he called for them, just as the clock which hung over his bed struck noon.

"'Right now,' he said, 'just as the clock is striking twelve, the child has felt better. When he has completely recovered bring him to me so that I can bless him.'

"My mother came home, and anxiously asked one of the servants how her child was faring.

"'Nothing has changed,' she was told, 'except that instead of lying motionless as he had been doing the whole time, he woke up at twelve and asked for water.'

"A few weeks later,' concluded the aged count, 'I was completely well. I was brought to the rebbe, who gave me his blessing, and told me that I should always treat Jews with kindness. I have kept my promise, and now, in my old age, I desired to make the journey here to Rimanov in order to pray at his resting place."

Dravski wept profusely at that holy spot, and following the Jewish custom, left there a note — written in Polish.

In 1901 the German scholar Reb Aharon Marcus wrote in his *Der Chassidismus* that he had succeeded in securing that very *kvitl.* (The tzaddik's surname was Turm, and the signature at the end, giving the name of the supplicant's mother, follows the traditional Hebrew wording of such requests.) It reads as follows:

Ye souls of Abraham, Isaac and Jacob — pray for the soul of the late Mendel Turm! And you, Mendel, since you stand already in the presence of the Heavenly Throne, pray for the oppressed nations — the Jewish People and Poland — and pray too for me, for my children, and for my grandchildren!

Miechislav Dravski the son of Victoria

◆§ *Praise from a Stranger (iv)*

In Vitebsk, in White Russia, there lived a goodhearted nobleman from whose estates many Jews made their livelihood. The entire town of Chekhov belonged to him, and not only did he forgo the taxes of the poor Jews who lived there, but in addition he allowed the religious functionaries of the community — the *rav*, the *shochet*, the *chazzanim* and the *melamdim* — to pasture their cows and goats without payment.

This *graf*, however, was an ailing man, and as he grew older and weaker he would have to visit Dr. Bertenson in Vitebsk more frequently, leaving the administration of his estates, his castle and all of his business interests in the hands of his manager, who was a sworn anti-Semite. The Catholic parish church stood on the squire's estates, and on the instigation of its zealous new priest the manager began to deprive the local Jews of their livelihoods, and to exact taxes from even the poorest of them. This went on for some two years.

Now most of the Jews of the town were chassidim of Reb Shmuel of Lubavitch. When they visited him for a festival or a *Shabbos* they would listen to a chassidic discourse from his mouth, and when speaking to him individually at *yechidus* they would ask for his blessings for their children, for health and for their livelihood — and then they would travel home, certain that the Almighty would have pity on them. Not one of them thought it would be proper to trouble the rebbe with an account of what was happening to their sources of income, or with stories of some anti-Semitic parish priest.

One of the Jews whose business affairs had been connected for generations with the estates of this *graf* was called Reb Shmuel Isaacs — an honest, respectable and well-to-do merchant, who was moderately learned in both the revealed and the mystical aspects of the Torah, and who was known for his hospitality and generosity. When he visited Lubavitch for the festival of Shavuos in the year 1880 the rebbe asked him detailed questions about the state of the livelihoods earned by the Jews of the town, and the merchant told him the whole truth.

"I know of the condition of the *graf*," said the rebbe, "for Professor Bertenson has told me that it is precarious. But why did you not tell me all this time about the change in the policy of the administration towards the Jews on his estates?"

The rebbe spent some moments sunk in thought, and then said: "Travel home now, and at the first opportunity at which you see the *graf* tell him in my name that I know that his condition is dangerous, and that his physicians have despaired of saving his life. I promise him nevertheless that if he helps the Jews of Chekhov and the neighboring villages, the Almighty will give him one month's health for each family."

As soon as Reb Shmuel the merchant returned home he began to frequent the squire's courtyard in the hope of meeting him, but for days on end he was not to be seen outside because of his delicate health. One sunny day, though, his doctor advised him to prepare his carriage so that they could take a ride in the fresh air in a nearby forest. Reb Shmuel saw him being led out to his waiting carriage, frail and listless.

The *graf* saw him too, and invited him to join him in his carriage. No sooner did he hear what the rebbe had said than he asked Reb Shmuel to draw up a list of all the Jewish families in the region who could earn their living from his properties, after visiting them all either personally or by proxy — but no one was to know of his mission.

Reb Shmuel duly provided him with a list of more than one hundred and sixty families from the township, with an additional couple of dozen families from the surrounding villages. The Jews were once again enabled to earn a living — and the *graf* was restored to health. Reb

Shmuel became highly regarded around the castle, and every year the *graf* would send with him a *lulav* from his palm trees, together with sprigs of myrtle, as a gift to the rebbe in honor of the festival of Sukkos.

In this way he enjoyed fourteen years of uninterrupted good health — but then he suddenly felt very weak. He sent for Reb Shmuel and asked him to set out at once for Lubavitch, where he was to visit the resting place of the rebbe — for the tzaddik had passed away in 1882 — and to notify him that the *graf* felt weak, though according to his reckoning he was owed another year and seven months of life. Would the rebbe therefore honor his promise?

◆§ *Fellow Feeling*

וְהֵסִיר ה׳ מִמְּךָ כָּל חֹלִי
And God will remove all sickness from you (7:15)

Every night, before going to sleep, Reb Fishele of Strikov would pour himself a drop of vodka. After pronouncing the blessing over it he would taste it, and say: "*LeChaim,* Master of the Universe, Source and Life of all life! A very good night to you, Master of the Universe!"

He once explained that this custom of his was really a roundabout prayer for the speedy recovery of all his ailing brethren, whose suffering usually increased with the approach of night. For since it is written that בְּכָל צָרָתָם לוֹ צָר — "In all their affliction He is afflicted" — it follows that when the sick and ailing have a good night, the Almighty too is caused pleasure, so to speak. This nightly *LeChaim,* then, was Reb Fishele's way of hinting to the Almighty that He should so arrange things for those languishing in This World that He Himself should — in turn — also have a good night ...

◆§ *Sources of Income*

לְמַעַן עַנֹּתְךָ לְנַסֹּתְךָ
In order to humble you, to test you (8:2)

There were very few people indeed from whom Reb Menachem Mendel of Kotsk ever agreed to accept money. And the one wealthy and scholarly chassid who did support him was distressed one day to find that the tzaddik refused even *his* accustomed gift. Finding no rest, he finally asked the rebbe directly for his reason.

"Every livelihood," answered the rebbe, "has a cause, and the Almighty is the One Who activates these causes. It sometimes happens that He chooses to put a person to the test — to see whether he places his trust in the cause, or in Him Who *causes* the cause — and so He removes that cause. Now if that man had placed his trust in *it*, then his livelihood is cut off from Above, for by his thinking he made it *in fact* depend on the cause. If however he had placed his trust in Him Who *activates* the causes, then his livelihood continues undisturbed, and the Almighty brings other causes into play, for His emissaries are countless.

"Now in my case," he explained to his chassid, "the immediate cause of my income was — your support. So I thought: What if the Almighty wants to put *me* to the above test, and to remove my cause? Then you will have to become poor, so that you be unable to support me. I would therefore prefer to remove the cause myself, so that you will not have to be impoverished."

"Rebbe," cried the chassid, "I want to continue notwithstanding! And if the Almighty should want to put you to the test, and that involves my being left poor, then I accept that result willingly. Anything, so long as you do not remove the source of your income yourself!"

But only after he had repeated his entreaty many times did the tzaddik finally agree to accept his gifts as he had formerly done.

That same year, through some misfortune, the chassid lost his wealth and became a poor man, and was forced to seek employment as a *rav* and as the head of a rabbinical court in order to support his family.

☙ *The Vitamins that Count*

לֹא עַל הַלֶּחֶם לְבַדּוֹ
Not by bread alone (8:3)

Reb Shalom Yosef of Sadigora, the eldest son of Reb Yisrael of Ruzhin, used to eat exceedingly little, and there were times during which he ate almost nothing. One day soon after a meal had been served to him, his daughter Rachel Leah entered his study, and seeing that the food was untouched she began to weep.

"Why are you crying, my daughter?" he asked. "Do

you think that abstaining from food is going to weaken me?"

With that he picked up a heavy chair with two fingers, carried it about the room, and after returning it to its place told her: "If a man provides his soul with all its needs, then he can be strong even without eating!"

☙ *The Theory of Relativity*

וְאָכַלְתָּ וְשָׂבָעְתָּ
And you shall eat and be sated (8:10)

Reb Dov Ber, the Maggid of Mezritch, once asked a magnate who had come to visit him: "What do you eat every day?"

"Bread and salt, rabbi, like a poor man," was the reply.

The Maggid rebuked him, and told him that he should eat meat and drink mead every day, as wealthy men were accustomed to do. After he left, the disciples of the Maggid asked him to explain his instruction.

"If a rich man eats meat and drinks mead every day," reasoned the tzaddik, "then he will realize that a poor man needs at least bread and salt. If however he himself eats bread and salt, he will think that his poor neighbor can make do with a diet of stones."

☙ *A Meeting-Place of Souls*

וְאָכַלְתָּ וְשָׂבָעְתָּ וּבֵרַכְתָּ
And you shall eat and be sated, and you shall bless (8:10)

When Reb Yaakov Shimshon Shipitovka came to settle in *Eretz Yisrael* in 1799 he was so distressed by the conditions of famine in which the immigrants from Poland languished, that he decided to travel through Iraq and Egypt and other countries in order to collect contributions for their support. In one of the Oriental communities he came to the house of a *chacham,* the venerable sage who was the spiritual leader of the town. When he heard that his guest came from Poland he asked him if he knew a tzaddik by the name of Reb Baruch of Mehibuzh. Sensing that this *chacham* was a saintly man who knew of Reb Baruch through the gift of *ruach hakodesh,* Reb Yaakov Shimshon replied that he not only knew him, but regarded him as his unquestioned master. But when his host asked him to repeat some teaching that he had heard from his mouth,

Reb Yaakov Shimshon — for the first time in his life — could not recall a word, and they were both distressed at their loss.

Suddenly something came to mind, and he told the sage joyfully: "I have just recalled some little thing I heard from him. In the Grace after Meals we say: 'We thank you, O Lord our God, for having caused our forefathers to inherit ... , and for having brought us out of the Land of Egypt ... , and for Your covenant ... , and for Your Torah' — and so on. After all of this we say: וְעַל הַכֹּל ה׳ אֱלֹקֵינוּ אֲנַחְנוּ מוֹדִים לָךְ — *'And for all of this,* O Lord our God, we thank You.' Now on this passage Reb Baruch of Mezhibuzh commented as follows. We are obliged to thank God for each of the blessings we have listed. But וְעַל הַכֹּל — *more than* all of these reasons for gratitude — *'O Lord our God,* we thank You,' that is to say: We thank you for being the Lord *our* God; we are thankful that we have not strayed from You!"

The sage was overawed at these words.

"And is this what you call 'some little thing'?" he exclaimed. "Why, these are inspired words!"

With that he proceeded to expound them according to the mystical teachings of the Torah. For three whole days they explored these secrets together, divesting themselves of the shackles of the body, and spurning all food and drink. At length Reb Yaakov Shimshon feared that he could survive this ecstasy no more. He rose to leave — but only after he had asked the *chacham* where he had come to know Reb Baruch of Mezhibuzh.

"I saw him in the World Above," he replied, "for he is as familiar with the paths of heaven as he is with the paths of the World Below."

☙ *On Guard*

הִשָּׁמֶר לְךָ פֶּן תִּשְׁכַּח
Be on your guard lest you forget (8:11)

While speaking to a group of his chassidim Reb Moshe Zvi of Savran once quoted some expression from the Talmud. The head of the local rabbinical court was present, and pointed out that the Talmud never once used such a phrase.

"How much time has passed since you last studied the tractate to which I referred?" asked the tzaddik.

"Why, just half a year," answered the *dayyan*.

"I have not encountered this passage for seventeen years," said the tzaddik, "but allow me to show you that I am in the right."

When he had proved his point by consulting the passage in question, he turned to his chassidim and continued: "There is no cause here for surprise. The Torah, as you know, commands us to sanctify the *Shabbos* in two distinct verses. One tells us to '*remember* (זָכוֹר) the Sabbath day to keep it holy.' This mitzvah is fulfilled by reciting *Kiddush*, the blessing over a goblet of wine which expresses in words the sanctity of the Day of Rest. The other verse tells us to '*Guard* (שָׁמוֹר) the Sabbath day to keep it holy.' Who is obliged to recite or hear *Kiddush*? On this the Sages tell us: כָּל שֶׁיֶּשְׁנוֹ בִּשְׁמִירָה יֶשְׁנוֹ בִּזְכִירָה – Whoever is covered by the commandment of *guarding* (שְׁמִירָה) is also involved in the commandment of *remembering* (זְכִירָה).

"And I tell you too: כָּל שֶׁיֶּשְׁנוֹ בִּשְׁמִירָה – any person to whom *guarding* applies, who guards himself from the faintest shadow of sin, יֶשְׁנוֹ בִּזְכִירָה – will be one to whom *remembering* applies. Conversely, he who is not constantly aware of this *guarding* will not be blessed with *remembering* ..."

◆§ *To — or From?*

כֹּחִי וְעֹצֶם יָדִי
My power and the might of my hand (8:17)

Reb Levi Yitzchak of Berditchev once saw a man running breathlessly across the market place.

"Why are you running so fast?" he asked.

"What do you mean?" he panted. "I am rushing in pursuit of my livelihood!"

"And how do you know," asked the tzaddik, "that your livelihood is in front of you, and that you are running after it to catch up to it? Perhaps it is behind you, and you are in fact running away from it?..."

◆§ *Regrets of the Saintly*

לֶחֶם לֹא אָכַלְתִּי
No bread did I eat (9:9)

Reb Yaakov Shimshon of Kosov was once in exceptionally high spirits, and kept his chassidim enthralled with a colorful medley of chassidic stories from the conclusion of the morning prayers until the middle of the afternoon. Not a single one of them thought of going home for breakfast.

When his narration had come to an end one of his chassidim rose and said: "There is nothing remarkable about the statement of Moshe Rabbeinu, that while he was on Mount Sinai, 'No bread did I eat, nor water did I drink.' For he experienced such intense pleasure during those forty days in the World Above, with everything that his eyes saw and with the Torah that he heard from the Almighty Himself, that he was sated — just like in the World to Come, in which 'the righteous sit and bask in the radiance of the Divine Presence."

Reb Yaakov Shimshon saw the passage otherwise.

"It could be that these words do not express the *satisfaction* that Moshe Rabbeinu had at not eating and drinking, but on the contrary express his *regret*. For he considered how many divine sparks hidden in food and drink he could have liberated and elevated through eating and drinking with lofty intentions — and this food would yet file its claim against him for having thus deprived it from fulfilling its divinely appointed destiny!".

◆§ *Two Encounters*

לְיִרְאָה אֶת ה׳ אֱלֹקֶיךָ... וּלְאַהֲבָה אֹתוֹ
To fear the Lord your God...and to love Him (10:12)

Late in 1801, when Reb Shneur Zalman of Liadi was imprisoned for the second time in St. Petersburg, an offer was made to him by Rabbi Nota Notkin, a prominent *misnaged* from Shklov: he would exercise his connections in high places so that the authorities would free him, and in exchange for this, the tzaddik was to undertake to visit three renowned *misnagdish* scholars soon after he was released.

After resolving an exceedingly knotty scholarly problem posed to him by the first of these three opponents of Chassidism, Reb Moshe Cheifetz of Chavs, the rebbe proceeded to his second visit — to Rabbi Yehoshua Zeitlin of Shklov, who received him coolly. Seeing all his questions on Torah subjects handled deftly by his guest, the *misnaged* challenged him on a statement that appears in *Tanya,* the classic text on *Chabad* Chassidism written by Reb Shneur Zalman.

"On what authority do you claim in your book," he asked, "that the Torah must be studied with the love and awe of God, and that the study of the Torah without this love and awe does not rise heavenward?"

"This is an explicit statement in the *Zohar,*" replied the rebbe. "It is written there that 'Torah without awe and love cannot fly upward.' "

Rabbi Yehoshua objected: "But we do not decide according to the *Zohar* — only according to the Talmud!"

"This is to be found explicitly in the Babylonian Talmud as well," Reb Shneur Zalman assured him.

Since his host could not recall such a statement in the Talmud, Reb Shneur Zalman opened Tractate *Pesachim* at the following passage: "Rava pointed out a seeming contradiction. In one verse we read: 'Your lovingkindness is great *unto* the heavens.' In another verse we find: 'Your lovingkindness is great *above* the heavens.' How are we to reconcile these two texts? — The latter verse states the reward of those who study the Torah for its own good sake; the former refers to those whose service is not completely motivated by selfless intentions."

Rabbi Yehoshua was impressed with this reply, and gave his guest a respectful farewell.

From there Reb Shneur Zalman journeyed to Amchislav, where he was surprised at the greeting he was given by Rabbi Yoel: "Shalom Aleichem, my master!"

"And in what way am I your teacher?" asked Reb Shneur Zalman.

"When we were young, and we were both in Vitebsk," recalled Rabbi Yoel, "I asked you a certain question involving the passage I was studying in the Talmud, and you clarified it for me. And that is sufficient cause, the Mishnah teaches us, for me to respect you as my teacher."

"If that is the case," returned Reb Shneur Zalman, "why did you not go to St. Petersburg to ransom me? Is a man not obliged to ransom his teacher of Torah?"

"Believe me," answered Rabbi Yoel, "that if your

 release depended on money alone nothing would have held me back ..."

And after a long and friendly conversation and a respectful exchange of farewells, the tzaddik — having fulfilled his promise to be confronted by three famous antagonists of his teachings — went on his way.

◆§ No More Questions (i)

וְעָרְפְּכֶם לֹא תַקְשׁוּ עוֹד *And be stiffnecked no more (10:16)*

And you shall circumcise the foreskin of your heart, and your neck you shall no longer make stiff: For homiletical purposes, chassidic tradition is fond of repunctuating this verse, and in addition reading the final verb (תַקְשׁוּ) ambiguously. The verse then gives the following advice. וּמַלְתֶּם אֵת עָרְלַת לְבַבְכֶם וְעָרְפְּכֶם - לֹא תַקְשׁוּ עוֹד: If you wish to circumcise the foreskin of your heart and your neck, then *ask no more questions (Traditional).*

In the first years after Reb Shneur Zalman of Liadi became rebbe, the chassidic interpretations which he gave of Biblical verses and Talmudic quotations were often condensed into one sentence. On one occasion, for example, he took as his text a statement from the Mishnah: כָּל בַּעֲלֵי הַשִּׁיר יוֹצְאִין בְּשִׁיר וְנִמְשָׁכִין בְּשִׁיר. The context defines the restrictions applying to animals on *Shabbos* — under what circumstances may they move freely and be led from a private domain to the public domain. This particular sentence says: "And all animals bearing a chain or ring (שִׁיר) may go out wearing their chain and may be led along by it." Reading this same text on a mystical level, though, Reb Shneur Zalman gave the following interpretation: "*All the masters of song (*שִׁיר*)* — that is, the souls and angels who inhabit the World Above — *go out in song and are drawn in song,* that is, they may be either elevated or drawn down into This World through the outpouring of a worshiper's soul in melody."

When one of the chassidim who heard this from the rebbe's mouth repeated this thought to the few chassidim who then lived in Shklov, they are most distressed, in anticipation of the attack which the local *mis-*

nagdim would no doubt make on this seemingly bizarre interpretation of a straightforward legal statement. And in a short time their anxiety proved to be well founded.

In due course Reb Shneur Zalman had occasion to pass through Shklov, but since the local scholars had by now recognized that he was a luminary in the Torah world, many of them visited him and asked him various learned questions which had engaged their attention. He however offered no answers. They therefore decided to convene a gathering of scholars in the communal house of study that was known locally as "the cold *beis midrash*," and at this forum the visiting rebbe would be asked to deliver a learned dissertation, and to answer all the questions that had been put to him. Reb Shneur Zalman accepted the invitation.

Ascending the pulpit he said: "Instead of delivering a discourse and answering questions, I shall sing you a melody. For there is a Mishnah which says: כָּל בַּעֲלֵי הַשִּׁיר יוֹצְאִין בְּשִׁיר וְנִמְשָׁכִין בְּשִׁיר — that is, souls and angels from the World Above may be both elevated and drawn down into This World through the singing of a melody."

And with this he began to sing his haunting melody, and they heard in it the intense yearning of a lofty soul. A sweet stillness stole into the heart of every man there. In ways that they could not fathom, the thorny questions and problems that had brought them there all found their sure answers. With his melody lending voice to his *dveikus*, he refreshed their minds from the wellsprings of wisdom, and they could now gaze upon the Torah with a clearer eye.

One of their number, by the name of Rabbi Yosef Kolbo, had spent months of fatiguing exertion in an attempt to solve four near-insoluble problems that not even the sages of Vilna and Polotzk could master. But now, as if melted by the harmony of a soul searching and cleaving to its Source, the toughest of his problems resolved itself peacefully. Years later, when he had already become a steadfast disciple of Reb Shneur Zalman, this scholar recalled: "When those four problems resolved themselves in my mind, I felt like a small child."

❦ ❦ ❦

In 1804 an elder chassid of Reb Shneur Zalman by the name of Reb Avraham Sheines of Shklov told this story to the rebbe's grandson, Reb Menachem Mendel of Lubavitch. It was on the basis of this story that Reb Menachem Mendel later wrote his long chassidic discourse beginning with the words לְהָבִין עִנְיַן טְעָמִים which explains, among other things, the kabbalistic connotations of the musical cantillation symbols that adorn the printed Hebrew text of the Torah.

☙ No More Questions (ii)

In his youth the tzaddik of Pshischah once heard a dissertation delivered by Reb Moshe Leib of Sasov, in which he resolved an apparent textual difficulty by pointing out that one of the authorities involved presented his arguments in the reverse of the expected order.

After the lecture was over he said to his young guest: "I did not approach this subject with the express intention of solving that textual difficulty. The solution I proposed is no major matter, and in fact I did not even notice the need for it — until while I was studying, the rationale underlying my solution occurred to me, as a matter of academic interest. Once I had thought of it, I cast about for some problem to use it on, and this was the best I could find.

"To take this one step further, my son," he continued, "I would like you to know that Maimonides in his *Guide for the Perplexed* did not start out by posing philosophical problems and thereafter seek ways and means of solving them. For if this were the case, then whenever he was waiting for an answer — even if only for a moment — then *for that moment* he experienced separation from the Creator, God forbid. We are therefore forced to the conclusion that he had all the answers to start with, and not even for a single moment was his faith bothered by any philosophical objections. For the edification of his contemporaries, however, he was obliged to demonstrate that the learning that he had mastered could serve to answer certain philosophical problems. Today, however, if someone were to study the

Guide according to the sequence in which its arguments appear — first each question and then its answer — then for the moment that elapses between question and answer he is (God forbid) separated from his Maker!"

עקב

From that time on, whenever the tzaddik of Pshischah studied Maimonides' *Guide for the Perplexed*, he did so in this fashion: first the answer, then the question.

◆§ *Exemplary Virtue*

אֶת ה׳ אֱלֹקֶיךָ תִּירָא
You shall fear the Lord your God (10:20)

Reb Yaakov Yitzchak, the Yid HaKadosh of Pshischah, studied under Reb David of Lelov, under whose influence he was to become the disciple of the Chozeh of Lublin. He used to make the journey to Lelov with the clear intention of learning from Reb David how to fulfill a particular mitzvah richly — *ahavas Yisrael*, the obligation to love one's fellow Jew as oneself. To this end he made a point of accompanying his rebbe on his visits to the neighboring towns and villages, watching his every word and move.

Finding himself in this way in a certain village, he took an outdoor seat where he could rest after the journey, while Reb David visited one of the villagers to ask how he was keeping. The rebbe took so long over doing this that the Yid HaKadosh asked him what had delayed him.

"I found a man at home doing his work," said the tzaddik, "while his son abused him for being lazy. These were his words: 'You are so lazy that if I didn't fear God I would kill you!' Now when I heard words such as these, I stayed on: I simply couldn't leave the presence of a man so God-fearing!"

◆§ *Service of the Heart (i)*

וּלְעָבְדוֹ בְּכָל לְבַבְכֶם
And to serve Him with all your heart (11:13)

> *And to serve him with all your heart:* That is, with a service which is in the heart, namely, prayer *(Rashi).*

When he was at prayer the Baal Shem Tov used to tremble exceedingly. Once, in preparation for *Tefillas Geshem*, the prayer for rain which is chanted once a year on the festival of Shemini Atzeres, he robed himself in his white *kittel*. His disciple, Reb Dov Ber of

 Mezritch, stretched out his hand to straighten a wrinkle which he had noticed on the shoulder, but at the mere touch of the *kittel* he began to tremble so much that he took hold of the table that stood in front of him, and it too shook. On another occasion the Baal Shem Tov became engrossed in prayer while standing next to the eastern wall of a dwelling, and the grain in the barrels which were ranged against the opposite wall was seen to tremor.

The tzaddik once said: "Whoever wants his prayer to ascend to heaven, let him say his prayers with me, word by word."

A certain disciple undertook to do this, and for a long period he would echo the prayers of his rebbe, one word at a time, from the first to the last. One *Shabbos*, while they were making their way through the morning prayers in this way, the Baal Shem Tov came to the verse: שֶׁקֶר הַסּוּס לִתְשׁוּעָה — "A horse is a vain thing for salvation" — which he repeated over and over again. The disciple repeated it once only, according to his custom, and then was left to wonder: On what mysteries could his rebbe now be concentrating? He consulted the relevant books but could find no possible explanation, so he decided to stop praying with the Baal Shem Tov.

He did visit his house some time later, though, and when the tzaddik asked him why he had decided to stop, he told him the truth. Whereupon the tzaddik explained the circumstances of that *Shabbos* morning: "On his way home from a journey some distance from here a certain Jew found that he would be unable to reach the nearest settlement before the eve of that *Shabbos*, and had no alternative but to spend the holy day out in the fields. A highwayman nearby came to hear of this, and leaped on to his horse in order to kill him and rob him of his possessions. But when I said that verse he lost his way, and the lone traveler was left in peace."

☙ *Service of the Heart (ii)*

Reb Dov Ber, the Maggid of Mezritch, was accustomed to praying alone, but every morning, when toward the end of the service he came to the rhymed paean of praise which begins with the words אֵין כֵּאלֹקֵינוּ — "There is none like our God" — he would ask someone to call together the quorum of ten men required for congregational prayer, and conclude his devotions with this *minyan*. One day, one of the ten happened to be a young man called Reb Yaakov Yitzchak Horovitz, who was many years later to become renowned as the Chozeh, or Seer, of Lublin. The Maggid asked to have someone else brought in his place, for this young man, he said, was a *batlan*, an impractical good-for-nothing. No one else happened to be available at the time, however, so it was decided to proceed with those present.

The Maggid barely managed to proclaim: "There is none like our God!" — when the young man fainted, and only with difficulty did his friends manage to bring him to.

"Didn't I tell you that you should not let this young man be here because he is a *batlan?*" said the Maggid when he had concluded his prayers. "All I said was: 'There is none like our God,' and as soon as he saw all the hosts of heaven, he straight away fainted from fright. If someone else had been here instead of him, he would have seen nothing, and would therefore have had nothing to be afraid of."

◆§ *Service of the Heart (iii)*

The disciples were spending the Days of Awe with their rebbe, Reb Dov Ber of Mezritch. When they had concluded the prayers of Rosh HaShanah, the New Year, the rebbe stood looking out of the window for a long time, instead of going home to recite *Kiddush* over a goblet of wine. So long did he tarry that finally Reb Menachem Mendel of Vitebsk approached him and asked him why he did not go home.

"What can I do about it," replied the Maggid, "if Reb Pinchas of Korets is still at his prayers, setting up a clamor in all the heavens!"

◆§ Service of the Heart (iv)

A few chassidim once asked Reb Pinchas of Korets why when he prayed his voice could not be heard, nor could one see any hint of ecstasy.

"The essence of prayer," he explained, "is *dveikus*, cleaving to the Creator, and the essence of *dveikus* is *hispashtus hagashmius*, divesting oneself of one's corporeality. This is something like the departure of the soul from the body. Now the departure of the soul from the body at the end of a man's lifetime – in the words of our Sages – sometimes resembles the dragging of a rough cable though a narrow hole, while at other times, resembling a kiss, it is like drawing a wisp of hair out of the milk. During prayer, likewise, in some people the temporary elevation of soul from body is as tortuous as the hauling of a ship's cable; in others, it is more like a kiss."

◆§ Service of the Heart (v)

"A thought once beset me," said Reb Mendel of Bar, a chassid of the Baal Shem Tov, "right in the midst of the ecstasy of prayer: 'How dare you pray to the Almighty, when you are so full of sin?'

"I felt duly contrite, and for a long time was unable to rid myself of that thought, which I believed was motivated by a holy source. But then I considered: If this is indeed a holy thought, why does it not come to disturb me while I am *eating*?

"And I banished it!"

◆§ Service of the Heart (vi)

A certain freethinker who lived in Berditchev was always scoffing at Reb Levi Yitzchak and his chassidim.

"If you were in the synagogue when our rebbe is at his prayers," they assured him, "then you too would be prompted to repent."

The *apikores* laughed and said: "I'll go along, just to show you that it will make no impression on me whatever!"

True to his word, he visited the *shul* and waited from the beginning of the morning prayers until the end of *Shemoneh Esreh*, and then snickered as if to say: "What did I tell you?"

But within minutes the tzaddik came to the words: וּבָא לְצִיּוֹן גּוֹאֵל וּלְשָׁבֵי פֶשַׁע בְּיַעֲקֹב – "And a Redeemer will come unto Zion, *and to those among Yaakov who return from sin.*" The very depths of his soul cried out, as over and over again he spoke these last words. This the visitor could not withstand. Touched to the heart, he resolved there and then to tackle life afresh, to become one of those who return from sin.

☙ *Service of the Heart (vii)*

Reb Levi Yitzchak of Berditchev once came to Reb Yisrael, the Maggid of Koznitz, and told him that he intended to make the journey to Vilna in order to argue in defense of Chassidism with the *misnagdim*, its opponents.

"Then let me anticipate their first question to you about your own conduct," said Reb Yisrael. "If you do not read out of a *Siddur*, then why, in seeming neglect of the Code of Jewish Law, do you recite the *Shemoneh Esreh* prayer with your eyes open?"

The Berditchever addressed him with his favorite Russian term of endearment. "*Serdtse* ('my beloved heart')," he said, "do you think I *see* anything at the time?"

"*I* know that you don't see," said Reb Yisrael, "but what will you answer *them?*"

☙ *Service of the Heart (viii)*

In the course of their prayer, certain chassidim of the *Chabad* school pause at appropriate intervals to meditate on those tracts of chassidic philosophy that illuminate the particular passage which they have reached.

It was with this mode of worship in mind that Reb Shneur Zalman of Liadi, the author of *Tanya*, once asked his son, Reb Dov Ber of Lubavitch: "With what are you currently praying?"

Reb Dov Ber replied: "With the discourse that begins

 with the words: וְכָל קוֹמָה לְפָנֶיךָ תִשְׁתַּחֲוֶה — 'And all those who stand shall prostrate themselves before You.' "

He then went on to ask his father in turn: "And with what do *you* pray?"

"With the floor and the bench," he said.

❀ ❀ ❀

This exchange has also been handed down in another version.

The father asks: "With what did you pray last Rosh HaShanah?"

The son answers as above. Then, in response to his question, Reb Shneur Zalman answers: "With the *stender* ('lectern') — for all of the material creation comes into being through the Creator's infinite essence (הִתְהַוּוּת הַגַּשְׁמִיּוּת הִיא מֵעַצְמוּתוֹ)."

◆§ *Service of the Heart (ix)*

Chassidim, as everyone knows, are sometimes to be heard singing quietly to themselves while they are at prayer. In an analysis of this custom as it is practised among chassidim of the *Chabad* school of thought, Reb Shalom Ber of Lubavitch once distinguished between a number of modes of *niggun* — including melodies of joy, melodies of contriteness, melodies of spiritual yearning, and melodies that sing of the worshiper's rapturous love of God. Common to them all, he explained, is a characteristically *Chabad* kind of intensity, that is, an ecstasy anchored in measured meditation, and finding expression in *dveikus* — a cleaving to the Creator that encompasses the whole being.

Reb Shalom Ber went on to recount: "Reb Moshe Vilenker and Reb Pinchas Reizes were among the first disciples of Reb Shneur Zalman of Liadi, the *Alter Rebbe*. When they first came to him, and had been examined in their studies, he directed them to Reb Moshe Zalman Feldman, who was to teach them *niggunim*. This chassid was a middle-aged scholar who spoke little, but was a gifted singer; on the festivals and during the Days of Awe it was he would led the congregation in prayer in the *minyan* with which his rebbe prayed. During the languid summer days he liked to stroll out to the fields beyond the outskirts of the town, with a large volume under his arm, and spend tranquil hours in lone study and pensive song. In fact it was this custom of his that gave him his surname — Feldman, which is Yiddish for 'man of the fields.'

"One day," continued Shalom Ber, "Reb Shneur Zalman entered the small *beis midrash,* where he found his two new disciples, Reb Moshe and Reb Pinchas, deep in their studies together with several of their friends. He took a seat at their table, and after some moments during which his soul seemed to have soared elsewhere, he roused himself and said: בַּמֶּה בְּהֵמָה יוֹצְאָה בְּשַׁבָּת — 'The Mishnah discusses the question, *With what* [appurtenances] *may an animal go out* [from a private domain to the public domain] *on Shabbos?'* Reb Shneur Zalman saw in this a mystical hint toward the service of the Creator, and interpreted these words as follows: 'The prayer-time of each weekday is its own *Shabbos.* And during this prayer-time, בַּמֶּה בְּהֵמָה יוֹצְאָה — *With what does the animal go out?* That is: through what kind of service in his prayer can a man drive out his animal soul? And the Mishnah goes on to speak of various kinds of animals — the camel, the she-camel, the donkey and the horse. So, too, each level of the animal soul necessitates its own distinctive manner of divine service' — and here Reb Shneur Zalman went on to explain them all. Then he continued: 'But what is common to all these kinds of service is hinted at in the statement of the Mishnah: כָּל בַּעֲלֵי הַשִּׁיר יוֹצְאִים בְּשִׁיר וְנִמְשָׁכִים בְּשִׁיר. [Literally: All animals bearing a chain or ring (שִׁיר) may go out wearing their ring and may be led along by it.] *Going out* and *being drawn along* hint respectively at רָצוֹא וָשׁוֹב, two of the primal forces in the dynamics of the human soul — in turn seeking to *wrest itself free* from the body and to cleave to its Source, and then *resigning itself* to the discipline of inhabiting a physical body and illuminating it from within, for this is its divinely-appointed mission. And singing [שִׁיר] during his prayers can help a worshiper separate and distill the elements of holiness hidden within his animal soul, and arouse him to pray with devout intent.'

"With this teaching," Reb Shalom Ber concluded, "Reb Shneur Zalman of Liadi implanted in his chassidim a devotedness to the service of the heart, and endowed them with the ability to be aroused to worship singlemindedly through the power of a melody."

◆§ *Service of the Heart (x)*

Reb Yitzchak, the Chozeh of Lublin, once asked his disciple, the Yid HaKadosh: "My dear Yid, why do you snatch the words of your prayers so hastily?"

The disciple from Pshischah answered: "I find them so delicious that I want to swallow them quickly!"

"And don't *I* relish the words?" asked the Chozeh.

"Rebbe," the Yid replied, "the words of *your* prayer are like fiery flames, so it's hard to gulp them down ..."

◆§ *Service of the Heart (xi)*

Reb Yaakov Yitzchak, the Yid HaKadosh of Pshischah, was once asked from heaven whether he desired to undergo suffering; he replied that he was willing to do so for one hour. He was at once visited by such grievous pain that he was unable to bear it.

"A time like this is a good time to say my prayers," he thought, "for prayer involves הִתְפַּשְׁטוּת הַגַּשְׁמִיּוּת — divesting oneself of one's corporeality, and in that way I will not feel the pain."

And with that he began to recite the afternoon *Minchah* prayer.

◆§ *Service of the Heart (xii)*

Reb Uri of Strelisk once visited a town, and while in its synagogue prayed at length with the ecstatic abandon that earned him the reverent nickname "the Saraph," or fiery angel.

After the service the local *rav* asked him: "Do you not consider the possible inconvenience to the waiting congregation? For the Talmud tells us that when Rabbi Akiva prayed alone, his prayer was so ecstatic that a person might leave him in one corner of the room and find him later in another. When he prayed with the congregation, however, he used to pray briefly, in order to spare them inconvenience."

"But Rabbi Akiva," replied the tzaddik, "had twenty-four thousand disciples, and amongst them there must have been at least ten men — enough for a *minyan* — who did not find their rebbe's prayer burdensome. Why, then, did he not pray with them, and then he would not have to cut his prayers short? We are therefore forced to understand his practice as follows. When he used to pray *with* the congregation — that is, when the congregation prayed with devotion, as he did — then his prayer was accepted at once, and there was no need for him to pray at length. But if within that vast congregation he prayed *alone* — he alone prayed as one should — then because of the necessity of raising aloft and refining all the prayers of the whole congregation, Rabbi Akiva was forced to pray at length ..."

◈§ *Service of the Heart (xiii)*

Reb Yisrael of Ruzhin used to take a long time over his prayers; Reb Shalom of Belz would recite his prayers hastily. On this one of their contemporaries commented that both of them cherished every word of the prayers: the former loved them so much that he could not bring himself to part with them, while the latter — for the same reason — could not restrain his eagerness to make them his.

◈§ *Service of the Heart (xiv)*

The mode of worship traditionally favored by chassidim of the *Chabad* school of thought which flourished in Belorussia is characterized by the unhurried and systematic contemplation of themes in chassidic philosophy which underlie the prayer at hand; Polish chassidim, by contrast, are accustomed to reading their prayers ecstatically, but quickly.

Two chassidim once met — one a devotee of this school of thought, one of the other — and discussed the worshiper's task of warding off any extraneous thoughts which may interfere with his concentration during prayer.

Said the Polish chassid: "Suppose a farmer decides to put up a fence in order to keep his swine out of his vegetable patch. If he binds the canes close to each other, without leaving spaces between them, then he will achieve his aim; if he leaves spaces between them, then the pigs will certainly find their way in ..."

"You are right," said the *Chabad* chassid. "But this is only true if they are not yet in the garden. If, however, they are already inside, and one needs to drive them out, then if the canes of the fence are placed *too* closely together, there will never be any chance of driving them out at all!"

◆§ *Service of the Heart (xv)*

Another *Chabad* chassid once brought his plaint to Reb Hillel of Paritsh, the celebrated elder chassid of Reb Menachem Mendel of Lubavitch. When he studied chassidic writings in preparation for prayer, his soul was afire; when he then proceeded to read the daily prayers, this spiritual zest left him, and he was unable to pray as he should.

"We have a rebbe," said Reb Hillel. "Ask him."

"But is it possible to make the journey to the rebbe for every question that comes up?" objected the chassid.

"So if the festival of *Sukkos* came and you haven't got a *lulav* and an *esrog* with which to carry out the mitzvah of taking the Four Species in your hand," said Reb Hillel, "do you make do with a stick and shake it instead?"

The chassid was persistent nevertheless and entreated Reb Hillel to advise him what to do, until he finally obliged and said: "So what does it matter to you if you pray *before* you say your prayers?"

◆§ *Service of the Heart (xvi)*

Weary and famished after a long journey, Reb Zelig of Shrintzk once arrived at the home of his grandson, Reb Yechiel Meir of Gostynin. Not wanting to keep him waiting until after he had said his morning prayers so that they could eat together, Reb Yechiel Meir asked his grandfather to eat his breakfast at once, alone. At first the older man insisted that he would wait, but finally he agreed to eat alone — for does the Talmud not teach that a guest is obliged to accede to the requests of his host?

When Reb Yechiel Meir joined him at the table after having finished his prayers in another room, Reb Zelig said: "Here, let us say there is something I want to tell you which I learned through the inspiration of *ruach hakodesh* ... Today you did not pray with a settled mind. In fact you did not even take note of the words you were saying!"

Amazed, his grandson asked him how he knew.

Reb Zelig answered: "Rabbeinu Bachya writes in *Chovos HaLevavos* that he who prays without *kavanah,* without devout intent, is like a man who gives another a meal but does not eat with him. Since you gave me breakfast but did not eat with me, it is certain that you prayed without *kavanah.*"

◆§ *Service of the Heart (xvii)*

Reb Zalman Zlotopolski was a chassid who enjoyed the rare distinction of being held in such esteem by his rebbe, Reb Shmuel of Lubavitch, that he had entire chassidic discourses delivered exclusively to himself, in private. In 1878, in the midst of such a discourse, the rebbe quoted the well-known Talmudic dictum: "Rabbi Eliezer used to give a coin to a pauper, and then he would pray." Prayer, explained the rebbe, should be characterized by liveliness. When one gives alms to a poor man and thereby enlivens him, one's own prayer thereafter gains greatly in vitality — and to emphasize his point, Reb Shmuel threw his arms upward, as he was wont to do on such occasions.

As soon as Reb Zalman returned home to Kremenchug he repeated his discourse to Reb Chaim Dov, a chassid who was renowned for the depth of his grasp in the more profound reaches of chassidic philosophy. Starting the very next morning, Reb Chaim Dov made it his custom to provide vodka and cake on the table at the back of the *beis midrash* in order to enliven the spirits of all the poor folk who passed through the town.

When word of this came back to Reb Shmuel in Lubavitch, he commented: "Do you think that Reb Chaim Dov's erudition comes from his study of *Shaarei Orah* or *Ateres Rosh* [abstruse philosophical tracts of the speaker's grandfather, Reb Dov Ber of Lubavitch]? Not at all! It owes its success to the cake that he gives the underfed before he prays."

◆§ *Telling Half a Story*

פֶּן יִפְתֶּה לְבַבְכֶם... וְעָצַר אֶת הַשָּׁמַיִם
Lest your heart be beguiled... then will He close up the skies (11:16-17)

A man complained to Reb Yitzchak of Vorki that he was not earning enough to make a living. After the tzaddik had answered whatever he answered, he commented to one of his chassidim, Reb Feivl of Gritza: "This man was ashamed to repeat the first half of the quotation to me, so he only quoted the second half."

The other chassidim who were present did not understand this comment, but Reb Feivl later explained them Reb Yitzchak's meaning. "The rebbe," he said, "was alluding to a statement in the Mishnah: 'I have conducted myself wrongly, and I have ruined my livelihood ...' "

◆§ *The Land of the Living*

לְמַעַן יִרְבּוּ יְמֵיכֶם
That your days... may increase (11:21)

In order that your days ... may increase on the Land which God swore to your forefathers: Thus is it written — but not outside the Land *(Talmud, Tractate Berachos).*

Reb Eliyahu Yosef of Drivin was one of the elder disciples of Reb Dov Ber of Lubavitch and, after his passing, of Reb Menachem Mendel of Lubavitch, both of whom used to direct students to learn chassidic philosophy from his mouth. After he had moved from Drivin he became the *rav* of Polotzk, where he became dangerously ill, and his doctors despaired of saving his life. Now the disease from which he suffered is the subject of a conflict of opinion in the *Shulchan Aruch,* the Code of Jewish Law. If an animal were to contract this disease, Rabbi Yosef Caro holds it to be still kosher, while Rabbi Moshe Isserles holds the animal to become *trefah,* in which case it must be discarded.

Said Reb Eliyahu Yosef: "I known what I will do. I will go and settle in *Eretz Yisrael,* where Rabbi Yosef Caro — from his time onward — is the *mara de'asra,* the ruling legal authority for that region. In *Eretz Yisrael,* the law will be settled in accordance with *his* view!"

He set out at once for the Holy Land, where he lived on for over twenty years more. At length he passed away on the twelfth of Tammuz 1865 in Jerusalem, among whose hills he was brought to rest.

סדר ראה
Sidra Re'eh

◆§ *Life-Giving Waters*

כִּי תְאַוֶּה נַפְשְׁךָ לֶאֱכֹל
For you will desire to eat (12:20)

Towards the end of a fast which was to extend from one *Shabbos* to the next, Reb David of Lelov was out on the road when he experienced the most fearful thirst. The sudden sight of a spring bubbling with cool, clear water intensified his suffering so acutely that he was on the point of breaking his fast and drinking. He stood still for a moment to consider the matter briefly, and found the strength in himself to master his burning thirst.

Continuing on his way, he soon found himself overcome by a surge of unutterable joy: he had succeeded in vanquishing his Evil Inclination! A further moment's thought, however, taught him otherwise.

"This joy could not derive from the Good Inclination," he told himself. "It no doubt came from the Other Side. The Evil Inclination is contriving to trap me into becoming conceited!"

And in order to avoid becoming thus ensnared, Reb David returned to the spring, and drank his fill of its waters.

◆§ *A Healthy Appetite*

Reb Yitzchak Meir of Ger, accompanied by Rabbi Dov Meisels of Warsaw, once visited a wealthy individual in the capital city in order to ask him to utilize his connections with the authorities for some matter involving the public good.

When they were shown into his house they found him enjoying his lunch of non-kosher food. The tzaddik of Ger promptly gave him the customary greeting: "Good appetite!"

"Rebbe," said their host, "if you knew that I was now eating forbidden food, you would not have wished me such a good appetite!"

"Quite the contrary," said the rebbe, "I intentionally wished you just that, in the hope that in the eyes of heaven you would be classed only as a *mumar leteiavon* — an apostate who acts out of uncontrolled desire, rather than as a *mumar lehach'is* — an apostate who is motivated by wilful rebelliousness ..."

◆§ *A Matter of Taste*

A wealthy Jew from Pest, who did not observe the Sabbath and the festivals and who ate non-kosher food, happened to be present at a chassidic gathering presided over by Reb Chaim of Zanz. According to the custom at the *tish* in certain chassidic circles, the rebbe partook of the food which was served to him, and then offered the remaining portion *(shirayim)* to his disciples, each of whom tasted a morsel. Reb Chaim offered a little of the food to this individual too — but as soon as he reached home he complained of a stomach ailment, and from then on lost his appetite so completely that he balked at the sight of food. Since he steadily lost weight and the doctors were baffled, his family seized upon the suggestion that some passerby offered them — that they should seek the advice of a certain tzaddik who happened to be nearby at the time. His name: Reb Chaim of Zanz.

The tzaddik heard their story,and advised them to break all the *trefah* kitchen utensils in the house or to sell them to gentiles, and replace them with new ones, and to begin to conduct a kosher kitchen. The head of the house would soon be well.

As soon as these instructions were carried out the

waning patient began indeed to recover his appetite, and as he regained his former strength, the reason for his ailment became clear to them all: once he had tasted the *shirayim* which the tzaddik had offered him, he developed an instinctive aversion to any *trefah* food.

◆§ *Feed the Body, Feed the Soul*

Rebbitzin Rivkah, the wife of Reb Shmuel of Lubavitch, developed such a serious lung condition that her doctors declared her case to be beyond hope.

Her father-in-law, Reb Menachem Mendel of Lubavitch, heard this and said: "On the verse וְרַפֹּא יְרַפֵּא — 'and he shall surely heal,' the Sages of the Talmud comment that 'from this we learn that the Torah permits a doctor to heal.' *This* is what the Torah permits — but when it comes to pronouncing the opposite verdict, God forbid, that is no affair of his at all."

He then instructed her to make a breakfast of bread and butter every morning immediately after washing her hands when she woke up — without observing the usual order of first saying her morning prayers — and gave her his blessing for long life. After some time she decided to allow this instruction to lapse, and told her father-in-law that she now hurried through the morning prayers, and immediately after that sat down to breakfast.

"It is better to eat in order to be able to pray," he said, "than to pray in order to be able to eat."

◆§ *One Man's Meat*

While Reb Shmuel of Lubavitch was on a visit to St. Petersburg for some communal matter, one of his chassidim came to him with a complaint: "Rebbe, in this city it is hard to come by meat that is really strictly kosher."

"And who says that one has to eat meat altogether?" asked the rebbe. "Have not the Sages of the Talmud taught us that 'an ignoramus is forbidden (אָסוּר) to eat meat'? Now this word אָסוּר at root means *bound*. That is to say, an ignoramus feels *bound* to eat meat ... One can survive *without* such meat that one lusts to eat."

◆§ In the Eyes of God and Man

וְזָבַחְתָּ... כַּאֲשֶׁר צִוִּיתִךָ
And you shall slaughter...as I have commanded you (12:21)

Reb Nachum of Chernobyl was making one of his accustomed rounds of the Jewish towns and villages collecting money for the ransom of captives. Arriving one morning at the outskirts of a certain village he asked one of the local citizens: "Where does your *shochet* live?"

Now the man he met was in fact the local *shochet* himself, but because he was dressed in tattered clothes he did not want to introduce himself as such to the visitor, who was obviously a man of stature. He therefore gave him instructions as to how to reach the house of the *shochet* — by a roundabout route, while he himself took a short cut home, and changed his clothes before the prominent guest arrived.

Some time after Reb Nachum found the house he explained to his host — gently and apologetically — that it was his custom, wherever he traveled, to ask to be shown the knife of the ritual slaughterer, in order to satisfy himself as to its unblemished sharpness and validity. After his prayers, could he therefore be shown his host's knife?

While the tzaddik was praying, the *shochet* took out his own knife, examined it, and found it to be in excellent condition. "Nevertheless,' he thought, "since I am about to show it to someone, perhaps I might as well sharpen it just a little bit more?"

But this thought was immediately replaced by another: "Now let us see. If someone were to ask me right now to slaughter for him, would I not use this knife right away, exactly as it is? Is it not then unthinkable that in the sight of the Almighty the knife is valid, but if it is to be submitted to the scrutiny of flesh and blood it needs to be sharpened *just a little bit more?"*

He therefore decided to do nothing more to it, and simply to show it to the tzaddik as it was.

After Reb Nachum had finished praying, and his host presented him with his knife for examination, the tzaddik said: "If in the eyes of the Almighty your knife is valid, then it is most certainly so in my eyes too. Take it and use it: there is no need for me to examine it."

◈ Not Gone, but Returned

בָּנִים אַתֶּם
You are sons
(14:1)

In most congregations it is customary to add to the number of seven statutory worshipers who are honored by being called to the Torah during the *Shabbos* morning service in the synagogue. Reb Henich of Alisk, the son-in-law of Reb Shalom of Belz, used to make a point of never making any such additions until the first six worshipers had each been called to their allotted passages. He himself was customarily called up in the sixth place and only thereafter, if at all, were additional passages allocated.

In the year 1884, however, on the *Shabbos* on which the weekly Portion of *Re'eh* is read, he gave instructions in his synagogue that the first part of the weekly reading should be divided into sections shorter than usual, so that the sixth man — himself — should be called to the reading of the passage which opens with the words בָּנִים אַתֶּם — "You are sons to the Lord your God."

None of those present understood this change of policy — until on the following Friday the tzaddik passed away. The chassidim then lighted upon a telling interpretation of that very verse in *Or HaChaim,* the Biblical commentary of Rabbi Chaim ben Attar. This Oriental scholar writes as follows: "One needs to understand why these words appear immediately before the words לֹא תִתְגֹּדְדוּ — the prohibition against gashing oneself in token of mourning. It would seem that the Torah is hinting here that a man's death does not imply a loss to the deceased. He is, rather, like a son whose father sent him off to do business in a distant city, and then in the course of time sent for him. True enough, the son is now no longer present at the place of his sojourn — but he is still alive. Moreover, the son is pleased to be able to return to his father, who is the source of life. For this reason, the Torah reminds us first בָּנִים אַתֶּם — that we are sons to the Almighty, and then teaches us a corollary of this: לֹא תִתְגֹּדְדוּ — that we are not to gash ourselves and to cut bald patches in our hair, nor to give vent to any of the other once-common manifestations of violent grief."

◆§ Discernment

לֹא תְאַמֵּץ אֶת לְבָבְךָ
You shall not harden your heart (15:7)

It sometimes happens that a man is in two minds as to whether or not to give alms. For this reason is it written: "You shall not harden your heart" *(Rashi).*

A chassid once brought a gift of three hundred rubles to Reb Nachum of Chernobyl, who was a poor man all his days. The family was overjoyed — but most of all the chief *gabbai,* who was relieved that now the household would at last be able to pay off some of the debts which were owed to the baker and the butcher and so on.

Soon after that chassid had left, the rebbe received a few dozen visitors at *yechidus*, and made a break for the evening prayer. He then closed himself in his study for a time, and later resumed the series of private interviews, which continued until late into the night.

When the last visitor had left, the chief *gabbai* — who was responsible for the household expenses — called on the rebbe in order to receive the long-awaited money needed to settle the accounts. In fact as soon as he had heard of the three hundred rubles he had prepared a list of all the creditors, and had calculated how much he would now be able to give each of them in part payment. The tzaddik opened the drawer of his table and asked the *gabbai* to take whatever was there. Seeing only sundry silver and copper coins, but no sign of the bills that made up the gift of three hundred rubles, the *gabbai* stood still in unquestioning silence.

Seeing how his face had dropped, the tzaddik asked: "Why do you look so sad? Has He Who provides bread for all creatures not shown us — in His lovingkindness — undeserved generosity?"

The *gabbai* could no longer restrain himself. The debts and the privation that hung over the rebbe's household caused him anguish, and he spoke out in words that came straight from the heart: "But were are the three hundred rubles which that chassid brought? That sum could have helped us pay off some of our debts!"

"It is true," conceded the tzaddik, "that he brought

me three hundred rubles. My first reaction was to wonder why I deserved such a large sum, and then I was happy that I had found favor in the eyes of the Almighty and that He had chosen to sustain my family and myself with a generous hand. But when I thought into the subject a little more deeply I became distressed, lest He had given me material benefits instead of spiritual riches. Now among the chassidim who visited me soon after that gift arrived was one who poured out his troubles to me: for a whole year he had not paid the village *melamed* for his children's tuition; the local squire had threatened to drive him out of his house because of his arrears on the rental of the millstones; and to make the situation even more acute he now had to arrange a wedding for his eldest daughter.

"So then I thought that perhaps the Almighty had given me the special privilege of being the agent for the disbursement of charity in a way that would earn me three mitzvos at once — the support of his children in their Torah study, the saving of a family from homelessness, and dowering a poor bride. I asked him how much he needed, and he said that three hundred rubles would solve all his problems. I decided therefore to present him with the whole amount I had received.

"But then another thought came to mind: an amount such as this could bring relief to a considerable number of poor families. This view too seemed to be right — and I could not decide between them. And that is when I closed myself in my room so that I could weigh both arguments. After a little while I arrived at the conclusion that these two views came from the Good and the Evil Inclinations, and that the view which proposed dividing up the amount for several families did *not* come from the Good Inclination. How did I know that?

"Because if this had been the view of the Good Inclination, then as soon as the money reached me he should have expressed his opinion, as follows: 'Nachum! Here, take the three hundred rubles and divide it up into six parts. Give away five to the needy, andd keep one for yourself.' But he did *not* say that. Only *after* the Almighty had made it my privilege to heed the Good Inclination, and I had decided to give the whole amount to that poor chassid, only *then* did this voice come along and try to speak to me craftily.

"I therefore took the advice of the Good Inclination – I called in that poor fellow and gave him the whole amount."

❀ ❀ ❀

When Reb Yosef Yitzchak of Lubavitch told this story, he commented: "From this we learn that *discernment* is more essential to the practical aspects of divine service than is comprehension or emotional involvement. Even an accomplished tzaddik, even God-fearing Jews, even Torah scholars – all need to apply intellectual discernment to their practical service of the Creator."

◆§ *Someone Agrees With You*

Reb Menachem Mendel of Kosov had a simple and honest brother by the name of Reb Yitzchak – a poor man, who was supported by the tzaddik as part of his household.

Now the rebbe was visited one day by an individual who had won notoriety as an antagonist of his. This man brought his sorry situation to the rebbe's attention – his daughter had reached marriageable age – and since he was penniless he sought advice as to how he could earn some money. In response to the rebbe's question he said how much he needed, whereupon Reb Menachem Mendel emptied out his drawer and handed him its contents – a few hundred gold rubles.

When Reb Yitzchak heard of this he was incensed. Whenever his brother was asked for money to cover his own household expenses he said he had none, and now – for his antagonist, mind you! – he suddenly had plenty.

He went straight off to ask his brother: "How could you do such a thing?"

"My dear brother," answered the tzaddik, "only a few minutes ago someone was here, and he said *exactly* what you are saying now. But I took no notice of him – for reasons best known to myself – nor do I intend to take notice of you."

"Who was this who agreed with me?" asked Reb Yitzchak.

Replied his brother: "Satan — the Evil Inclination!"

◆§ To Humor a Fool

דֵּי מַחְסֹרוֹ
Sufficient for his need (15:8)

Reb Menachem Mendel of Kotsk once received a rabbinic guest with all the traditional trappings of respect, including a festive meal in his honor. His chassidim were surprised, for they knew that their rebbe did not at all hold this pretentious guest in esteem.

When they asked him for an explanation of his conduct he said: "In defining the financial support which the Torah obligates us to give or lend a poor man — דֵּי מַחְסֹרוֹ: 'sufficient for his need' — the Talmud says that these words imply 'even a horse on which to ride, and a servant to run before him.' Now the first half is understandable: perhaps our poor man is too weak or sick to walk, so he needs a horse. But 'a servant to run before him'?! Why, if he desires such a thing, it is sheer foolishness. Why should we be obliged to give it to him?

"But from this we may learn that even to humor the whim of a fool counts as the mitzvah of charity..."

◆§ Self-Serving Charity

וְלֹא יֵרַע לְבָבְךָ בְּתִתְּךָ לוֹ
Let your heart not grieve when you give to him (15:10)

On his way home from a business trip to Danzig before he became a rebbe, Reb Simchah Bunem of Pshischah passed through a town called Sheps. As soon as he arrived at his lodgings he sent for one of the local chassidim, a poor man by the name of Reb Zalman, and asked him to arrange a festive meal in his home in honor of the guest from Pshischah, as chassidim are accustomed to do. In order to make this possible he gave him ample money to buy fish and chickens and all kinds of delicacies besides.

When Reb Zalman had gone off to begin his purchases, Reb Simchah Bunem sent his attendant to summon a furrier to his lodgings. To the fur hat and coat that he bought from him he added shoes, and generous lengths of white material which could be made up according to need. He wrapped it all up into one outsize bundle, and sent it off with his sturdy attendant to the cottage of the destitute family. When the messenger brought back word of how ragged the whole family looked, Reb Simchah Bunem promptly dispatched him with enough money to buy them all the clothes they could conceivably need. And that was not all — for after the festive meal Reb Simchah Bunem asked his host to treat all his guests to vodka, and for this too he gave him more money than was needed. In a word, Reb Zalman was left with money to spare.

When the guest of honor was about to leave, he offered his host a substantial sum as a parting gift.

"But from all the money that you have given me until now," protested Reb Zalman, "I have quite an amount left over, apart from the clothes and other goods that you bought me." And he refused to accept it.

"In giving us the commandment to give *tzedakah* to the poor," answered Reb Simchach Bunem, "the Torah tells us the following: 'You shall surely give him, and let your heart not grieve when you give to him.' That is to say...' — and here the tzaddik lent an interpretation of his own to the plain meaning of the above verse — "...that whoever gives alms to a pauper out of compassion, because his tender heart cannot bear to look upon the sufferings of the poor man, has not given *tzedakah* at all. For such a man is in fact serving his own interests, alleviating his own distress. *Tzedakah* should be given in such large amounts that one reaches the point where 'your heart will not grieve when you give to him' — when one no longer feels compassion for his situation. Only then does one fulfill the commandment of giving *tzedakah.*

"Now in my case, too: once I had given you whatever you lacked my heart was no longer pained by your condition. Now, therefore, I can finally fulfill the mitzvah of giving *tzedakah* as one should. For all the trouble I went to in giving my previous gifts was only a preparation that would enable me to do this mitzvah now. If at *this* stage you refuse to accept this gift from me, then (God forbid!) all my efforts until now will have been in vain..."

In response to this explanation Reb Zalman accepted

the gift with good grace, and they parted company amidst warm expressions of friendship.

☙ The Joy of Giving

Reb Chaim of Zanz is widely remembered for the way in which he distributed charity with an open hand. Once his son, Reb Baruch of Gorlitz, asked him to help bear the financial burden of marrying off his daughter.

"I have no money now," said Reb Chaim.

A few days later a number of wealthy chassidim visited Zanz and made him a gift of a large sum of money. His son was pleased to hear of this: surely he would now be given what he had requested. Instead, however, the tzaddik sent for a certain poor townsman who had a whole line of daughters to marry off, and gave him the entire amount.

When the son came to speak to his father and was told what had happened, he wept and said: "Why should I be less eligible to receive help than some other poor man? Don't I also need money to marry off a daughter?"

The tzaddik explained his reasoning: "You, my son, will be able to go traveling about in places where you are known, and our brethren will no doubt help you out generously. But as for this obscure pauper — if *I* don't give him money, who will look after him?"

❀ ❀ ❀

Reb Chaim once asked: "Among the tzaddikim whom I visited in order to learn from their various ways was Reb Zvi Hirsch ('the Beadle') of Rimanov, to whom I went in order to learn how *tzedakah* is to be given — but in this I did not succeed. For when he had money he gave it all to the poor, leaving himself nothing; if he did not have money he was still just as happy as if he had it and as if he was giving it to the poor. But as for me, if I haven't any money to give the needy I pine away from distress."

☙ The Wheel of Fortune (i)

כִּי בִגְלַל הַדָּבָר הַזֶּה יְבָרֶכְךָ

Because for the sake of (בִּגְלַל) *this thing (i.e., charity), He will bless you:* Fortune is a wheel

(גַלְגַל) that turns in the world *(Talmud, Tractate Shabbos).*

Because for the sake of this thing He will bless you (15:10)

Hearing that Reb Feivish of Zabriza was going to spend *Shabbos* in Skole, his young disciple Reb Menachem Mendel of Kosov set out to greet him — on foot, because he could afford no other way. As evening fell on Thursday a village inn came in sight. He had not tasted a morsel of food all day long, and he was weary from trudging across the Ukraine, so he asked the innkeeper if he could spend the night in his hostelry.

"You may certainly sleep here," was the answer, "but I have nothing to give you for supper. I have not even got a slice of bread left to give my little ones. There is no income from this inn, and if I do not pay the owner of this village what I owe him for the lease within a few days, he will throw me and all my family into his dungeon. And I have not a solitary coin to start paying with."

Reb Menachem Mendel was so distressed to hear this story that he could not sleep all that night. In the morning he said farewell, gave the poor man his blessing that the Almighty should help him, and resumed his slow tramp along the highway.

A carriage soon overtook him, and as it slowed down the Jew sitting within called out to him: "Young man! Where are you heading?"

"To the rebbe of Zabriza," answered the walker.

"In that case," said the owner of the carriage, "come and join me up here, because I am headed in that very direction."

"But I will not travel with you," stipulated Reb Menachem Mendel, "unless you give me twenty silver coins."

"It is not enough that I offer to take you in my carriage without charging any fee!" fumed the other. "On top of that you demand payment?!" Then he added: "I shall give you a respectable contribution — but not such a large sum as that!"

"Believe me," said Reb Menachem Mendel, "that I do not need the money for myself. My request is made for the benefit of others — and for your benefit, too."

The rich man in the carriage now wanted to know what benefit he could expect to derive from his contribution, apart from having earned a mitzvah.

"Who knows what ups and downs each new day can bring?" said Reb Menachem Mendel in reply. "For life is a wheel that turns in the world ..."

These words had their effect. The rich man took out twenty silver coins and handed them to his prospective passenger, who said: "Now I shall not move from here until you return with me to the nearest inn, so that you will be able to see with your own eyes what a great mitzvah you have fulfilled."

The rich man agreed, and they rode back together along the highway until they reached the village they sought. Reb Menachem Mendel handed the innkeeper the money he had just been given, sent him off to town to buy up a stock of vodka for his inn, and assured him that from that day on he would prosper in all his affairs.

He now turned to the owner of the carriage and said: "As you know from the words of our Sages, 'One mitzvah brings another in its train.' Let us stay here for the morning prayers, and in the meantime, if you give your coachman some money, he will be able to go and buy bread so that our host's children will have what to eat, and we will be able to eat some of it for breakfast."

This was done, and there was enough bread left over for *Shabbos* meals for the whole family, as well as for provisions to last the travelers for the remainder of their journey.

As they were about to leave, Reb Menachem Mendel whispered in the ear of the innkeeper: "From now on you will prosper more and more, and in the course of time my rich companion will utterly lose his fortune. When the time comes, remember to repay one kindness by another!"

When they arrived at Zabriza they were unable to make their way through the bustling throngs of chassidim, until Reb Feivish himself called out: "Make way for the people who have just performed a mitzvah!"

In response to Reb Menachem Mendel's account of how his traveling companion had saved an entire family from starvation, the tzaddik — borrowing the words of the patriarch Yaakov — said: "I know, my son, I know. But did you tell the innkeeper how he is to act when the time comes?"

"I told him," said Reb Menachem Mendel, "and he undertook to discharge his obligation."

After *Shabbos* the rich man drove off in his carriage, a contented man. In due course, however, he was tossed by the tempests of time and fortune. Every transaction was a disappointment, every investment was a failure. He was left literally penniless. Dire necessity drove him to wander from town to town, knocking on the doors of the well-to-do in quest of alms. During this same period Reb Menachem Mendel became renowned as the rebbe of Kosov — and the innkeeper became a prosperous man, just as his young guest had promised him long ago.

In the course of his years on the road, the destitute wanderer arrived at Kosov. He did not know that the tzaddik who had made the name of the town famous was the same young man to whom — in such different circumstances! — he had once given twenty silver coins. The itinerant paupers who knew Kosov from previous visits now told the newcomer: "Let us come along and visit the local rebbe. *There* is a man who knows how to provide for the likes of us!"

Recognizing him at once, the rebbe called him aside and said: "Take my advice, my friend, and may God prosper your path. I will give you a letter to a certain wealthy individual, and through him you will be helped."

The pauper wondered at these words, but was too weary to ask for an explanation. With the letter in hand he set out in the direction he was told to take, and eventually found himself treading the length of the long-forgotten dirt track that meandered its way to a certain remote village inn. The innkeeper did not recognize him after his fifteen long years of privation, but before he opened the envelope he said: "I know this letter is from the rebbe of Kosov, for this very night he appeared to me in my dream and told me that the time had come for me to repay one kindness by another."

He then reminded the wanderer of their first encounter, and told him what it was that their mutual friend had whispered in his ear at the time. For the first time in years, a smile now warmed the strained features of the dusty traveler.

The innkeeper went on: "Be my guest until I make an honest reckoning of all the prosperity with which the Almighty has blessed me. Then we will travel together to Kosov, and we will do whatever the rebbe tells us."

It is not known what instructions were given by the tzaddik for the settling of their accounts, but one thing is certain — the innkeeper made the wanderer an exceedingly generous gift, the tzaddik blessed him with success, and when he re-established himself in business he prospered in every venture.

◆§ *The Wheel of Fortune (ii)*

One of the chassidim of Reb Avraham Yehoshua Heschel journeyed to Apta to tell his rebbe to what wretched straits he was reduced.

"I will give you a letter to one of my people," said the tzaddik, "instructing him to give you two hundred rubles on my account. He is a very wealthy man."

When the poor man arrived at the home of the addressee, he merely told him that he had been sent by the rebbe, and was received warmly. Only after he had enjoyed his host's hospitality for several days did he hand him the letter. At the sight of it the rich man went purple with rage.

"I don't know what business affairs the rebbe has with me that he should take it upon himself to instruct me to give you such a large sum on his account!" he protested. "I can give you a certain amount — but definitely not two hundred rubles!"

The guest argued that it would not be proper for him to disobey the rebbe's orders by receiving less. In the end he left empty-handed, and returned to Apta to repeat his sad story.

"Very well," said the tzaddik, "I will now give you a letter to another one of my chassidim. This man is not so rich, so I will tell him to give you only one hundred rubles."

This letter received a different welcome altogether.

"My brother," said this chassid to the stranger at his door, "please stay in my house for a few days until I manage to put together the amount that the rebbe named."

After he had handed it over with a happy heart, the poor man took his leave and brought this story, too, back to the tzaddik.

Now the recipient of the first letter noticed after a short time that his fortunes were steadily waning. He even came to a stage at which he was compelled to beg for bread from the houses of the rich. In the course of his wanderings he came to Apta, and the mere sight of the town reminded him of the letter he had received from the tzaddik who lived there. As the misfortunes that had overtaken him since then came to mind one by one, he could not forgive himself for not having obeyed the rebbe's instruction unquestioningly — for he saw his own willful disobedience at the time as the root of all his sufferings since then.

He begged and pleaded to be admitted to the rebbe's presence for an audience, but the rebbe had left orders that this was not to be. Seeing him weep day and night, one chassid advised him to stand outside the rebbe's window, where the tzaddik would be able to hear his anguish for himself. The rebbe in fact asked his attendants whose voice this was, and when they told him, they added that he was full of regrets for his earlier conduct.

Said the tzaddik: "If he has any claims against me, I am willing to appear with him at a hearing before a rabbinical court."

A *beis din* of three rabbinical judges was duly constituted — one of their number was Reb Moshe Zvi of Savran — and the tzaddik stated his case: "This is the background to the story. When I was due to come down to This World, the Almighty entrusted me with the amount of gold and silver that I would need for the discharge of my divine service in the course of my lifetime down here. I divided it up, and distributed it amongst the disciples with whom I came in touch. Now all the property that this man ever owned — was mine. When he refused to give that pauper two hundred rubles on my account, I claimed my own, and gave it over to the other chassid, the one who followed my instructions."

After due deliberation the court ruled that the man could not reclaim his property, for it was not his. Nevertheless, compassion dictated that he be awarded sufficient for his upkeep, provided that he regretted his earlier action and made amends with the rebbe.

The verdict became fact. Throughout his days he earned sufficient for his support, but left no estate behind him; the other chassid prospered in all his affairs and became a wealthy man.

☙ Open Your Hand (i)

פָּתֹחַ תִּפְתַּח אֶת יָדְךָ

You shall surely open your hand (15:11)

Therefore do I command you, saying, You shall surely open your hand: As if to say, "I would like to give you some sound advice" *(Rashi).*

Reb Shneur Zalman of Liadi, the author of *Tanya,* used to make a point of conducting his household frugally, and would explain his attitude by saying: "Our Sages observe that the Torah is wary of spending the money of Israel — and since the upkeep of my household depends on the support of the public, it follows that I should be sparing in my expenses."

Indeed, when one of his children or grandchildren wore a costly garment, they did not do so in his presence, lest he object.

One day his young grandson — Reb Menachem Mendel of Lubavitch, who later became renowned as the author of *Tzemach Tzedek* — wore an expensive belt, and forgot to take it off when his grandfather called for him unexpectedly.

"Tell me," opened Reb Shneur Zalman, "how much did that belt cost?"

"Fifteen rubles," answered his grandson.

"And are you such a rich man," protested the tzaddik, "that you should be wearing such an expensive item?"

The grandson was silent, and the tzaddik continued: "How much was the dowry you received from your bride's father?"

"Two thousand silver rubles," was the answer.

"And what do you intend to do with this sum?"

"I will hand it over to a trustworthy merchant, and earn something on it."

"But perhaps he will return you neither the capital nor the interest?"

"This man is very wealthy, and utterly reliable"

"So what if he is very wealthy now," persisted the tzaddik. "In time he can become very poor."

"What, then, should I do with the money?" asked the grandson.

"My firm advice," said the tzaddik, "is that you should put the entire sum into this box, and that way it will certainly be preserved in its entirety."

The box, it should be mentioned, was a charity box... The grandson's first thought was that Reb Shneur Zalman was joking — until he heard him speak on: "I really meant that I would like you to give the money away to *tzedakah*, and then both the capital and the interest will remain intact — whereas if you give it to some wealthy merchant, I fear that you will lose even the capital."

The grandson heard what was being said, but soon left the rebbe's study nevertheless, and decided to entrust the money into the hands of a scholarly and utterly trustworthy merchant of means. Some months later all the possessions of this man were destroyed in a fire, and he was literally reduced to poverty.

In due course Reb Shneur Zalman asked Reb Menachem Mendel: "Well, did you earn anything through your investment?"

And when he was told of the total loss that had befallen him, he continued: "But why did you not heed my advice? Had you put all your money in this box, then both the capital and the interest would have remained intact. Why does each man here not trust the advice of his rebbe like the people of Volhynia, who are great believers? Let me tell you what I mean.

"I was once on my way home from Mezritch during a bitterly cold winter, and by the time we reached our wayside inn, I was so stricken by frostbite that the coachman carried me indoors from the wagon. The innkeeper, an elderly and God-fearing Jew, rubbed my feet with snow and vodka until I recovered.

"I then asked him: 'How long have you been living here?'

" 'More than fifty years,' he said.

" 'And do you have a *minyan* of ten men with whom you can pray according to the Law as part of a congregation?' I asked.

" 'No,' he answered. 'Only on the Days of Awe do I go to a nearby township to worship with the people there.'

" 'Now tell me,' I said, 'do you think it is right that an elderly man should pray all his life without a congregation, and hardly ever be able to say *Kedushah,* and *Barechu,* and all the other responses which a solitary worshiper cannot make? Why should you not go to live in the town?'

" 'And from what will I earn my livelihood over there?' he asked.

"So I asked in return: 'How many householders live in that township?'

" 'I should say around a hundred,' he replied.

" 'In that case,' I concluded, "we see that the Almighty can find a livelihood for a hundred families. Tell me — don't you think He can manage the same for one man more?'

"Then I added: 'By the way, I am a disciple of Reb Dov Ber, the Maggid of Mezritch.'

"He left me at once. Half an hour later I saw a number of wagons drawn up in front of the inn, loaded high with household goods and chattels of every description.

" 'What is this?' I asked him.

" 'Why,' he said, 'I am on my way to settle in that township, just as you told me to do.'

"You see, then," — Reb Shneur Zalman wound up his talk with his grandson — "how strong was the faith of that old man. I was still a young man at the time, but as soon as he heard that I was a disciple of the Maggid of Mezritch he dropped everything at once, including the dwelling and the livelihood which had supported him respectably for over fifty years. And you heard from me twice that there was a risk that you would lose both the capital and the interest — yet you did not believe!"

◈ Open Your Hand (ii)

A number of chassidic leaders once convened in Berditchev to discuss some grave threat which hung over the Jews of Russia. The meeting was presided over by Reb Shneur Zalman of Liadi, who proposed that the funds needed to save the situation should be raised by the imposition of a tax of a quarter of a ruble on every Jew — or, according to another version, by the payment of a quarter of their dowries by every bridegroom.

A knock was heard at the door which was behind the speaker's back. He said: "The grandfather has arrived." (Reb Aryeh Leib of Shpola was known since his infancy by this Yiddish nickname — *der Shpoler Zeide.)*

Reb Aryeh Leib came in, and was invited by Reb Shneur Zalman to wash his hands for bread and to join the company at the table for a meal. The new arrival walked up and down the room, but gave no answer.

When he ignored the invitation a second time, Reb Levi Yitzchak of Berditchev said to Reb Shneur Zalman, who was his relative by marriage: "*Mechutan*, do you not know that the Zeide fasts from one *Shabbos* to the next?"

Reb Shneur Zalman nevertheless turned to the Zeide a third time, inviting him to eat — and this time the invitation was accepted.

There was another knock at the door.

"The emissaries of Reb Baruch of Mezhibuzh are here," said Reb Shneur Zalman.

And when they entered they turned to him and said: "Our rebbe sent us here to tell you that in the days of Mordechai and Esther people were not told to contribute quarters: other measures were taken!"

"Do you hear that?" Reb Shneur Zalman said to those at his table. "Reb Baruch [who was known as an outspoken critic of his] holds that I am the Mordechai of this generation!"

He then turned to the emissaries and said: "I would ask you to tell Reb Baruch that there are three modes of repentance — fasting, prayer, and charity. The first was the means appropriate to the city of Nineveh; the second was practiced by Mordechai and Esther; the outstanding means which is the especial task of our generation is *tzedakah*, charity."

◆§ *Open Your Hand (iii)*

Two of the disciples of Reb Shneur Zalman of Liadi who were known for their grasp of the revealed and hidden aspects of the Torah, and for the manner in which they served their Maker, were particularly outstanding in the mitzvah of *tzedakah*. These two philanthropists were called Reb Zalman of Dubrovna and Reb Pinchas of Shklov. A note in the will of Reb Zalman says that on the Day of Judgment he sees no merits on which he will be able to rely — apart from the mitzvah of *tzedakah*, and the power of his rebbe.

He was a wealthy man, and kept his copper, silver and gold coins in separate boxes. When a poor man visited him with a request for alms he would estimate what sum would be appropriate, and then dip his hand into the box required; whatever came up in the first handful he would give away.

Reb Pinchas was also wealthy, and he made the journey to Dubrovna for the express purpose of learning from Reb Zalman how to go about performing the mitzvah of *tzedakah*. Some time after he had learned to give alms in the same way he visited their rebbe, Reb Shneur Zalman of Liadi, and told him: "I have learned a new way to give *tzedakah* from Reb Zalman."

Then, when he had described it, he added: "But there is one difference between us. Reb Zalman does not open his hand to see how much is in it, whereas I — even though I too give the pauper whatever comes up in my hand — still open it first just to catch a glimpse."

◆§ *Open Your Hand (iv)*

Like many Jews of his time, the father of Reb Menachem Mendel of Rimanov earned his livelihood as an *arendar* — by leasing the rights to an inn from the squire who owned the village.

One day the squire came to him with a proposition:

"Moshke, I want to move to a distant province, so I have to sell all my property here. I know you to be an honest and trustworthy man, and have grown to like you. If, therefore, you will pay such-and-such an amount — which is only a tenth of the real value of all my estates around these parts — then I am willing to sell you my entire property, on condition that you pay me this amount in cash within a few days."

The leaseholder's first reaction was to rejoice at the rare opportunity that had been brought his way to become so wealthy without exertion — but he soon realized that even the price the squire had quoted was well beyond his means.

His wife offered the following suggestion: "We do have a house, with some silver utensils and gold ornaments. If we sell all of these we will have ready money, and whatever is still lacking we will be able to borrow from our friends and relatives. Then we will not have to forgo the good fortune which the Almighty has sent our way."

Having followed this advice, he set out cheerfully for the squire's mansion with his purse of money, ready to finalize the details of the transaction.

His spirits were suddenly chilled by an agonizing shriek. He looked around and ran towards a dilapidated cottage that stood alone not far from the road. Opening the door, he saw the corpse of a man lying on the floor. It was surrounded by a distraught woman and her seven ragged children, all wailing in despair. They had obviously been left without food or clothing, so the leaseholder turned to the poor woman and said: "Here, take this purse. It's for you and all your little ones."

She could not believe her ears. Could he be joking at her expense? At first she refused to accept it, and only after some time did he succeed in convincing her that this was a gift offered in earnest.

This little encounter fired all the heavens with excitement. Here was a Jew who had given away everything he owned for the sake of a mitzvah! Not only had he forgone the vast wealth which was within moments of his reach, but he had left himself utterly destitute, for in order to raise the money which he had just given this widow he had sold his home and everything in it!

No sooner had the Heavenly Court decided to reward him handsomely than word of the verdict reached the grudging ears of Satan. He hastened to appear before the Court and argued as follows: "Before any of your tzaddikim are given a gift from heaven they are always put to a test. I will therefore plummet down to That World and test this mortal too. Only then shall he be granted whatever reward you have decided upon!"

At that moment there appeared from the opposite direction the Prophet Eliyahu, of blessed memory.

"If there must be a test," he said, "then it is I that shall go down to administer it. For if the Adversary is entrusted with the task, who knows if in his zeal he will not impose more than even this saintly man can bear?"

And the Heavenly Court accepted his view.

The leaseholder, in the meantime, realizing that he now owned nothing but the shirt on his back, thought to himself: "What point is there in going home the way things are at the moment? I had better take up the staff of the wanderer and visit one town after another. Who knows? Perhaps the Almighty in His mercy will bring a bit of good fortune my way... "

By evening he had already reached a certain town, and made his way to the local *shul*. He resolved that he would ask no mortal for bread to eat nor for a nook in which to sleep. If one of the worshipers invited him home to eat, he would follow him; if not — he would do without. The prayers came to an end, but not one solitary person approached him to ask the stranger in their midst whether he had a place where he could satisfy his hunger and lay his head to rest. He was weighted down by fatigue, and hunger, and thirst — but his spirit was strong, and he allowed no second thoughts to tarnish the noble decision of that morning. On the contrary, he said: "Whatever happens, I thank God, Who gave me the opportunity of carrying out such a great mitzvah!" And with that the famished wanderer took down a tall volume from the synagogue shelves, and nourished his soul with the study of the Torah.

A dignified presence appeared now before him, and addressed him in these words: "May peace light upon you, man blessed by God! From where do you come, and what brings you here?"

And as the wanderer unfolded his story to the patient listener, he came to the episode of that morning.

"Listen to what I have to tell you, my friend, "said the venerable stranger. "Since the Almighty has blessed me with great wealth, please accept from my hand a certain sum — enough to support your family throughout your entire lifetime. In exchange for this, sell me the merit of the mitzvah which you performed today. And if God makes your affairs prosper, you will be able to perform many more mitzvos like this one."

This tantalizing offer roused a tremor of eager anticipation in the heart of the wanderer — but only for a moment. His strength of purpose did not fail him, and he replied emphatically: "No! Since the Almighty gave me the rare privilege of doing a mitzvah at such cost — with *mesirus nefesh,* one might even say — I will not sell my mitzvah for all the money in the world!"

"Very well," said the aged stranger, "then sell me only half of the mitzvah, and for that half I will give you the full amount I promised."

"I will not part with even half a mitzvah," the wanderer insisted.

So eager was the old man to buy himself a share of that spiritual treasure that he went as far as to offer the whole payment for even one hundredth part of the other man's mitzvah. Even this offer was rejected outright.

Seeing before him a man of spirit, the venerable stranger said: "Know my son, that I am Eliyahu the Prophet, sent from heaven to put you to the test. Blessed indeed is your lot, for you not only earned a rich mitzvah, but withstood the temptation of selling even the tiniest fragment of it! One of three rewards is now yours: make your choice between them. Either you and your wife will be blessed with long life, or else you will be granted exceptional wealth, or you will be blessed with a son who will grow up to be a tzaddik."

"My sole wish is to be blessed with such a son," said the man without hesitation. "For what profit is there in riches and in long life if all those years we have not been blessed with a child?"

"The son whom you will beget," said the Prophet Eliyahu, "will be a man of such sanctity that his learning and his saintliness will illuminate the world. Be forewarned, though, that if this is to be so, then you and your wife will have to accept the lot of perpetual wanderers throughout your lives."

The man hastened home to consult his wife, and together they undertook to pay the price of their reward with loving patience. In the fullness of time a son was born to them, and they called him Menachem, which means "the consoler." This infant grew up to be Reb Menachem Mendel of Rimanov, who proved indeed to be a shining light of learning and saintliness, and comfort to his People.

May the merit of his beautiful life protect us and all of Israel!

◆§ *Open Your Hand (v)*

It was not a new problem, but it was nonetheless urgent: a chassid by the name of Reb Ben-Zion of Ostrov, with not a penny of his own, had to marry off his daughter. He hired a wagon and set off to Ger in order to consult his rebbe, Reb Yehudah Aryeh Leib, the author of *Sfas Emes*.

"Since you will be passing through Warsaw," said the tzaddik, "call on Reb Bunem Eybeschuetz, and ask him to endeavor to put together the amount you need."

Reb Bunem, who was a chassid of means, gave him a royal welcome in true chassidic style — a long table in his honor laden with refreshments, around which a melodious company of scores of chassidim sat together into the wee hours of the night, exchanging stories of tzaddikim and choice tidbits of Torah lore. When Reb Ben-Zion told him of his request at breakfast the next morning, his host reassured him: "Do not worry. With God's help everything will work out smoothly."

The next day the guest said: "Since today is Thursday, I must set out already in order to reach my hometown in time for *Shabbos*."

Reb Bunem thereupon opened his safe and took out a thousand rubles, which he presented to his guest in the friendliest manner imaginable.

After taking his leave, Reb Ben-Zion decided to return to Ger in order to spend *Shabbos* in the company of his rebbe. When the tzaddik heard how things had worked out, he said: "I certainly did not intend that he should give the whole amount himself, but rather that he should persuade wealthy philanthropists to contribute the money."

"Rebbe," said Reb Ben-Zion, "that chassid in fact fulfilled your request — except that since he himself is a wealthy philanthropist, it was himself whom he persuaded to give the money."

◆§ *Forewarned is Forearmed (i)*

וּפָנִיתָ בַבֹּקֶר וְהָלַכְתָּ לְאֹהָלֶיךָ
And you shall turn in the morning, and go to your tents (16:7)

No harm befalls men who journey forth for a mitzvah, neither on their way out nor on their way home, as it is written, "And you shall turn in the morning, and go to your tents" *(Talmud, Tractate Pesachim).*

Reb Shneur Zalman of Liadi, the author of *Tanya,* used to dispatch his most prominent disciples to towns and villages in all directions, for the purpose of instructing their brethren in the teachings and life-style of Chassidism, and to arouse them to a service of God made alive by the experience of awe and the love of Him. At the same time, it was the task of these emissaries to collect contributions for the poor scholars who had settled in the Holy Land.

One of those upon whom such a mission was imposed was a celebrated chassid by the name of Reb Zalman Zezmer. He undertook to fulfill the rebbe's request, of course, and when he came to receive his farewell blessings, the tzaddik said: "Take extreme care not to spend the night in a house whose door faces east."

The chassid hired a wagon and set out. The Almighty made his mission prosper, so that he succeeded in stimulating hundreds of people to strive to new heights of piety. He likewise succeeded in raising substantial sums for the relief of the distressed scholars in far-off *Eretz Yisrael,* who looked for succor to the *maamad* funds which were thus replenished from time to time by their fellow chassidim in Russia.

On his way home, while he was enjoying the quiet satisfaction of having fulfilled the rebbe's command, he suddenly realized that the wagon had veered from the road and had lost its way in unfamiliar side-tracks. The wagon-driver too was alarmed, for in the pitch blackness of midnight they had no idea where they should turn. After continuing aimlessly for a short distance they suddenly spied a light in a distant house. They knocked on the door, and it was opened by an old man who greeted them with the traditional *Shalom Aleichem,* and invited them to rest in his house from their tiring journey.

Having washed his hands, Reb Zalman's first thought was to ask his host which wall was the eastern one, for this was the direction traditionally faced in prayer, and he had not yet had time for his evening devotions. But when the master of the house pointed at the eastern wall, Reb Zalman was seized with a fearful trembling, for that was the wall in which the door was to be found. His rebbe's warning was still fresh in his ears. He immediately ordered the coachman to load their chattels back on the wagon, to harness the horses, and to prepare for departure. The poor fellow could not begin to understand what had suddenly overcome his passenger, but Reb Zalman's voice was decisive, so he began to collect their bundles.

Their preparations were interrupted by a voice thundering from the doorway. It was their host, and his words struck terror in their hearts: "I take guests *into* my house; I do not let them *out.* You two are staying here!"

With that he strode out, and bolted and locked the door behind him. In the moment of shocked silence that followed, the two prisoners were startled by the raucous shouts and curses of a fearsome gang of ruffians who clattered their way into an adjoining room.

"Tell me, whose carriage is that out in front?" asked one of the voices. "Did you manage to trap us a fancy bird today?"

"Such a rare catch we haven't made for a long, long time," returned the voice of their host. "They've got a whole stack of bundles, and you can even hear the shiny coins clattering in their boxes."

"Let's go in and see them for ourselves!" shouted another voice.

The door burst open, and the chassid and his wagon-driver found themselves facing six bloodthirsty savages, who leered at them and said to each other: "First things first! Let's fill up our bellies before we get down to business. These birdies won't escape from the cage!"

Reb Zalman looked the robbers squarely in the eye and said: "I was sent out to do a mitzvah by a holy man who knows hidden secrets. He foresaw that I would fall into danger and ordered me not to spend the night in a house whose entrance faces east. The owner of this house is my witness that as soon as I became aware that this door faces that direction I tried to flee — but I did not succeed. Listen now to a warning: you had better let us out of here, for my holy master will avenge our blood!"

Uproarious laughter burst forth from all sides — except from the mouth of the householder, who fell silent and thoughtful.

Throughout the night Reb Zalman and his coachman poured out their hearts over verses from the Book of *Psalms.* Before dawn they heard hushed footsteps approaching their room. It was their host, who whispered to them: "Quick! Follow me! I will help you escape from here."

This was hard to believe, but there was no time to pause, and without a word they followed him to their wagon. As they clambered up to their seats he whispered: "I saved you because of your rebbe!" — and with that he gave Reb Zalman a bill of fifty rubles for the tzaddik.

When they reached Liadi the rebbe said to his chassid: "I did not sleep all that night because of you."

And he took the fifty-ruble bill and stuck it into a crack in the wall.

Years later a pauper came to Liadi and asked to be admitted to speak with the rebbe. When the *gabbai* brought this message to the tzaddik, he declined to receive him. Instead, he took out the fifty-ruble bill from the crack in the wall and asked the *gabbai* to hand it to the man outside.

And no one there knew who that pauper was, except for two — the rebbe and the pauper.

סדר שפטים
Sidra Shoftim

⁂ Forewarned is Forearmed (ii)

צֶדֶק צֶדֶק תִּרְדֹּף
Pursue justice, only justice (16:20)

He who is neither lame nor blind nor crippled but feigns to be one of these will not die of old age without first becoming one of these, as it is written: "Pursue justice, only justice" *(Mishnah, Tractate Pe'ah).*

A chassid by the name of Reb Yosef Moshe, the son of Reb Avraham Yehoshua Heschel of Apta, once needed to travel to Jassy. He decided first to seek the opinion of Reb Yisrael, the Maggid of Koznitz, who gave his blessing to the journey.

One day before he left for Rumania he visited Koznitz again to take his leave of the Maggid, who in the course of their conversation said the following: "Now you are a man who spends a good deal of his time traveling. Tell me, what do you do when your carriage overtakes a poor man who is going in your direction on foot and asks to be given a ride?"

"Why, that is something that happens quite often," said Reb Yosef Moshe, "and my men of course have instructions to stop and take in the poor man, and to take him to his destination."

"And suppose you overtake a lame pauper leaning on a walking-stick — what happens then?" asked the rebbe.

"I would say that it is even more important to take such a man," said the chassid. "It must be hard to make a journey on foot when one needs the help of a cane."

"And I would say exactly the opposite," said the Maggid. "A healthy man depends on his legs. If a carriage comes by, so much the better; if not, he can always continue on foot. But if a man is lame, and needs a cane, how can he undertake a long journey and rely on the miracle of a carriage at the right moment that will be able to take him exactly where he wants? I would say that in such a case one should be wary in case he is only feigning lameness — and who knows what evil designs he has!"

The chassid was of course surprised to hear these words. Whatever could the rebbe be talking about?

He set out the next day according to plan, and being an old man, lay down in the carriage and fell asleep. On the way his companions saw a lame man who was somehow making his way along the highway with the help of two crutches. He begged them to stop and take him with them, so they called out to the coachman to draw rein and to wait until he caught up with them. Reb Yosef Moshe, awakened by the sound of their shouting, asked them why they had stopped. As soon as he heard the reason he recalled his visit to Koznitz and cried out to the surprised coachman at the top of his voice: "Quick! Gallop ahead as fast as you can!"

The coachman cracked his whip, and at the same moment the lame man called out to them: "Have pity! Wait for me!"

This made the chassid urge his coachman to drive off even faster. At this point the passengers who were facing the lame man saw him hold both crutches aloft in one hand and bolt furiously after them. Soon realizing that he would not be able to overtake them, he expressed his frustration by hurling one of his crutches at the carriage — but apart from a hole in the hood, he caused them no harm.

◆§ *Controversy*

דִּבְרֵי רִיבֹת בִּשְׁעָרֶיךָ
Matters of controversy within your gates (17:8)

A delegation of the chassidim who lived in a certain town once called on Reb Avraham of Sochatchov, the author of *Avnei Neizer,* with a complaint. They claimed that the *rav* of their town had ruled with undue leniency in a certain question involving the dietary laws, and since they were therefore reluctant to accept his ruling in any other ritual question that should arise in the future, they requested that their rebbe send them some other *rav* who would be able to serve as a reliable and competent authority on the *halachah.*

Replied the tzaddik: "Even according to your claim, what this *rav* did was to pronounce as permissible something that the Sages of the Talmud have ruled to be prohibited — an *issur derabbanan*. But what you yourselves are about to do is to transgress an *issur de'oraysa*, for according to all opinions to sustain a controversy is explicitly forbidden in the Torah itself. Not only that, but through engaging in controversy people come to err, and to transgress other prohibitions which appear in the Law."

Now there is a verse in the Torah which is addressed to the judges of the rabbinical courts: "If there should be a matter too obscure for you in judgment, between blood and blood, between plea and plea,... matters of controversy within your gates ..." In concluding his audience with the dissident delegation, Reb Avraham gave this verse a novel interpretation by inserting a few explanatory words of his own: "If there should be a matter too obscure for you in judgment, between blood and blood, between plea and plea,... *it is because there are* matters of controversy within your gates ..."

◆§ *In Lonely Majesty*

שׂוֹם תָּשִׂים עָלֶיךָ מֶלֶךְ
You may appoint a king over you (17:15)

A certain individual who lived in Lublin used to buy up a stock of combs every Friday and then hand them out in the communal bathhouse that afternoon to whoever wanted them. When word of this original custom reached Reb Yaakov Yitzchak (the Chozeh) of Lublin he spoke very warmly of the practice, citing it as an instance of the *mitzvah* of *gemilus chassadim*, doing a favor to one's fellow. Report of the tzaddik's reaction was brought to the attention of Rabbi Azriel, the official *rav* of the city, whose admirers nicknamed him "the iron-headed" on account of the solid logic which he applied to the study of the Talmud. This scholar was known to be an opponent of Chassidism in general and of the Chozeh in particular.

"The chassidic rebbe," he commented, "has forgotten an explicit statement in the Talmud, where it is said: 'When King David entered the bathhouse he realized that he was naked and said, *Woe is me that I should be left bare of any mitzvah!'* Now if what the rebbe praises so highly were in fact a mitzvah, then King David too could have bought up stocks of combs and distributed them to all comers in the bathhouse ..."

This comment in turn was brought back to the ears of the rebbe.

"My learned colleague," he said, "has overlooked an explicit statement in the Mishnah, where it is said: 'Nor may one see the king when is having his hair cut, nor when he is naked, nor when he is in the bathhouse, as it is written, *You may appoint a king over you;* stand in awe of him.' It follows, then, that it was impossible for King David to have performed this mitzvah ..."

☙ The Succession

נָבִיא אָקִים לָהֶם...כָּמוֹךָ
I shall raise them up a prophet...like you (18:18)

In 1826, when one of the emissaries of Reb Uri of Strelisk returned from his travels, he told the rebbe that a certain chassid had begged to be excused for not having visited Strelisk for the festival of Shavuos as he always did, and planned instead to come for Rosh HaShanah.

"Fool that he is!" said Reb Uri. "If he comes here for Rosh HaShanah, who will answer him?"

Soon after came the *Shabbos* on which the weekly Portion of *Shoftim* is read. The tzaddik read aloud from the Torah Scroll in the synagogue, according to his custom, with Reb Yehudah Zvi of Stretyn at his right and his own son, Reb Shlomo, at his left. In the course of his reading he came to a verse which gives the words of the Almighty to Moshe Rabbeinu: "I will raise them up a prophet from among their brothers, like you, and I will put My words in his mouth, and he shall speak to them all that I command him." But instead of reading "from among their brothers, *like* you" (מִקֶּרֶב אֲחֵיכֶם כָּמוֹךָ), he read "from among their brothers, *from* you." (מִקֶּרֶב אֲחֵיכֶם מִמְּךָ). Reb Yehudah Zvi read out the word to him as it appears in the Torah, but though Reb Uri repeated the whole verse, he again read as before. This was repeated once more, and again a third time. But now, still seeking to correct him, Reb Yehudah Zvi showed the rebbe the printed text so that he could see it for himself.

This time Reb Uri began the verse afresh, and read as follows: "I will raise them up a prophet from among their brothers, *like you, like you, like you!*" And, having said כָּמוֹךָ three times, he placed his hands on the head of Reb Yehudah Zvi and said the word once more, with a burning intensity — *"like you!"*

It was clear to all the chassidim present that this elder disciple of the tzaddik had just been ordained his successor.

Less than three weeks later, on the twenty-third day of the month of Elul, Reb Uri returned his fiery soul to heaven — one week before the Rosh HaShanah to which he had once made reference...

His son, Reb Shlomo, expressed himself soon after: "I do not know how it is possible to live after a father like that" — and within four months he had joined him.

☙ *No Academic Question*

הוּא יָנוּס אֶל אַחַת הֶעָרִים הָאֵלֶּה וָחָי
He shall flee to one of these cities, and live (19:5)

If a disciple is exiled, his rebbe is sent into exile with him, for it is written, 'and live' — to teach us that he is to be afforded a source of vitality *(Talmud, Tractate Makkos).*

Reb Simchah Bunem of Pshischah once asked his disciple, Reb Menachem Mendel of Kotsk: "If in the World Above they order me to go to *gehinnom,* what shall I do?"

Reb Menachem Mendel answered not a word. After a pause of a few moments, his rebbe said: "If that happens, I will ask them to bring me my teachers, Reb Yaakov Yitzchak (the Chozeh) of Lublin,and Reb Yaakov Yitzchak (the Yid HaKadosh) of Pshischah. For does the Talmud not say: 'If a disciple is exiled, his rebbe is sent into exile with him'?"

"Rebbe," said Reb Menachem Mendel, "to you this rule is not really a matter of interest. But I stand to gain by it ..."

☙ *Natural Justice*

לֹא תַסִּיג גְּבוּל רֵעֲךָ

A poor widow earned her livelihood from the lease which she held on an inn — known among East

You shall not move your neighbor's landmark (19:14)

European Jews as an *arenda* or *michyah* — until along came some other villager, offered the local squire a higher fee, and displaced her. The widow had him summoned to a lawsuit which was to be heard before the local rabbinical court on a charge of *hasagas gvul* — "moving one's neighbor's landmark," the Biblical metaphor which means not only depriving one's neighbor of his land rights by moving a fence or landmark, but also the prohibition of encroaching unfairly on another's source of sustenance. The newcomer refused to appear.

Hearing that he was a frequent visitor to the court of Reb Shalom of Belz, the widow persuaded her local *rav* — whose summons this man had ignored — to write to the tzaddik, asking him to order his follower to appear before the court. She arrived at Belz with the letter in hand and delivered it to the tzaddik, but was shocked to see that he ignored both her request and the letter from her *rav*. Returning home, she told the *rav* of her disappointment. He was so incensed that in his indignation he made some very critical remarks about the tzaddik's motives: he no doubt sought to flatter his moneyed follower rather than ruffle his relations with him. In a more sober moment some time later, he came to regret having spoken this way about the holy man, and resolved to make the journey to Belz to request forgiveness of the tzaddik.

"I bear no grudge against you," Reb Shalom reassured him. "You should know, however, that flattery plays no role with me. I did not accede to your request because justice is on the side of the new innkeeper. You see, the grandfather of this *arendar* held this same lease many years ago, until the father of this widow's late husband offered the local squire a higher fee, and displaced him. Left penniless, that old man eventually had to find some other place to live, and since he and his family left your region so long ago, the whole connection of his family with that inn has been completely forgotten. But, as the Psalmist says, 'the steps of man are ordered by God' — and through the unseen workings of Divine Providence things so worked out that this very man, the grandson of the original lessee, succeeded in hiring the same inn which had been held by his own forebears. This livelihood is his by right: would it be proper to wrest it from him?

"The facts of the case, by the way, may be checked to your own satisfaction."

The *rav* took up this offer, and found that this was indeed the history of the inn.

סדר כי תצא

Sidra Ki Seitzei

◆§ Lost and Found

הָשֵׁב תְּשִׁיבֵם לְאָחִיךָ

You shall surely return them to your brother (22:1)

A stranger once walked into the *shtibl* frequented by the chassidim of Chernobyl who lived in Berditchev, and asked them if they were chassidim of the tzaddik of Chernobyl. Hearing that they were, he gave them money for *tikkun*, and asked them to prepare a festive meal at his expense.

When they were all seated together around the table he said: "Do you people know who your tzaddik is, Reb Aharon of Chernobyl? I have just come from him now. Let me tell you what happened to me, and then you will know what manner of man he is.

"When I happened to be here in Berditchev a few years ago, a certain businessman who worked on a commission basis came here to buy up various goods for the shopkeepers of his town. Even after he had paid for them he had quite a sum left. Anyway, his wallet fell from his pocket unnoticed, and I picked it up. I wavered for a moment whether to return it or not, but the stranger was already on his way. I followed him at once, but lost him in the crowd and could not find him. I went about my affairs, and in the course of time the Almighty prospered my way and I became a rich man. But when that agent came home to his town his creditors gave him no peace, for the money he lost was theirs. In addition he lost his livelihood, for the shopkeepers were no longer willing to trust him. He died in misery soon after, leaving his wife in wretched poverty, and his sons illiterate — for there was no one to pay their tuition fees.

"After some time he appeared to me in a dream. 'Why did you kill me?' he said. 'And worse still, look at the state my widow and children are left in — all because of you! I now demand that you appear with me in a lawsuit to be heard here in the World of Truth!'

"I woke up in alarm. But then I told myself: 'Does the Prophet Zechariah not teach that *Dreams speak falsehood?* And does the Talmud not tell us that *A man is shown in his dreams only that upon which his heart ponders by day?* It is only because I have thought of this incident so often that it figured now in my dream!'

"But when the same dream repeated itself the next night, and the next night again, and so on I saw that this was no joking matter. So one night I answered him in my dream: 'Very well, I agree to the lawsuit — but not in the World of Truth. For what will you gain from it if my wife and children will be widowed and orphaned too?'

" 'In that case,' he replied, 'tell me where the hearing should take place.'

" 'Give me time to think it over,' I said, and he agreed.

"First thing in the morning I set out to consult Reb Aharon of Karlin, but he said that he couldn't get involved in a matter of this sort, and recommended that I go off to see Reb Aharon of Chernobyl. Your rebbe, Reb Aharon, told me that when this man came to me again in a dream I should tell him that the hearing would be held before him. I returned home, and when I passed on this suggestion at the next opportunity the plaintiff agreed, and I set out at once for Chernobyl.

"I appeared at the date and time set by the tzaddik, and he opened the hearing by inviting the deceased to state his claim. Not a word of what was said reached my ears, but after a few moments the tzaddik turned to me and said: 'The deceased has various well-founded claims against you — that you brought about his death, and so on. What do you have to say in your defense?'

"I explained that I had in fact wanted to return the wallet, but had lost him in the crowd; and since I had no idea who he was, what was I to have done?

" 'Will you agree to accept whatever verdict I hand down?' the tzaddik asked me.

"I said I would, and the tzaddik said the plaintiff was also agreeable.

" 'This, then, is my verdict,' he said after a pause. 'You are to return home and to make an honest stocktaking of whatever you own in money and property, down to the last thread and shoelace. Half of the total you may keep for yourself. As to the other half, you are to make the journey to the township where this man's widow lives, and hand it over personally to her. While you are there, hire competent tutors to teach her children. In addition, you are to set aside a certain proportion of your half and distribute it as *tzedakah* to the needy.'

"Stage by stage I did exactly as I was told — first at home, then in the widow's hometown — and then I made another journey to Chernobyl to express my gratitude to the tzaddik for having looked after the whole affair for me. I am now on my way home from there, so I thought that since I was passing through Berditchev, I would like to drop in here and hold a thanksgiving meal in the company of you folk.'

◆§ *Whispers from Another World (i)*

לְמַעַן יִיטַב לָךְ *That it may be well with you (22:7)*

> *That it may be well with you* — in the World in which all is good; *and prolong your days* — in the World which is endless *(Talmud, Tractate Kiddushin).*

When he had reached a ripe old age, one of the respected citizens of the community of Uman sold all his belongings and set off to live out his remaining years in *Eretz Yisrael.* He wanted to be buried in the soil of the Holy Land when his time came — "after a hundred and twenty years," as people say.

After only a few days there he decided to leave *Eretz Yisrael,* and a few months after having farewelled him, his old friends were surprised to see him back in his hometown. He was showered with questions from all sides: What made him go? What made him return? But he gave no answer whatever, and the whole episode remained a puzzle in the eyes of his townsmen.

A short while later he took ill, and called for the officials of the *Chevrah Kaddisha,* the voluntary burial society of the town, for he had something of importance to tell them. They hastened dutifully to his bedside, but when they arrived he merely made conversation on all manner of trifling subjects. The officials were surprised, and left his room. The next day he summoned them again, and though their first impulse was to ignore him, they finally decided to accede to his request. Once again he took up their time on inconsequential small talk, as if he were out of his mind, and they eventually left him in annoyance. When he called for them again on the third day they refused outright to be bothered in vain, but when he received this message he sent word that this time he would explain his invitations; he earnestly requested that they not take offense, but come to see him.

They took up seats around his bed, and the pale little man said: "The time has come to reveal a certain episode from the story of my life.

"When I was a young man I used to travel to various fairs and markets, earning my living from merchandising. Most of my business was in the region of Berditchev, and every time I passed by the town I would spend a day or two there in order to be able to see the tzaddik who lived there, Reb Levi Yitzchak.

"On my way from a certain fair one morning, I passed through Berditchev and went straight to the house of the tzaddik. He was walking up and down his study, robed in his *tallis,* and whispering the preliminary passages of the daily prayers in an ecstasy that was beautiful to see. I did not dare to disturb him at a moment like this, of course, so I waited in the adjoining room, and listened to his voice. Suddenly an angry little knot of noisy men and women brushed past me and stormed their way straight into the rebbe's study, where they kept up their raucous arguments. It was clear that they had come to the *rav* with a lawsuit, and as I heard their bitter claims and counter-claims, I pieced the story together.

"It transpired that a poor Jew had made a bare living by working as a money-changer. Having no capital of his own, he conducted his entire business with money which he borrowed from acquaintances. Every so often he would pay his debts from his meager earnings, and so continue. Now during the previous night this man had lost three hundred rubles — all of it borrowed money. He was in great consternation: he would lose his entire means of support, and be spurned as a bad debtor as well. He suspected the maid of his household, but despite her protestations of innocence he abused and cursed her, and even beat her in order to persuade her to return the money. She reported this treatment to her parents. They of course descended upon his house in a fury, and now, at the height of their violent dispute, they had all decided to bring it to the rebbe for adjudication.

"After listening to all parties the rebbe said: 'I can see that the maid is utterly innocent. This was an unfounded suspicion. At the same time it is clear that the money was in fact lost, and that this man did not simply invent this story in order to cast aspersions on her. As to where the money is — that, I am afraid, I do not see.'

"And Reb Levi Yitzchak walked up and down his room in distress, not knowing how to find a way out of this confused situation.

"Suddenly he stood still and said: 'If some person were to be found who would give me three hundred rubles so that we could make good this man's loss, I would promise him a share in the World to Come!'

"Hearing this from the adjoining room, I walked straight into his study and said: 'Rebbe, are you prepared to give this promise in writing?'

'I am,' he said.

"I took three hundred rubles out of my pocket and gave them to the tzaddik, who handed them directly to the money-changer.

"Then he said to the maid: 'Because you were suspected in vain, I give you my blessing that you will make a good match.'

"And to the man he said: 'And as for you — you have my blessing that you will never again suffer a loss.'

"The little group left the rebbe's presence in good spirits, and I retired to the waiting-room, allowing him to proceed with his morning prayers.

"When he was ready I entered his study again and reminded him about the written promise. He immediately asked his *gabbai* to bring paper, pen and ink, and sat down to write a note. As he folded it up he said: 'Here is your note, but take care never to open it or read it all the days of your life. When your time comes, and you sense that your last day in This World has arrived, hand over the note to the officials of the *Chevrah Kaddisha,* and ask them to place it inside your grave.'

"I took it joyfully from his hands, and of course took good heed of his instructions. Moreover, in order that it should be preserved safely, I decided to hide it in a special place: I had it bound by a bookbinder into the cover of my *Siddur.*

"When I left for *Eretz Yisrael* I forgot that prayer book in all the excitement of my preparations, and only when I arrived there did I realize that I had left it behind me, here in Uman. I lost no time in deciding what to do, and left the Holy Land at once. So you now understand that I did not leave there because of confused thinking. Now two days ago, when I fell ill, and thought my time had come, I called for you. By the time you arrived I felt somewhat better. I saw that this was not yet my last day, so I had to start talking on some other subject. The same thing happened yesterday. Today, however, I feel that my end is in fact drawing near. Gentlemen, here is the note. I beg of you to fulfill the instruction of the tzaddik. Place it in my grave."

He stretched out a wrinkled hand, and in exchange for their solemn promise, entrusted them with the folded note. A few hours later the man was no more.

After his passing the officials said to one another: "It was only this man alone whom the tzaddik forbade to read the note. There is clearly no prohibition on our reading it, now, after his death."

Accordingly, before carrying out their promise to the deceased, in a funeral that showed all honor to his memory, they unfolded the tiny note and read these words: *Open for him the gates of the Garden of Eden. — Levi Yitzchak the son of Sarah.*

◆§ *Whispers from Another World (ii)*

A once-prosperous merchant who had lost his entire fortune came to Reb Avraham Yehoshua Heschel of

Apta with the request that he intercede in heaven on his behalf, and advise him as well what to do: he had a daughter of marriageable age, and hardly a penny left to his name. The tzaddik asked him how much he needed and how much he had, and he answered that he needed a thousand rubles for the wedding and the dowry, and in his pocket he had exactly one ruble.

"Go in peace," said the tzaddik, "and take up the first offer of a transaction that comes your way. May God make your way prosper!"

A strange instruction, indeed: business without capital? ... But after this first thought the man relied on his faith in the words of his rebbe and set out on his way.

He arrived at an inn which he found was frequented by dealers in gems. He approached the table around which a group of them were crowded, and examined the diamonds that were set out on it.

"What are you looking at here?" asked a Jewish dealer. "Are you perhaps interested in buying one of these diamonds?"

"I am," replied the man.

"And how much money do you have, if I may ask?" said the dealer.

"One ruble," was the reply.

The whole group burst out in uproarious laughter.

The dealer continued boldly: "Listen here! I've got a deal for you that needs only one ruble. Buy my share in the World to Come!"

"I am agreeable," said the new arrival, "on condition that you confirm the sale in writing, and sign it according to law."

The gem dealer agreed, and egged on by the derisive laughter of his friends, he wrote out and signed a contract of sale, which he duly handed over to the purchaser in exchange for his last ruble. Having nothing more to do in the company of these people, the traveler found himself a quiet corner, took out of his pack the volume of the Talmud that he always carried with him, and was soon deep in thought.

While they were still chuckling with scorn at the hapless *batlan* who had just paid out his last ruble for a commodity that did not yet exist, in walked the wife of that gem-dealer. As it happened most of his gems in fact belonged to her; in fact, his whole wealth had come to him through an estate which she had inherited. She asked what they were snickering about, and they told her.

Incensed, she turned upon her husband: "So just in case you *did* have a share in the Next World coming to you, did you have to go and sell it, and remain naked like some heathen? I'm not going to live with a pagan like you! Come along with me to the *rav* and give me a bill of divorce!"

He stammered out an attempt at an excuse: he had only meant the whole thing to be a joke, and so on. His wife remained unconvinced. *She* was not going to be the wife of a pagan who had no share in the World to Come!

Her husband begged one of the employees of the inn to search around urgently for the new arrival.

When he joined the distraught couple, the dealer addressed him as follows: "Listen here, Reb Yid. I'm sure you realize, don't you, that everything that passed between us was one big joke? Here take your ruble back, and return me the contract. Okay?"

"Not at all," said the traveler. "Business is business. *I* certainly had no joke in mind!"

"If so," said the gem-dealer, "I'll let you make a profit of a few rubles on the deal, and you can sell me back again what you bought from me."

"The profit I demand," said the traveler, "is one thousand rubles."

"Are you out of your mind?" shouted the dealer, red with rage. "For some miserable little bit of paper that I gave you, you're demanding such a fortune?"

At this point his wife chimed in decisively: "Even if he demands five thousand rubles you must ransom your share in the World to Come."

The dealer quietly offered the stranger a hundred rubles, but he refused.

"I would like you to know," he said, "that I am not the impractical *batlan* that you and your friends take me for. I too was once a businessman, except that I lost my fortune, and it was the *rav* of Apta who advised me to accept the first offer of a transaction that presented itself

— because I need a thousand rubles with which to marry off my daughter. And I am not going to forgo one solitary kopek out of that one thousand rubles!"

Two hundred, three hundred — each successive offer received the same answer: not a kopek less than one thousand rubles. Words were never going to make any impression on a man as stubborn as this, and in the end the gem-dealer had no option but to give him that whole sum in exchange for his bill of sale.

His wife now turned to the stranger: she would very much like to see the tzaddik of Apta.

"My pleasure," he said. "Allow me to direct you to him."

When they arrived there, the woman said to the tzaddik: "I am of course pleased that through my agency such good fortune should come the way of that poor fellow. But I have one queston of you, rebbe. Is my husband's share in the World to Come in fact worth one thousand rubles?"

"At the time of the first sale," replied the tzaddik, "when he sold his share in the World to Come for the price of one ruble, his share in it was not worth even that one ruble. But at the time of the second sale, when he bought back his share in the World to Come for a thousand rubles and helped to marry off the daughter of a poor fellow Jew, his share in That World was worth far, far more than a thousand rubles. No money can measure its worth."

◆§ *Whispers from Another World (iii)*

When Reb Menachem Mendel of Rimanov was a young man, before he became known as a tzaddik, he married the daughter of a prominent householder from Fristik who supported the young couple at his table for some time after their marriage, according to the custom. During this period, the young man devoted himself to the service of his Maker through study and prayer by day and by night. He indulged as well in ascetic practices, such as fasting for long periods, and rolling in the snow in the bitter winter mornings. When his father-in-law saw that nothing else interested him, and that he neglected to provide for his young wife, he ordered his daughter to demand that her husband give her a bill of divorce. She refused this demand outright. Her father reacted by driving them out of his house, and cutting them off utterly from any share in his inheritance.

The young couple found themselves a humble dwelling of their own, where they lived in unrelenting privation. The young woman suffered all in silence, and with whatever work she could get in sewing and embroidery supported herself and her husband on the barest of rations.

It once happened that for three days on end she earned nothing, and they were left without even a loaf of bread to eat. So she said to herself: "If we sit here in silence, we will both die of hunger. I'll go along to the baker. Perhaps he will give me a cake on account, something that I can take along to my husband. The poor tzaddik has been fasting in the *beis midrash* for three days now!"

The baker refused her request, and she left him in tears. He called her back immediately and said: "If you give me your share in the World to Come, I will give you the bread."

She was in a dilemma, and pondered her situation earnestly. Finally she said to herself: "Whatever happens to me, I'm not going to let my husband die of hunger."

Turning to the baker, she said: "Give me the bread, and some cheese as well — and I am now giving you my share in the World to Come."

He gave her what she requested, and she made her quiet way to the *beis midrash*. She spread out a little tablecloth for him, laid out the bread and cheese, and remained standing there — not according to her usual custom of retiring modestly from the House of Study once she had brought him his meal.

He washed his hands in preparation for the breaking of bread, pronounced the benediction, and ate what she had brought him. Then he said: "Tell me, what makes you stand here still?"

"My dear husband!" she wept. "You know what toil and suffering I have undergone in order to make my soul worthy of enjoying the bliss of the World to Come — and now I have lost my share in it!"

When he had heard the whole story from her innocent lips he consoled her: "Do not regret what has happened, for a moment before you came I was seized by a fainting fit. If you had not brought me the bread I would have died. That means that with this loaf of bread you have earned yourself a *new* share in the World to Come, for the Sages teach us — do they not? — that 'Whoever saves the life of one fellow Jew, it is as if he saved an entire world!' Why, then, do you need your *old* share in the World to Come?"

◆§ *Whispers From Another World (iv)*

The old man languishing on his sickbed was clearly about to breathe his last: it was time to call the members of the *Chevrah Kaddisha* brotherhood, according to custom, so that they could help him utter the words of *Vidui,* the confession which is recited by one who is about to return his soul to his Maker. The sick man suddenly turned in bed to face the wall. A moment later he turned to face the men of the fraternity, and said: "You may go your separate ways. My time has not yet come."

The next evening, after the twilight Third Meal, when *Shabbos* was drawing to a tranquil close, he called for them once more. When they arrived he told them quietly: "The time has now come for me to take my leave from This World."

"How do you know that?" they asked — and they leaned over the wan face to hear the urgent whisper of an old man straining to tell his last story.

"In my youth," said the old man, "I was a servant in the household of a villager who was the father-in-law of the tzaddik Reb David of Lelov. Before daybreak one bitterly cold morning my master sent me to have a ram slaughtered by the local *shochet.* On my way I was shocked to see a man lying on the frosty ground with arms and legs outstretched. I came closer, and saw who it was — the tzaddik Reb David, almost killed by the cold. He had broken the ice to immerse himself in the nearby river, and on coming out of the water had fainted from sheer cold. I quickly took off my fur coat and put it on him, hoisted him on my shoulders, and carried him to his home. There I boiled a kettle and gave him tea, and laid him in his bed. After he had regained his strength he made me swear that I would not reveal what had happened until my time came. Then he added these words: 'In return for the great favor that you have done for me, I owe you some reward. You may choose between wealth — and a share in the World to Come.'

"When I told him that I chose the latter reward he said: 'Before you pass away from This World you will see me while you are awake. But so long as you do not see me, even if you appear to be breathing your last, you may be certain that your time has not yet come.'

"And that, my friends, explains why yesterday evening I turned my face to the wall. I thought my minutes on earth were counted, and was therefore certain that I would see the tzaddik, as he had promised. I did not see him, however, and there is a reason for that. For when in the World Above they called for Reb David and told him that the time had come for him to fulfill his promise and visit a certain old man on his deathbed, he said: 'I am now enjoying the bliss of the Sabbath day. Now is no time to be sent down to the coarse materiality of the World Below! Let me go after *Shabbos* has passed.'

"Just now, a moment before I summoned you, the tzaddik appeared to me. I saw him clearly, so I am certain that within a very short time I will depart this life. My friends, help me say my last *Vidui* on earth!"

Word for word they pronounced the solemn confession; word for word he mouthed it after them. His time on earth had come to a close, and he was now in a World which is beyond the bounds of time.

◆§ *Whispers From Another World (v)*

In Helochov in the 1870's there lived a chassid called Reb Chaim Yehoshua, who was eighty-seven years old. For a week he had felt his strength waning, though his mind remained clear and unwavering. Sensing that his days on earth were coming to an end, he requested that the inner circle of elder chassidim in the town should assemble at his bedside, and when they arrived, he asked that they invite as well a distinguished chassid who was then in their town — Reb Dov Ze'ev of Yekaterinoslav, an emissary of Reb Shmuel of Lubavitch.

"One request I have of you all," he told the venerable gathering, "but first I must tell you of a singular incident that once befell me.

"In 1833 or 1834 I spent all of the eight days of the festival of Channukah in the court of Reb Menachem Mendel of Lubavitch. In the course of that time I heard three chassidic discourses from his mouth, all of them based on the idea that the struggle of the Maccabees against the Seleucids was a spiritual battle. It was a revolt against the desire of the invaders to impose Hellenism on the People of Israel, as expressed in their proud demand: 'Inscribe it for yourselves on the honor of an ox that you have no share in the God of Israel!' And it was only through the self-sacrifice of our ancestors for their faith they ousted the invaders. The rebbe then spoke at length in praise of this *mesirus nefesh* shown by our forefathers for the sake of sanctifying the Divine Name.

"I was forty-odd years old at the time, and lived with my four brothers and two brothers-in-law in a village near Kalisk in the Vitebsk region. Our father, Reb Avraham Yisrael — a chassid of Reb Shneur Zalman of Liadi and then of his son Reb Dov Ber of Lubavitch — had settled there, and brought us up as farmers with a particular zest for fulfilling the mitzvah of hospitality.

"Late one night during the winter of 1835 or 1836 I heard a knock on the door. I got out of bed and opened the door, and saw before me two Jews wearing heavy fur coats and covered in snow. I extended my hand in the traditional greeting of *Shalom Aleichem,* and invited them to come inside and warm themselves by the stove. When I had prepared them hot tea, and a meal of bread and butter and milk, I left them to eat alone, and went out to the cowshed. On the way there I thought I heard the wailing of a child. At first I dismissed it as the meow of a cat, but as I came nearer, it was unmistakable.

" 'Who is that crying over there?' I asked.

"'It's me, Binyamin,' answered a trembling little voice.

"I soon traced the sound to the covered wagon which my two guests had stood at the far end of the farmyard. I climbed up to see, and my blood froze — for inside lay two small children trussed up in ropes, one asleep, and the other crying.

"Those were the days of the *chapers*, brigands who used to kidnap Jewish children. They would sell them to farflung communities who were forced by the authorities under fearful threats to hand over a certain number of children to the terrors of conscription in the Czarist army. So these were the guests who were supping so placidly in my kitchen! My first thought was fear lest they kidnap our own children likewise. I quicky unbound the ropes from these two shivering little waifs, and took them in my arms to the house of my brother Michael, which stood among the trees in our orchard. My brother was already awake, so I quickly told him what was happening and hastened home.

"Entering my kitchen I saw that one of the guests was making conversation with one of our children. I excused myself, woke up the rest of the family, and whispered to them what we should be wary of. When I came back to the kitchen the same man said to me: 'What a nice, good boy this is! But I have been punished by heaven with two crazy children who talk nonsense. In fact, I had to tie them up with ropes, and I am now on my way to take them to a very important doctor in Vitebsk.'

"My brother Michael had managed meanwhile to give the two little prisoners a solid breakfast, and to hide them away in a safe place in his house. He now stormed into my kitchen in a rage, and addressed my guests: 'A very good morning to you, kidnappers that you are! Either you leave this very minute, or you will suffer a bitter end!'

"The child-snatchers did not yet realize that they had been caught redhanded, so one of them said to the other, in tones of righteous indignation: 'Let us pick up and leave this place. You can see that we have fallen among heartless people who do not even have pity for an unfortunate fellow like yourself who is taking his mentally-disturbed children to see a doctor. You see' — he continued, turning now to my brother and myself — 'I too live in a village, just as you do. But when I saw that my dear friend who lives in the nearby forest has this most unfortunate problem with his dear children, and there was no doctor in our district who could deal with such an illness, I felt sorry for him. I quickly harnessed my horses, and I am now taking him to consult a very important doctor in Vitebsk.'

"The kidnappers left the house with long faces that expressed offended sensitivity. A moment later, though, when they saw that their passengers were no longer in their wagon, they ran back to us, shouting and cursing. It did not take them long now to realize that this would not be at all to their advantage, so they turned around soon enough, and galloped out of our village as fast as they could.

"A month later, when my brother Michael paid one of his periodic visits to Reb Menachem Mendel of Lubavitch and told him of this episode, the face of the tzaddik beamed with joy. He blessed us all and told us to watch over the children for a year, and only then to return them to their homes. We of course followed his instructions. For a whole year they studied together with our own little ones, and did very well indeed.

"From that time on, I was overcome by a burning desire to do what I could for the ransom of captives. In fact I even made the journey to Lubavitch especially to tell the rebbe of my wish, and he told me how I should go about doing this mitzvah. Three or four months of every year — partly in summer, partly in winter — I would travel to various places and ransom children such as these, who are known in these parts as 'Cantonists.'

"This went on for seven years — until one day I was trapped by a vicious ambush. I was a hairsbreadth from death. When I was eventually freed I again traveled to see the tzaddik, who chose Helochov as the place I should live in, and gave me his blessing for long life. In addition to that, he gave me his promise that when my time came to go up to the Other World, I would be — and these were his very words, which he took from the Talmud — עִמִּי בִּמְחִיצָתִי, 'with me, in my abode.'

The old man drew a deep breath, and let it out slowly.

"My masters," he said, speaking now more deliberately, "either today or tomorrow my soul will return to its Creator. My parting request to you is that after the soil will have filled my grave, a *minyan* of ten men should stand next to it, and say these words: 'Reb Menachem Mendel, son-in-law of Reb Dov Ber, and grandson of Reb Shneur Zalman! Your servant Chaim Yehoshua the son of Esther is dead. Before his passing he appointed us his agents for the mitzvah of informing you of this, and of reminding you of your promise to Chaim Yehoshua the son of Esther that by virtue of the mitzvah of the ransoming of captives, he would be *with you, in your abode.*' "

They all promised together to fulfill his request, and the next morning — after he had completed all of his usual morning devotions — Reb Chaim Yehoshua returned his soul to his Maker with a clear mind, his last words being *Shema Yisrael.*

❦ ❦ ❦

The whole of the above episode was recorded by the emissary from Yekaterinoslav, Reb Dov Ze'ev, who concluded his account as follows: "On the same day Reb Chaim Yehoshua was brought to rest. When his grave had been filled by soil, we stood around it together, all ten of us, and — in the very words that we had been given — faithfully reminded the departed rebbe of his promise to his chassid."

◆§ *Responsibility*

וְלֹא תָשִׂים דָּמִים בְּבֵיתֶךָ
You shall not bring blood upon your house (22:8)

Reb Menachem Mendel of Rimanov was once presented with a costly table as a gift. His little boy and one of his playmates from the neighborhood immediately began a game of chasing each other noisily around it. In the midst of all the excitement the neighbor's child knocked his head against one of the corners of the table and began to cry. A moment later he was laughing again, but nevertheless, since someone had come to harm by it, the tzaddik decided at once to remove the stumbling-block from his house by having the corners of the expensive table cut off.

☙ For the Sake of Peace (i)

כִּי יִקַּח אִישׁ אִשָּׁה
If a man take a wife (22:13)

The bridal party was ready, the *chuppah* was standing in place, but the distinguished guests were kept waiting — for the bride's father, Reb Yaakov Yitzchak of Lublin, was spending far longer than usual over his afternoon prayers. No one thought it proper to ask for an explanation, but at the wedding breakfast the Chozeh himself raised the subject.

"You are no doubt surprised," he said, "that I took so long this afternoon over the *Minchah* prayer. Well, here is the reason. As you all know, the Talmud teaches that 'Forty days before the formation of an infant a heavenly voice proclaims: *The daughter of so-and-so is destined to marry so-and-so* — and at the same time they announce in what year the marriage will take place, as well as the week, the day, the hour, and the moment. Now if the parents of a young couple in their eagerness to perform a mitzvah arrange to hold the ceremony *before* the time announced years earlier, then some kind of dispute is bound to come up in order that the *chuppah* take place at the required time. As our Sages say: 'There is no marriage contract — *kesubbah* — that does not involve some controversy.'

"Now since I knew that the moment fixed in heaven had not yet arrived, I deliberately took my time over the *Shemoneh Esreh* prayer, in order to spare us from that other method of filling in the last few minutes ... "

☙ For the Sake of Peace (ii)

In his fourteenth year Reb Avraham of Sochatchov married the daughter of Reb Menachem Mendel of Kotsk. When they were already in the carriage on the way to the *chuppah*, his father — Reb Ze'ev Nachum of Biala — suddenly realized that in all the bustle of the wedding preparations he had completely forgotten to remind his son to prepare a learned dissertation. This would have to be delivered, according to custom, at the reception held in honor of the bridegroom immediately before the ceremony.

"Do you have something prepared?" he asked his son. But he too had overlooked the matter.

"What will you do now?" his father asked in distress. "You can be sure that all the most prominent scholars will have assembled at Kotsk for the occasion, and without a doubt they will be expecting to hear some profound *pilpul* from you!"

"Don't worry, father," said the little fellow. "I still have time to prepare while we are traveling."

With that he opened up the volume of the Talmud that he had with him, and after a quarter of an hour of intense concentration he cried out happily: "No worries — I now have a good *pilpul!*"

What with all the clatter and lurching of the carriage his father had no opportunity to hear the discourse before its delivery; he had no option but to rely on his son.

On their arrival in Kotsk the young bridegroom amazed the learned multitude by the breadth of his erudition and the brilliance of his analytical acumen. His discourse lasted several hours, and was appropriately based on a Mishnah in Tractate *Nedarim* that deals with the marriage of the daughters of scholars.

While the marriage contract was being drawn up, the bride's father, Reb Menachem Mendel, said to the father of the bridegroom, Reb Ze'ev Nachum: "*Mechutan,* I am told that you have provided your son with expensive clothes. Now tell me: is it right to spend so much money on clothes that will soon be outgrown by a bridegroom who can still draw himself up to his full height — and even spring up on tiptoe for *Kadosh! Kadosh!* — while standing under the table?

"Since, as you recall, the Talmud assures us that 'There is no marriage contract that does not involve some controversy,' *this* is the subject on which I have chosen to have a difference of opinion with you!"

◆§ *The Honor of Your Presence*

In honor of the marriage of his daughter to the present Lubavitcher rebbe in 1929, Reb Yosef Yitzchak Schneersohn of Lubavitch delivered a *maamar* — a discourse on the teachings of the *Chabad* school of chassidic philosophy — based on the words *Lechah Dodi:* "Come, my beloved, to greet the bride."

In introducing his discourse, the rebbe addressed the distinguished assemblage in the *Tomchei Temimim* yeshivah in Warsaw as follows: "As is widely known, the forefathers of a bridal couple come as guests from the World of Truth to grace the ceremony with their presence. In the House of Israel at large, as many as three generations come to a wedding. There are those who are honored by even earlier generations, each according to his spiritual level. Now, by way of invitation to the tzaddikim who were our forefathers to join us at the *chuppah* and to bestow their blessings on the bride and groom, let us now open with a chassidic discourse; its content is partly from Reb Shneur Zalman of Liadi, partly from his son and successor Reb Dov Ber of Lubavitch, partly from his nephew and successor Reb Menachem Mendel of Lubavitch, partly from his son, my grandfather Reb Shmuel, and partly from my father, Reb Shalom Ber. And, as our Sages remind us, 'He who quotes a teaching in the name of a sage, let him see that sage in his mind's eye standing before him!' "

◆§ *Man, Wife, and Tzaddik (i)*

וְכָתַב לָהּ סֵפֶר כְּרִיתֻת
And he shall write her a bill of divorce (24:1)

In 1740 the greatest scholars of Slutsk and all that district went out to greet the Baal Shem Tov, who had come to the city on a visit. Among them was the aged scholar Reb Uri Nasan Nata, who as a youth was known as the Ilui ("prodigy") of Karinik, a township near Brisk. One of the wealthy householders of Brisk had taken him as a son-in-law, and after he was left a widower he had moved to Slutsk.

His son Reb Shlomo had been educated by him at home, and then at the age of fourteen he had left home to seek a scholarly environment — first in Vilna, then in Horodna, and then in Cracow. There he had encountered a prominent scholar by the name of Reb Menachem Aryeh, who was a hidden tzaddik, and grew to be his close disciple in the study of the teachings of Chassidism — though on condition that their connection be kept secret. At the age of about twenty-two he returned to Slutsk. His father was overjoyed with his progress in learning, and arranged a match for him with the daughter of a leaseholder who lived in a villager nearby. Half a year after their marriage, however, the young wife lost her sanity, and since she was in no state to accept a bill of divorce, he was of course unable to remarry. When the Baal Shem Tov now visited Slutsk, the young man's father brought their sad plight before him, and the unfortunate woman's father likewise asked the tzaddik for advice and a blessing for her recovery.

The Baal Shem Tov then invited both fathers to meet him together and asked them if either of them bore a grudge against the other. The bridegroom's father, Reb Uri Nasan Nata, spoke first. He was full of praise for his *mechutan,* the bride's father. Here was a man who despite the pressure of business fixed times for the study of Torah, maintained a hospitable house which was open to all comers, supported Talmudic scholars generously, and maintained his son-in-law in the most respectable manner. Since the young man had been mentioned, Reb Eliyahu Moshe now spoke most highly of his noble character. He was clearly proud of his assiduous son-in-law, who throughout his stay in the village always found time on weekdays to conduct study circles for the simple farming folk who lived round about, teaching them *Chumash* with Rashi's commentary, and the moral lessons of *Ein Yaakov;* and on *Shabbos* he would read for them from the Midrash and the Ethics of the Fathers. While teaching he imbued them with a comradely love for each other, explaining to them that no man's profit ever came at the expense of that which Divine Providence had destined for another. In a word, he was well loved by the villagers from all around. They were saddened by his present plight, and prayed that his young wife would be restored to complete health, and that he would return to teach them as in happier times.

The Baal Shem Tov listened attentively to them both, and then said: "With God's help, I will be able to heal the young woman completely, and restore her mind to its original clarity — but only on condition that when this happens the young couple do not live together, and when several days have passed, and she is in a fit state according to the Law to accept a bill of divorce, she accepts such a document from her husband with a willing heart."

The *mechutanim* were stupefied at these words. The aged father of Reb Shlomo proposed various legal objections to such a divorce, and Reb Eliyahu Moshe argued that his daughter would be grieved by such a procedure, since she respected her husband highly. He was certain that his son-in-law would likewise be distressed. He himself was prepared to contribute an enormous sum to charity — in the merit of which he begged the tzaddik to pray for her recovery, but to allow the young couple to rejoin each other in the love and harmony to which they were accustomed. The Baal Shem Tov answered unequivocally — that if they did not agree to the condition that he had stipulated, he would not be able to help them.

A few days later they called on the tzaddik together with the young Reb Shlomo, and told him that they accepted his condition — though of course they could not guarantee that the young woman would agree. The Baal Shem Tov heard their reply, and told Reb Eliyahu Moshe to go home and tell his ailing daughter that the Baal Shem Tov had come to Slutsk and asked her to come to speak with him about a matter of importance.

The *mechutanim* looked at each other in amazement.

"But for the last six years," Reb Eliyahu Moshe protested, "she has not uttered a syllable! She has found herself a nook between the stove and the wall, and can barely be fed. In a word, the poor young woman is utterly out of her mind. How can I possibly speak to her?'

The Baal Shem Tov gave no answer.

Making his way homeward with a heavy heart, Reb Eliyahu Moshe remarked to his *mechutan* that if the tzaddik had seen the state in which his daughter was to be found, he would not have spoken as he had. And from the very depths of his heart, Reb Uri Nasan Nata sighed in sympathy with the sufferers from all sides. Not so his son, Reb Shlomo. For when before his marriage he had been a disciple of Reb Menachem Aryeh, he had felt an intellectual affinity with the teachings of the Baal Shem Tov. Now that he had met him, and had heard his teachings from his mouth, he became attached to him with all his heart. He therefore told his father-in-law that he held that they should follow the instructions of the Baal Shem Tov implicitly. His father added that since they had already accepted a far more difficult condition, they should certainly fulfill an instruction which required merely that they attempt to speak to the young woman.

Opening the door Reb Eliyahu Moshe found his daughter sitting in her accustomed corner behind the stove. He began at once to tell his wife what the Baal Shem Tov had said, adding that he was widely reputed as a wonder-worker. To their amazement, their daughter rose from her place as soon as she heard her father's words. She approached them quietly, and in a voice they had not heard for six years, asked who this was who worked wonders. They told her that the man about whom they were speaking was a renowned tzaddik, and she answered that before hearing any more she first wanted to immerse herself in a *mikveh* for purification.

Fearful lest the Evil Eye reverse this unbelievable transformation, her parents bolted their door fast. The young woman ate and spoke and slept as if completely normal, though she felt very weak. On the third day they saw that she had contracted malaria, and in her delirium spoke partly about the Baal Shem Tov. When her father heard her crying and asking to be taken to the wonder-worker, he was suddenly reminded of what this cataclysm in his life had made him forget — that the tzaddik had asked to see her. She was visibly happy to receive the message, and on the very next day, accompanied her parents, she made the journey to Slutsk.

Reb Shomo had heard by now of his wife's recovery, for his father-in-law had sent a special messenger with the news. He now began to speak with his father about the principles of Chassidism taught by the Baal Shem Tov, for he considered this to be a teachable moment. He explained the emphasis which the tzaddik gave to the mystical teachings of the Kabbalah; the workings of Divine Providence not only on humanity but even on the mineral and vegetable kingdoms; the intrinsic worth of even the simplest fellow Jew; the central role of the obligation of *ahavas Yisrael;* and so on. The aged scholar pondered these matters all that day and throughout the following night. On the next day he set out to tell the Baal Shem Tov what his son had told him of these principles, and added that he would dearly love to become a disciple of his. At the same meeting he told the Baal Shem Tov of the good news which had just reached his son. To this the tzaddik replied that on that same day the young woman was again unwell, but that when her father would carry out his mission she would recover and come to see him.

When the young woman and her parents arrived at Slutsk, she and her husband entered the room of the tzaddik, who told them that they would have to divorce. With bitter tears the unfortunate young woman told the Baal Shem Tov how highly she respected her husband for his refined character. If the tzaddik decreed that they should divorce, he must surely know that she was unworthy of so righteous a husband, and she felt it her duty to obey. Reb Shlomo, likewise moved, told the tzaddik that his wife exemplified all the noble attributes by which the Sages define a good wife. If, however, the tzaddik ordered that they divorce, he too would be agreeable.

The Baal Shem Tov arranged to see them four days later; he would then arrange the legalities required.

The next three days the young couple and their parents spent in fasting and prayer. When on the fourth day they made their cheerless way to the tzaddik, they found a *rav,* a scribe and two witnesses already waiting. The Baal Shem Tov asked them if they agreed wholeheartedly to the divorce. They answered that they believed that whatever the tzaddik told them would be for their good, and since they loved each other, each of them was willing to proceed with the divorce — for the good of the other.

The Baal Shem Tov retired for some time to another room.

When he returned he said: "Six years ago a threat of fearful suffering hung over your lives because of the accusations of the Prosecuting Angel. The verdict was then issued that you should each undergo what you have gone through these last six years. Now that your faith in the instructions of your rebbe has been so strong that you were even willing to proceed with a divorce on account of it, this very faith has at this moment freed you from the continuing sentence of the Heavenly Court. The charge against you has been annulled. Live on happily together, and you have my blessing that your house be filled with sons and daughters, and that you both live to a ripe old age."

The young couple remained in Slutsk for three years, after which they moved to Minsk, where Reb Shlomo became one of the pillars of the chassidic community. They then settled with their family in Bayev, until Reb Shneur Zalman of Liadi moved to Liozna, where Reb Shlomo and his family joined his circle of chassidim. Finally, in 1796, they settled in *Eretz Yisrael* where they lived on for another fifteen years — until Reb Shlomo was some ninety-nine years of age.

◆§ *Man, Wife, and Tzaddik (ii)*

When a man divorces his first wife, the very altar sheds tears for him *(Talmud, Tractate Gittin).*

A wealthy chassid once came to Lubavitch to ask Reb Menachem Mendel to recommend a fine young man as a match for his daughter. The rebbe sent at once for one of the students then at the yeshivah, and in introducing him said: "Here is a good match for her."

Without hesitation the chassid invited the young man to his home, and within a short time the young couple were betrothed and married.

Not long after, the young woman began to complain that this husband of hers was not to her liking. After a period of unrest and various attempts at restoring harmony, she insisted on a divorce.

Her father set out at once to consult the rebbe on this step, and he answered: "God forbid! This is her match."

Returning home the father exerted himself to bring peace into the lives of the young couple, but it did not last. His daughter was soon demanding a divorce as before, so he made the journey to Lubavitch once again.

The rebbe answered him sharply: "Did I not tell you that they should not divorce?"

After the father had again attempted to restore domestic harmony his daughter repeated her demand more insistently than ever. She would not even allow her father to visit the rebbe, for, as she said: "Is the rebbe some kind of governor-general that he should order me to spend my life with someone whom I do not want?"

She had her way, and she and her husband divorced.

Some time later she married a God-fearing widower, and for a long period they lived in peace. Their marriage, however, was not blessed with children. The husband did not feel the lack so acutely, for he had children from his previous marriage — but his wife suffered intensely. Consequently, when one day he had occasion to make the journey to Lubavitch, she asked him to mention her name to the rebbe with the request that she be granted a child.

When he duly raised this question at the conclusion of his *yechidus*, the rebbe said: "Am I some kind of governor-general, that I can give the order for children to be born?"

The husband found this answer unintelligible. When repeated he it at home, however, his wife understood it all too well.

◆§ *Not Quite a Mitzvah*

וְהָיָה אִם בִּן הַכּוֹת
And if he be worthy of stripes (25:2)

At the time that Reb Yitzchak of Vorki succeeded Reb Avraham Moshe of Pshischah as rebbe, he lived in a village near Warsaw that belonged to a lady by the name of Tamar'l, who was renowned for her philanthropy, and whose estates he managed.

On one occasion a large group of chassidim who came to consult him there made their way to his house by way of the surrounding fields, and on their way caused damage to the grain crops through which they passed.

One of the owner's employees responsible for these farms was a chassid by the name of Reb Moshe Plotzker. Seeing the damage caused by the visitors, he stormed into the rebbe's room and exclaimed: "It would be a mitzvah to beat them!" — for this was the custom among the gentile landowners of the time.

Reb Yitzchak gave no answer. Assuming that the rebbe concurred with his view, the angry man strode out to give the offenders their deserts.

But the tzaddik called him back and said: "When a man is about to perform a mitzvah, he usually articulates his lofty intention by first contemplating and pronouncing the evocation that opens with the words *LeSheim Yichud*. If he is a chassid, then even before that he usually purifies himself in preparation for the holy act by immersing himself in the waters of a *mikveh*. In that case, you should first go to the *mikveh*, then say *LeSheim Yichud* devoutly, and only then go ahead to perform your mitzvah ..."

◆§ *To Preserve a Name*

וְלֹא יִמָּחֶה שְׁמוֹ
That his name not be wiped out (25:6)

While speaking to Reb Avraham of Sochatchov, a well-meaning chassid commented about a certain freethinker: יִמַּח שְׁמוֹ — "May his name be wiped out!"

The tzaddik reacted abruptly: "Do you know what the Law prescribes in the case of an apostate who dies without leaving children, God forbid?"

The chassid was silent.

The tzaddik went on: "The Jerusalem Talmud explains that the widow of such a man is obliged to undergo *chalitzah*. This ceremony, as you know, takes the place of *yibbum*, the obligation which the Torah places upon a deceased man's brother to marry the widow *for an express purpose* — in order 'that his name be not wiped out from Israel.'

"So you see that the Torah is concerned that even the name of an apostate should not be erased — and you take the liberty of saying what you said about this freethinker?!"

◆§ *Weight-Watchers (i)*

אֶבֶן שְׁלֵמָה וָצֶדֶק יִהְיֶה לָּךְ
A perfect and just weight shall you have (25:15)

Once a month, on the eve of Rosh Chodesh, it was the custom of Reb Menachem Mendel of Rimanov to send out two supervisors to all the shops in town to see whether the weights and measures being used were sound. One of those sent on a certain occasion was Reb Zvi Hirsch, who was later to succeed his rebbe. Arriving with his partner at the shop of a certain wealthy businessman who had once dabbled in scholarship, he found an undersized liquid measure. When Reb Zvi Hirsch rebuked him for his carelessness, the shopkeeper answered that it was not used for measuring.

"But there is an explicit law on the subject," said Reb Zvi Hirsch. "Our Sages teach us that a man is forbidden to have an oversized or undersized measure in his house, even if it is used as a pail for garbage."

The shopkeeper's retort was brazen. Borrowing a phrase remembered from the Book of *Samuel,* he asked: " 'Is Shaul also one of the prophets?!' Does our Reb Zvi Hirsch too go about laying down the Law?"

In reaction to this, Reb Zvi took the measure in hand, and trampled on it.

When he returned from his day's rounds and was asked by the rebbe if everything was in order, Reb Zvi Hirsch concealed that incident, being afraid that the wrath of the rebbe would be kindled against the arrogant offender. But Reb Menachem Mendel got to hear of the story from the man who accompanied him.

He immediately instructed his *shammes* to announce that the townsmen should all assemble in the synagogue to hear a sermon, but though he was to knock with his cane on all the shutters according to custom, he was to ignore the house of that offender. The shopkeeper heard that the rebbe was speaking on the subject of weights and measures, and realized that this whole tempest was brought about on his account. He went to the synagogue of his own accord, and as a sign of contriteness removed his shoes in preparation for begging forgiveness of the tzaddik. Reb Menachem Mendel promised to forgive him on condition that by way of a fine he undertake to donate fifty gold ducats to charity.

Before the shopkeeper arrived at the synagogue to humbly make amends, someone noticed that the lips of Reb Zvi Hirsch were muttering something. Asked what he was saying, he replied: "Only a little prayer that the man should not be punished before he comes to make peace with the rebbe."

◆§ Weight-Watchers (ii)

"I was once in the house of Reb David of Lelov at dawn," recounted Reb Yitzchak of Vorki. "He was garbed in *tallis* and *tefillin,* ready to begin his morning prayers. Suddenly a gentile walked in and asked the tzaddik to sell him half a gallon of beer. No other member of the family was in the house at the moment, so Reb David went ahead with amazing alacrity and measured out the beer himself. At this point, though, the gentile wanted to buy it more cheaply, so he asked the tzaddik to measure him out an additional quantity for the same price. Reb David cut the conversation short, poured what was in the container back into its barrel, returned to his study and began his prayers.

"I was baffled by the entire little episode. What made him start? What made him stop? And if he had already decided to get himself involved in selling beer to the gentile, why did he not come to an agreement with him on the price, and settle the matter?

"So Reb David explained it all to me. 'Listen, my friend,' he said. 'My guiding principle is בְּכָל דְּרָכֶיךָ דָעֵהוּ — *Know Him in all your ways.* Before a man begins any action he first needs to know what pleasure the Almighty will have from it. When I first went to measure out the beer, I intended thereby to fulfill the mitzvah of keeping just weights and measures, and so I did it energetically. But from the moment I saw that our encounter had become no more than plain commerce, I withdrew from it. For what do I have to do with him? And what pleasure would the Almighty now derive from our encounter?"

◆§ The Wife of One's Youth

וְאֵשֶׁת נְעוּרִים כִּי תִמָּאֵס
Can the wife of one's youth be reviled? *(Haftarah)*

In the household of a certain chassid there lived a maid whose husband had been conscripted into the Czarist army at the outbreak of the Russo-Turkish war of 1877, and had never been heard of since. She therefore asked her mistress to ask her husband to raise the subject when he next visited his rebbe, Reb Shmuel of Lubavitch.

The rebbe was riding in his carriage just outside Lubavitch, as he often did, and when he saw this chassid approaching, he invited him to join him. The chassid utilized the opportunity well.

"Rebbe, I have been given a message for you," he said, and went on to tell him all about the unfortunate *agunah,* who neither knew whether she had a husband alive nor was able to remarry.

"My father," said the rebbe, referring to Reb Menachem Mendel of Lubavitch, "was good at these things — but I know nothing. Let me tell you a somewhat similar story that involved my father.

"My father had a relative whose husband had deserted her, claiming that she was ugly and an evil woman. She came to our household, and my mother took her in as a house-help. She asked my mother several times to raise the subject with my father, but every time my father would get out of it. Once, before the Days of Awe, my mother insisted, and said: 'Is it not written וּמִבְּשָׂרְךָ לֹא תִתְעַלָּם — *And hide yourself not from your own flesh?'*

" 'You too?' my father replied. 'Haven't I got enough heartache from all the people who come here with their bundles of woes, that you have to add some more?'

" 'Then make up your mind,' countered my mother. 'If you are unable to help, then tell that to all your chassidim so that they will stop coming to see you; if after all you *are* able to help everyone, then why don't you give an answer to our relative?'

" 'But the Dnieper is not on fire,' said my father.

" 'Very well,' said my mother, 'then fix a time.'

"And my father told her that after the coming festivals — within a few weeks — he would see what could be done.

"During the Ten Days of Penitence between Rosh HaShanah and Yom Kippur my father called his *gabbai* and told him that if a certain leaseholder from the region of Orsha should arrive during the Intermediate Days of the festival of Sukkos — since every year this man came to Lubavitch especially for the last days of this festival — he should send him to see him at once.

"He was duly called to see my father, who said: 'I have a mission for you involving a mitzvah — to pass on a letter to a man called Chaikl who lives about twenty miles from your home.'

" 'It will be my pleasure to obey, God willing,' said the leaseholder, 'immediately after the festival.'

" 'No,' said the rebbe, my father. 'What I meant was that you should set out immediately, and spend the last days of the festival at home.'

"The man was not exactly overjoyed at the prospect, after all the trouble he had gone to in order to be able to spend those very days in the company of the rebbe and all the chassidim — but for him this was an order, and he felt obliged to obey. But no sooner had he left the study with the letter in hand, than my father called him back and said: 'Remember, do not fail your mission!'

" 'God forbid!' replied the man. 'Of course I will fulfill it faithfully.'

"Back at his lodgings, he told his fellow chassidim of his hard luck — he had come all the way here for *Yom-Tov,* and the rebbe was sending him back home. His comrades cheered him up. This was, after all, a mission to be undertaken for the sake of a mitzvah, and surely there must be some profound reason behind it. If anything, they told him, he should rejoice that he was the one fortunate enough to be chosen to undertake this urgent task. In brief, they set the table with whatever refreshments they could afford, were happy themselves and made him happy as well, and he set out cheerfully in an open carriage drawn by two horses, accompanied by his gentile wagon-driver. It was the eve of Hoshana Rabbah, a little over twenty-four hours before the final days of the festival. As soon as they set out they were drenched by a continuous downpour of rain, and the first thing the chassid did on his arrival home was to change his clothes and warm himself over the enormous built-in stove. A short time later his driver came in to tell him that one of their horses had died.

" 'So let it be an atonement for my sins,' said the leaseholder, dismissing the incident as insignificant.

"A little later the gentile came in to say that the second horse had died too.

" 'What can be done?' the leaseholder consoled himself. 'The Almighty will make good my losses.'

"But then the gentile came in a third time — the mill-house was on fire. Something jogged the man's memory.

" 'What on earth has happened to me?' he cried. 'What have I done with the rebbe's letter?'

" 'What letter?' his family wanted to know — and when he went through the pockets of his drenched clothes he found it. Without losing a moment he instructed his coachman to set out on horseback to deliver the letter to Chaikl. He refused at first, being wet and tired from their journey, but the leaseholder offered him payment for his pains, and poured him a glass of vodka to warm him up. Before he set out he was given a covering letter as well, in which the leaseholder solemnly warned Chaikl that he should fulfill the rebbe's request without delay; he himself had already received his just deserts for not having acted promptly enough.

"Chaikl opened the rebbe's letter. Without any delay, he was to send off the miller who worked for him, in time to spend the last days of *Yom-Tov* in Lubavitch. The miller was promptly summoned, but being a simple coarse fellow, he merely answered: 'What is there for me to do over there? What business has the rebbe got with me?'

"Seeing that pleading did not help, Chaikl threatened to dismiss him if he did not oblige — and on Hoshana Rabbah the miller arrived in Lubavitch.

"When he walked in for *yechidus,* my father took hold of him and said: 'Young man! Why have you deserted your wife for these last three years?'

" 'Rebbe,' said the miller in alarm, 'I can't support her.'

" 'Then I will write to your employer and tell him to increase your wages so that there will be enough for the two of you,' said my father.

" 'But rebbe, he protested. 'She is an evil woman!'

" 'No doubt her only *evil* is that she doesn't cook meals that are good enough for you,' said my father. 'But now that you will be able to afford to give her more money for household expenses, you can be sure she will cook better.'

" 'But she is ugly,' complained the miller.

" 'So what *would* suit you — a countess?!' said my

father. 'Come with me to the kitchen, please.'

"Then, when they arrived there, he continued: 'Here is your wife. Go along happily, the two of you, and live in peace together according to the Law of Moses and Israel.'

"And that, for the rest of their lives, is exactly what they did."

Reb Shmuel had concluded his story. "That kind of thing," he said to the chassid who accompanied him in his carriage, "my father was able to do — but not me."

"If I may ask," ventured the chassid, "what answer can I take home to that unfortunate maid who does not know her husband's whereabouts?"

Replied Reb Shmuel: "Write to the army headquarters in St. Petersburg, and ask them to investigate."

An answer eventually arrived from the capital to notify the young woman that her husband was dead. A rabbinical court was set up, and after due deliberation it pronounced her free to remarry.

סדר כי תבוא
SIDRA KI SAVO

◆§ *The Art of Giving (i)*

וְעַתָּה הִנֵּה הֵבֵאתִי
And now, behold I have brought (26:10)

If one brings a gift to a sage, it is as if one made an offering of the First Fruits in the Temple *(Talmud Tractate Kesubos).*

Reb Mordechai of Nadvorna once felt a deep desire to perform the mitzvah of offering the First Fruits of *bikkurim* in the only way possible since the Destruction of the Temple — that is, in the spirit of the above teaching of the Sages. He therefore bought a lamb and had it slaughtered. Its meat he distributed to needy families in honor of *Shabbos,* and gave part of the wool to an upright chassid who was little steeped in the vanities of This World, with the request that he spin it into yarn from which *tzitzis* could be made. He then wrapped up the bundle of long woolen threads, hired a special messenger, and personally sewed the precious little package into a safe pocket in the man's overcoat. The messenger was then dispatched to deliver the gift to Reb Chaim of Zanz.

On his arrival in Zanz, he explained to the tzaddik that Reb Mordechai had sent this gift in fulfillment of the mitzvah of bringing the First Fruits to the Temple.

Reb Chaim was radiant with joy. He not only untied the gift from its hiding place with his own hands, but — as the messenger was later to relate — he even preserved the paper in which the tzaddik of Nadvorna had wrapped it.

◆§ *The Art of Giving (ii)*

It was a principle with Reb Tzadok HaKohen of Lublin not to accept gifts from anyone, not even a *pidyon* from his chassidim. The only payment he would ever agree to accept was the money paid by the father of an infant in the ceremony of the Redemption of the Firstborn, *pidyon haben*, for the Torah explicitly made him entitled to it as a *kohen*, a descendant of the priestly clan. And even this money he used only for the purchase of sacred literature, never for any other purpose.

His daily living expenses were paid out of the income which his *rebbitzin* made in her secondhand clothes shop. When she passed away his chassidim wanted to support him generously, but he flatly refused to accept any help. However, when one of his chassidim asked to be allowed to reopen the shop, he agreed — but only on condition that he would be given no more than his daily needs. These were modest enough, to be sure — one meal every evening, which consisted of tea and a bun, or a little porridge.

Despite all this, one chassid got it into his head that he would like to present the tzaddik with a bottle of pure olive oil and a costly package of fish. Realizing that nothing would ever be accepted as an outright gift, he tried to outwit the tzaddik, and said: "I am bringing First Fruits" — and he quoted the teaching of the Sages, that "If one brings a gift to a sage, it is as if one made an offering of the First Fruits in the Temple." Reb Tzadok was overawed, as always, by the mere quotation of words from the Talmud, so he accepted.

On the following *Shabbos*, however, he opened his discourse to the chassidim at his table by quoting the same statement: "If one brings a gift to a *talmid chacham*" and so on. Then he continued: "But *am* I a sage? One cannot say that one has not studied, because one has. But what if one *has* studied? For in *Proverbs* it is written: 'Why is the price of wisdom in the hand of a fool, seeing he has no sense?' And the Sages teach us that this verse refers to those who study the Torah but do not observe it..."

When the *tish* was over and the chassidim had dispersed disconsolately, one of his elder disciples approached the tzaddik and said: "Rebbe, we were all shocked to hear such words from your mouth!"

"And is that a good enough reason for me to be a liar?" returned Reb Tzadok. "If I received the gift from that man, that implies that I am a Torah scholar worthy of being called a *talmid chacham*. Now I do not hold that to be the case, so I was obliged to state the truth in the hearing of you all."

◆§ *The Art of Giving (iii)*

On his way to *Eretz Yisrael* in 1929, Reb Yosef Yitzchak of Lubavitch passed through Alexandria. The moment his train drew up at the railway station, the door of the carriage burst wide open and a man leaped inside. His arms were loaded with a basket full of exotic fruit, and his eyes were streaming with tears of joy.

"Rebbe!" he exclaimed as soon as he was able to catch his breath. "When I was a little boy in Russia my grandfather took me along with him to visit your grandfather, Reb Shmuel of Lubavitch, so that he should give me his blessing. My grandfather brought the rebbe a basketful of fruit as a kind of *bikkurim*, a gift of First Fruits.

"You, rebbe, were also a little boy at the time, and you were playing in your grandfather's study. So when he received the gift, Reb Shmuel said to my grandfather: 'May it be God's will that your grandson will one day bring First Fruits to my grandson.'

"Many long years have passed since that meeting, and in the meantime my business affairs brought me here to settle in Egypt. But when the other day I heard that you, rebbe, would be passing through the city, that blessing of Reb Shmuel's came to life in my memory, and I thought: 'The time has come!' I bought this fruit and I hurried here to see you.

"I thank God for granting me the privilege of seeing Reb Shmuel's blessing come true!"

◈§ *It's the Thought That Counts*

הַקְּלָלוֹת הָאֵלֶּה
These curses
(28:15)

People who came to see Reb Shlomo of Radomsk in request of a blessing were sometimes shocked to discover that instead of kindly sympathy or advice he showered them with curses. Those whose *kvitl* was received in this manner were always pleased to discover later, however, that their affairs prospered exceedingly — whether by natural means, or by means beyond the predictable.

A learned and wealthy chassid once came from Pietrikov to consult with the rebbe about an important forthcoming transaction. Using plain logic and business sense, the rebbe gave him a piece of advice which produced such a vast profit that the businessman sent one of his friends to inform him of it. This messenger was himself a man of learning, and when he saw how pleased the rebbe was with the news he had brought he ventured to begin: "I hope you will not mind, rebbe, if I take the liberty of asking you one question. It is clear that in this case you gave my friend a piece of advice which can be comprehended by pure reason. Why, then, do you often help people through curses, if you can achieve the same result by blessing them?"

Replied the tzaddik: "My rebbe, Reb Meir of Apta, used to act this way, and would explain himself as follows. 'It is very probable that in the World Above they will punish me for cursing my fellow Jews — but I have no option in this matter, and the Torah absolves those who act under duress.'

"In fact we have a hint of this situation in the words of Moshe Rabbeinu: 'Not a single donkey have I taken from them, nor have I done evil to a single one of them' — for one cannot be helped by a tzaddik except by either of two means: either the tzaddik has to accept the gift of a *pidyon*, or he has to curse the supplicant. And this is what Moshe Rabbeinu is arguing here to the Almighty — since he has neither accepted as much as a donkey from the Children of Israel, nor has he said as much as a harsh word to them, it is impossible for him to help them."

The messenger had not expected to hear such a rationale for the tzaddik's bizarre behavior, and he hastened to pass it on to his fellow chassidim.

In his book *Tiferes Shlomo*, the tzaddik gave a further explanation of the use of harsh words. He opens by asking why the rebukes and curses of *Parshas Ki Savo* are read in the synagogue on the *Shabbos* preceding the last week of the outgoing year, the week during which the penitential prayers of *Selichos* are said. His answer is based on an analogy with the promise in the Book of *Hosea:* וּנְשַׁלְּמָה פָרִים שְׂפָתֵינוּ — "With our lips we will compensate for oxen" — a reference to the replacement of the sacrificial service by prayers. Reb Shlomo cites the assurance of the Sages that "He who studies the passage in the Torah concerning the burnt offerings is considered to have actually sacrificed a burnt offering." Applying it to the above-mentioned rebukes and curses of the *Tochachah* passage, he argues that even if Israel were found punishable by the sufferings described there, the reading of the words alone is no doubt accounted by the Heavenly Court as if they had already undergone them — and with that the tribulations which had been prescribed for the passing year, but which never materialized, are struck off the list.

☙ *Classified Information*

יַכְּכָה ה׳ בְּשִׁגָּעוֹן
God will smite you with insanity *(28:28)*

One weird delusion obsessed the deranged mind of a certain unfortunate fellow. He was somehow convinced that the commander of the local gendarmerie was Eliyahu the Prophet, and that the governor of the city was the Messiah himself. His family were sorely vexed by this, because he never tired of telling all and sundry of his singular discovery. They decided therefore to take him along to Reb Simchah Bunem of Pshischah.

The poor man had barely opened the door of the rebbe's study when he excitedly gave him the news: "The Prophet Eliyahu and the Messiah live in my city!"

"Who are they?" asked the rebbe.

"One is the military commander, and the other is the governor," explained the other.

"And who am I?" asked the rebbe.

"Why, you are the rebbe!" answered the visitor.

"Is it possible, then," asked Reb Simchah Bunem "that I — who am a rebbe — do not know that Eliyahu and the *Mashiach* are in your city?"

"Of course you know it," said the man, "and you know it well — except that you don't want to reveal it to anyone."

"Very well," said the tzaddik. "You too can know it, and nevertheless reveal it to no one — just like I do. Don't breathe a word of it to anyone!"

The man returned to his hometown and never raised the subject again — then at length he recovered his sanity completely.

◆§ *Hardly a Blessing*

הוא יַלְוְךָ
He shall lend to you (28:44)

A certain chassid asked Reb Menachem Mendel of Rimanov to pray that the Almighty should cause him to find favor in the eyes of a certain noble, from whom he wanted to borrow money.

"I cannot pray for that," said the tzaddik, "for it is with reference to the stranger in our midst that the Torah warns us of one of the punishments for our disobedience: 'He shall lend to you.' "

סדר נצבים
SIDRA NITZAVIM

◆§ *Melodies for the Ears of Heaven (i)*

מֵחֹטֵב עֵצֶיךָ עַד שֹׁאֵב מֵימֶיךָ
From the hewers of your wood to the drawers of your water (29:10)

It was the way of the Baal Shem Tov to show a particular fondness for simple, God-fearing folk, and many such people became his warm admirers. For the more intellectually sophisticated among his disciples this affinity was a bitter pill to swallow — nor did it become more palatable even after their rebbe had sent them to associate with such folk in order to learn from their example such desirable traits as unquestioning trust in the Creator, simple faith, and the love of a fellow Jew.

Among those who flocked to be near the tzaddik one *Shabbos* in summer were many such people — innkeepers, farmers, craftsmen, poultrymen, market stallkeepers, and the like. And it was these visitors to whom the Baal Shem Tov showed especial tokens of affection at his Friday night table. With one he shared the wine over which he sanctified the Sabbath; to another he lent his own *Kiddush* goblet; some were offered slices of the sweet *Challah* over which he had pronounced a blessing; and others tasted a morsel of fish from his plate. The inner circle of scholarly disciples who made up the holy brotherhood — the חֶבְרַיָא קַדִּישָׁא — wondered at the conduct of their rebbe.

The custom in the household of the Baal Shem Tov was that the guests who came to Mezhibuzh for *Shabbos* joined him at the Friday night *tish* and again at the twilight Third Meal on the following day, while the midday meal of *Shabbos* was reserved for the inner circle alone. This gathering strangers were not even allowed to watch from a distance. The unlettered folk who had come for that *Shabbos* therefore ate their midday meal at their lodgings, and then found their way back to the *shul* of the Baal Shem Tov, where they engaged in the only kind of divine worship that their meager schooling had given them — pouring out their hearts in singing the praises and entreaties of the Book of *Psalms*.

As the Baal Shem Tov took his place at the head of the long table, he first seated each of his disciples in a particular place, according to his custom, and then revealed to them such secrets from the world of the Torah that their hearts were aglow with spiritual delight. Their rebbe too was living through a moment of rare joy, and they thanked their Maker for having brought them into his radiant orbit.

But the hearts of a few were clouded by a critical thought. Why did their rebbe show such marks of favor to men so simple that they did not understand his teachings?

At once the face of the tzaddik took on a serious appearance. In a tone of restrained ecstasy and with eyes closed, he said: "In a place where penitents stand, the most righteous of men have no place. So our Sages teach us. There are two paths in the service of the Creator — the righteous service of tzaddikim, and the contrite service of *baalei teshuvah.* The service of simple folk belongs to the second level, the loftier level of the penitent — for they are lowly of spirit, regretting the imperfect past, and striving nobly to improve the future."

A haunting melody began imperceptibly from around the table, and those disciples who had harbored doubts as to their rebbe's conduct realized that he had sensed what they had been thinking. The music faded away. The Baal Shem Tov opened his eyes, gazed long and deeply into the faces of his disciples, one by one, and then told them each to rest their right hand on the shoulder of their neighbor. When they had sung quietly together for a further space, he asked them to close their eyes, and not to open them until they were told to do so. He then rested his right hand on the disciple who was seated at his right, and his left hand on the shoulder of the disciple seated at his left — and the circle was closed.

From that moment the sweetest of tender melodies stole into their ears, melodies that bore with them the heartfelt entreaties of honest souls.

"Ribbono shel Olam!" said one manly voice, appealing to the Maker of the Universe in gentle terms of his own, before going on to address Him in words first used by King David: "בְּחָנֵנִי ה׳ — Examine me, O God, and test me; refine ... my heart."

"Zisser fotter, father dear!" another voice prefixed his verse from *Psalms.* "חָנֵּנִי אֱלֹקִים חָנֵּנִי — Be gracious to me, O God, be gracious, for my soul trusts in You; and in the shadow of Your wings will I take refuge until woes are past."

"Father!" came the piteous cry of a storm-tossed life, desperately seeking anchorage in a haven of its own. "גַּם צִפּוֹר מָצְאָה בַיִת — Even the sparrow has found a home, and the swallow a nest for herself ..."

The holy brotherhood of learned chassidim trembled in the face of such innocent supplication. Their eyes were closed, but they shed tears of contriteness, and humbly envied the worship that was the daily portion of these simple singers of *Psalms*.

The Baal Shem Tov lifted his hands from the shoulders of the disciples, and the music vanished from their ears. He told them all to open their eyes, and again the brotherhood sang softly together.

One of that circle who was present on that *Shabbos* was Reb Dov Ber, the Maggid of Mezritch. Years later he told his disciple, Reb Shneur Zalman of Liadi, that at that moment he experienced a rapturous love of the Creator with an intensity that he had never before known. Indeed his whole being was seized by such a paroxysm of desire for *teshuvah* that his very slippers were soaked with perspiration and tears.

The singing had come to an end, and the brotherhood sat in pensive silence. For some time the Baal Shem Tov sat with his eyes closed in a trance of *dveikus*, then he looked again at his chassidim and said: "The music that you heard was the innocent singsong of the simple folk in the synagogue, intoning their verses from the *Psalms* from the bottom of their trusting hearts. Consider now. We mortals are made up of a body, which is not a thing of truth, and a soul, which is truth — and even the soul is only part of the Whole. Being thus creatures of imperfect truth, we are called *sfas emes*, 'the lip of truth,' a mere hint of truth. Nevertheless, even we are able to recognize and sense the truth, and be overwhelmed by it. How much more so must the Almighty — the ultimate Truth — recognize the truth in the psalm-singing of these simple men."

For a long time thereafter — so the Maggid of Mezritch told Reb Shneur Zalman of Liadi — he had been distressed by the fact that he had previously entertained doubts as to his rebbe's closeness with simple people. Though he had undertaken various penances to clear himself of this past guilt, he could find no rest — until one night he saw a vision which brought peace to his soul. In one of the palaces of the Garden of Eden, a group of little children were clustered around a long table, learning *Chumash*. At the head of the table sat their schoolmaster — Moshe Rabbeinu. They were studying the passage which speaks of the seeming disbelief of the Patriarch Avraham when he was given the divine promise that in their old age he and his wife would beget a child. One of the little students read aloud the verse: "And Avraham fell on his face, and laughed and said in his heart, 'Shall a child be born to him that is a hundred years old?" Moshe Rabbeinu thereupon explained them that all the Midrashic commentaries woven around this sentence were of course true — but at the same time, no verse in the Torah utterly leaves its plain meaning. As to the question of how it was possible to conceive of doubt in the mind of the Patriarch Avraham, the answer was that this doubt stemmed from the fact that he had a body — and even a holy body is flesh.

When the Maggid heard that by the mere fact of having a body a person can experience doubts that arise of themselves, he was no longer troubled by the recollection of his misgivings about his rebbe's conduct. At long last, his soul found response.

☙ *Melodies for the Ears of Heaven (ii)*

Reb Moshe Zvi of Savran was once on visit to Berditchev where he stayed at the house of his *mechutan*, a chassid by the name of Reb Moshe Yosef Chodorov. The craftsmen of the town at the time were busy deciding on the regulations which would govern their newly-found *Chevrah Tehillim*, a comradely fraternity whose chief aim was to bring together groups of artisans to chant the *Psalms* in unison. Once agreed upon, their regulations were entered for posterity in the *pinkas*, the community register. Most of the members of the fraternity were unlearned, though honest and God-fearing. And in case in any future communal situation they should require the services of someone more learned than themselves, they asked two of the respected young married scholars of the town to add their names to the list of members — and these two *talmidei chachamim* obliged.

When the founders of the *Chevrah* heard that Reb Moshe Zvi of Savran was in town they decided to send him the *pinkas,* with the request that he append his signature to their newly-inscribed regulations. And if he wanted to add or change anything they had written, they indicated that their agreement was assured in advance.

One of their two young scholarly members was chosen to be honored with this mission. When he arrived at the lodgings of the visiting rebbe he found that there was already an erudite caller sitting importantly there — a local heavyweight pedant, a veritable *lamdan.*

When this pillar of learning heard that the new arrival had joined the commoners as a member of their *Chevrah,* he turned to him in amazement and exclaimed: "What on earth are *you* doing in a *Chevrah Tehillim?* Leave *Psalms* for the artisans and the simple folk, who can do no better. You should be reserving your talents for the Talmud and the legal codes, not spending your time on *Tehillim!*"

"And since when should a Torah scholar not read the *Psalms?*" challenged the young man. "You recall what the Midrash says on the verse from *Psalms:* יִהְיוּ לְרָצוֹן אִמְרֵי פִי — 'May the words of my mouth find acceptance.' On this verse the Midrash elaborates that King David prayed that whoever read the *Psalms* should be accounted in the sight of heaven as of equal worth with him who engaged in the study of the laws of purity and impurity."

Replied the *lamdan:* "And I once heard from the mouth of a prominent scholar — *he* was no chassid, for sure! — that this Midrash says that King David made a request; it does not say that his request was *accepted.* In support of this view allow me to cite another case in which we see that King David made a request that was not granted. For we find in Tractate *Bava Basra* that 'There were seven people whose bodies were not overcome in the grave by worms.' And the Talmud goes on to say: 'There are those who say that the same applies to King David, as it is written, אַף בְּשָׂרִי יִשְׁכֹּן לָבֶטַח — *My flesh too dwells secure.* Another view holds that David prayed for this.' From this we see that this was only a *request* of his — but that it was not granted."

Reb Moshe Zvi of Savran had been listening quietly to this dialogue, but these last words of the *lamdan* were more than he could bear in silence.

"Who is it you say whose prayer was not granted?" he exclaimed excitedly. "Are you talking about David, King of Israel?! Woe is me, that I should hear such words! And besides, your learned colleague has misunderstood the meaning of that passage from the Talmud. The Sages had listed the seven people who were granted this privilege *without having requested it,* while 'David — prayed for this.' Because it came to him as the result of his request, his name does not appear among the seven. This passage, therefore, proves the very opposite of your thesis. The prayer of David *was* accepted."

With that he took the *pinkas* in hand, opened up at the page on which the artless worshipers had entered the statutes of their *Chevrah Tehillim,* and signed there with gusto.

◆§ *What Angels are Made Of*

Rebbitzin Mirl -- the wife of Reb Yitzchak Meir of Mezhibuzh, and the daughter-in-law of Reb Avraham Yehoshua Heschel of Apta — was a saintly soul. Once she was in synagogue, and hearing an unaccustomed bustle, she opened the door that led from the women's section to where the men were assembled, to ask what had happened. She was told that Reb Yaakov the wagon-driver had died.

"What?!" she cried aghast. "Is Reb Yaakov dead? Do you know who Reb Yaakov was?"

And when she had calmed down from her sudden anguish, she said: "It once happened that on a freezing winter's day I was left without a single splinter of firewood in the house. I went off to Reb Yaakov. He immediately harnessed his horse, drove off to the forest, and came back with a wagon stacked high with firewood. I stoked up the stove in the *beis midrash,* and dozens of people were then able to sit there and study Torah.

"On another occasion I ran out of water — not a single drop left. Again I went off to Reb Yaakov, and he brought me a huge barrel full of water, so that I was able to cook in honor of *Shabbos*.

"Master of the Universe!" she pleaded in conclusion. "May it be Your will that from every piece of wood that he brought, an angel be born — to speak up now on his behalf. And may all those drops of water be transformed into so many merits — to turn out and greet him as he arrives in the World Above!"

When the tzaddik came to *shul* a little later, the chassidim told him what his *rebbitzin* had said.

"I marvel at it!" he said. "Where did the woman get that divinely-inspired gift of *ruach hakodesh?* For what she said down here is exactly what they said in the World Above."

Unsung Heroes (i)

When at the circumcision of his son Reb Menachem Mendel of Lubavitch gave him the name Shmuel, no one present knew after whom the infant had been named.

At the festive meal which followed the ceremony the infant's grown brother, Reb Yehudah Leib — later rebbe in Kopust — asked his father: "After whom is the baby named? I don't know of anyone of that name in our family. Perhaps," he ventured in a whisper, "he is named after the Prophet Samuel?"

Replied his father, the Tzemach Tzedek: "The baby is named after a certain water-carrier in Polotzk who was called Shmuel."

Unsung Heroes (ii)

A chassid by the name of Reb Monye Monissohn, who was a wealthy dealer in gems, was once sitting in the presence of Reb Shalom Ber of Lubavitch. In the course of their conversation the rebbe spoke highly of certain unlettered folk.

"Rebbe," asked Reb Monye, "why do you make such a fuss of them?"

"Why, they have many noble qualities," said the rebbe.

"Well, I can't see them," said the chassid.

The tzaddik was silent. Later on, he asked Reb Monye whether he had brought his package of diamonds with him. The dealer said that he had, but he would prefer to show them to the rebbe a little later, not in the sunlight, so that they could be seen to their best advantage.

He later opened the package in a nearby room, arranged the gems carefully on a table, and pointed out a particular stone to the rebbe, saying: "This one is something really special!"

"I can't see anything in it," said the rebbe.

"Ah, but you have to be a connoisseur to know how to look at diamonds!" said the chassid.

"Every Jew too is something really special," said the rebbe, "but you have to be a connoisseur to know how to look at him."

◆§ *The Torah is For Mortals (i)*

לא בַשָּׁמַיִם הִיא
It is not in heaven (30:12)

Reb Yaakov Yitzchak of Lublin — known as the Chozeh, or Seer, on account of his clairvoyancy — was visited one day by a butcher. He wanted the tzaddik to advise him as to whether he should slaughter his cattle before the forthcoming festival, or sell them; he was afraid that after they were slaughtered and their vital organs examined they might be found to be *trefah*, in which case their carcasses would have to be discarded.

The tzaddik asked the butcher to write down a description of each of his animals, and then went through the list with him, telling him that this one was kosher, the next one *trefah*, and so on. About one of them he said: "I do not know — for when it is opened it will be found to involve a legal query. Whether the *rav* who is consulted will determine that this *she'elah* makes the animal kosher or *trefah*, I do not know. For it is on decisions on *halachah* that it is written that the Torah is 'not in heaven.' "

◆§ *The Torah is For Mortals (ii)*

In the summer of 1804, while Reb Nachman of Breslov was on a journey, his infant daughter Feige passed away. When he came home his family hid the news, which was possible because she had been staying in the home of a wetnurse in the nearby town of Ladizin.

Coming straight from his carriage into his house, the tzaddik found a large number of people there waiting for him, and began at once to deliver a mystical discourse which touched on the subject of mourning. His hearers sensed that he was aware through *ruach hakodesh* of what had happened, and those who had accompanied him in his carriage on the way home had received the same impression. After the discourse he asked after his daughter from his family, but they still kept the news from him. And the tzaddik observed none of the rites of mourning.

In that year, Rosh HaShanah fell on Thursday and Friday. At sunset on the following day, the chassidim were seated at the *Seudah Shlishis* meal in a room near his study, uncertain whether he would join them and deliver a discourse, for only on rare occasions would he sit with them at the Third Meal of *Shabbos.*

Suddenly Reb Nachman opened the door as if in alarm, to the surprise of all the assembled chassidim. He called for his elder daughter, and when she had joined him in his study he raised the subject of the passing of the little girl. When she began to speak evasively, he assured her: 'But I already know the truth myself.'

And then she was obliged to state the unfortunate fact explicitly. Reb Nachman did not join his chassidim for the Third Meal. Instead, after the Day of Rest had passed, he observed the rites of mourning for one hour, as the Law prescribes in the case of evil tidings which reach a person after thirty days have elapsed from the decease of a near relative.

No matter what a person may perceive through supernatural means, explained Reb Nachman, he may not observe the rites laid down by the Law until he is informed of the facts in the conventional way.

◆§ *Pastures that are Even Greener*

כִּי קָרוֹב אֵלֶיךָ הַדָּבָר מְאֹד
For this thing is very near to you (30:14)

Reb Chanoch Henich of Alexander used to repeat in the name of his rebbe, Reb Simchah Bunem of Pshischah, that anyone planning his first visit to a tzaddik should first know the story of an honest man from

Cracow by the name of Reb Aizik Reb Yekeles. This Reb Aizik lived in the days before surnames were invented; the appendage to his name tells us that he was the son of a certain Reb Yekele, in order to distinguish him from other people called Aizik who no doubt lived in the same courtyard. Until recent years there stood in Cracow the very synagogue that he built, and it was called — the *shul* of Reb Aizik Reb Yekeles.

This Reb Aizik dreamed several times that he should make the long journey to Prague, and there, near the royal palace, under the bridge, he should dig in the ground, where an unbelievable treasure was waiting for him. He set out for Prague, and headed straight for the bridge which stands near the palace. But he discovered to his consternation that the area was heavily guarded night and day by half a mounted regiment of burly hussars. How could a little Jew from Cracow sneak in under the gaping muzzles of their fearful muskets and blunderbusses, and start digging under the bridge for hidden treasure? It was a disappointing climax to such a fatiguing journey, and he would now have to make that whole exhausting journey home again — emptyhanded. All day long he walked up and down near that bridge feeling very sorry for himself, and when night fell he returned to his lodgings, where he tossed and turned until daybreak. His odd behavior day after day attracted the attention of the brass-helmeted officer of the guards, who called him across and demanded that he explain himself.

Reb Aizik told him the whole story of the dreams, and the bridge, and the treasure — and the brass hat exploded in laughter.

"Do you mean to tell me that on the strength of a dream you came all this long way? Who on earth believes the kind of nonsense they see in dreams? Why, I myself dreamed the other day that I should travel all the way to Cracow, where I would find some Jew called Reb Aizik Reb Yekeles; I was to dig under the fireplace of his house, and find an unbelievable treasure. Now I ask you: do you think it would occur to me to take notice of the kind of stuff you hear in dreams and to set out and make the long journey to Cracow?!"

At long last Reb Aizik understood why he had to come all the way to Prague. He went straight back to his own hometown, headed straight for his own house, dug away furiously under his own fireplace — and found an unbelievable treasure of hundreds of shiny gold coins. It was from this very fortune that he built the *shul* in Cracow that bore his name.

"And so it is," Reb Chanoch Henich would say in the name of Reb Simchah Bunem, "with anyone setting out to visit a rebbe. It should be clear in his mind that the purpose of his visit is to find out from the tzaddik that the treasure is to be sought not with the tzaddik but in his own house. And when he comes home, his task is to dig and seek the treasure in his own soul — *'for this thing is very near to you,* in your mouth, and in your heart, that you may do it.' "

◂§ *The Best Attorney*

Reb Shalom Ber of Lubavitch once entered the study of his father, Reb Shmuel of Lubavitch, to ask his advice on how to achieve a certain goal which he had set himself in the course of the divine service of self-refinement.

"Through meditating with profound concentration," was the answer.

"But the concept to be grasped is an exceedingly difficult one," said the son.

"If a subject really matters to a person," replied the rebbe, "then he comprehends it well. You will have observed the intellectual giants of each generation at work throughout the Talmudic and Rabbinic literature. In the course of solving questions of jurisprudence, they often construct hypotheses as to the kinds of involved arguments that could theoretically be put forward in court by the untutored women or ignoramuses who might be involved in the various kinds of legal disputes. Now the Torah is a Torah of truth. How, then, can one imagine such ingenious arguments coming from the mouths of simple folk who are unschooled and unlettered?

"The answer is simple. When a cause really matters to

people, then even the weakest intellects produce forceful lines of argument."

☙ How To Love Your Competitor

בְּפִיךָ וּבִלְבָבְךָ לַעֲשֹׂתוֹ
In your mouth, and in your heart, that you may do it (30:14)

A shopkeeper once complained to Reb Moshe of Kobrin that his neighbor, who sold exactly the same goods as he did, always did a lively trade, while he himself could not eke the merest livelihood out of his shop.

"I can promise a generous income to you, too," said the tzaddik, "but only on condition that when you see your neighbor making a handsome profit, you thank the Almighty for his success. Something like this: Thanked be the Lord, Who gives such a rich livelihood to a fellow Jew.' It may be difficult to say this wholeheartedly at the beginning, but as you train your mouth to say the words, then with time they will find their way into your heart as well — until you will in fact be saying them with all your heart. For, in the verse בְּפִיךָ וּבִלְבָבְךָ לַעֲשֹׂתוֹ — 'in your mouth, and in your heart, that you may do it' — we first find the words 'in your mouth,' and only later is it written 'in your heart.' "

☙ Ornament of God

הַעִדֹתִי... אֶת הַשָּׁמַיִם וְאֶת הָאָרֶץ
I call heaven and earth to witness (30:19)

The Russo-Japanese War broke out in 1905, the last year in the lifetime of Reb Yehudah Aryeh Leib of Ger, the author of *Sfas Emes*. Thousands of his young chassidim were conscripted and dispatched to the battlefields of the Far East.

In giving them his blessing and advice before they set out, he would begin by quoting a verse in the Torah which in ancient times was part of the announcement made to armies about to march forth: מִי הָאִישׁ הַיָּרֵא וְרַךְ הַלֵּבָב יֵלֵךְ וְיָשֹׁב לְבֵיתוֹ — "Who is the man who is afraid and faint of heart? Let him go and return to his house." He gave the verse a non-literal interpretation, however, as follows: "Who is the man who fears heaven? Let him return in repentance; and then," the rebbe would continue, "he will certainly return home from the battlefield."

So anxious was he for the welfare of these young soldiers that throughout the time they were at the Eastern front he did not once go to sleep in bed. He chose instead to sleep on the floor, lying on a single garment, which by morning was drenched with the tears he had shed over the anguish of his brethren.

And they in turn warmly reflected his faithful attachment to them. From out of the trenches they would write to him — hasty dissertations on fondly-remembered Talmudic themes, and touching descriptions of their daily lot.

One gifted scholar who hailed from Ostrov utilized every hour of respite in his bunker and wrote a long paper that discussed some learned comment of the medieval luminary Rabbeinu Yonah. After it had reached Ger, his rebbe wrote him a loving reply which opened with the words of a verse in the Torah: הַעִדֹתִי בָכֶם הַיּוֹם אֶת הַשָּׁמַיִם וְאֶת הָאָרֶץ. In the plain meaning of its context, this verse is spoken by Moshe Rabbeinu, and may be translated as follows: "I call heaven and earth to witness this day against you." In his letter, however, the tzaddik gave this verse too a non-literal interpretation. The verb הַעִדֹתִי is in fact related to the word עֵד, meaning "witness," but for the moment the tzaddik regarded it as if stemming from the noun עֲדִי, meaning "ornament."

Putting the words into the mouth of the Almighty, so to speak, he wrote the following: הַעִדֹתִי בָכֶם הַיּוֹם אֶת הַשָּׁמַיִם וְאֶת הָאָרֶץ — "With young Jews like yourself have I ornamented heaven and earth."

סדר וילך
Sidra Vayeilech

A Mere Child

וּבְנֵיהֶם... יִשְׁמְעוּ וְלָמְדוּ
And their children...shall hear and learn
(31:13)

And their children, who have not known, shall hear and learn: This refers to small children — not infants, but children of tender years *(Ramban).*

וילך

When Reb Menachem Mendel of Lubavitch was a child of four or five, he was often to be found in the study of his grandfather, Reb Shneur Zalman of Liadi. In fact it was known among the chassidim that when the tzaddik was praying, the toddler would take the toy *tefillin* which he had carved out for himself from two potatoes, tie them with string to his head and arm, sway his little body as if in prayer, and sing happily away. When his grandfather removed his *tefillin* at the conclusion of his morning prayers, he would mimic that action too. That done, he would run up and down and around the room as little boys do. Once, when the rebbe's door was left ajar, some chassidim peeked through the chink and saw that as the child was running around and dragging his potatoes along the floor, one of the strings was caught around the leg of the table. The rebbe bent down and disentangled it, and the boy played on as before.

On a certain occasion Reb Shneur Zalman delivered a chassidic discourse on the statement in the Ethics of the Fathers that "the world stands on three things." It was so abstruse that the chassidim did not fully grasp it, and asked the rebbe to repeat it. He promised to do so three days later after morning prayers, on condition that no more than thirty people would be present.

One of the fortunate ones was the distinguished chassid Reb Yitzchak Aizik of Homil, who later recounted: "When the rebbe began to repeat the *maamar*, I saw that his little grandson had made a path for himself right in the thick of the chassidim who were assembled there. I imagined that at any moment the strings that were attached to his toy *tefillin* would be caught up somewhere, and I was afraid that he might distract us during the repetition of the discourse. I was about to say something to him, and to ask him not to disturb me, but before I managed to open my mouth I was amazed to hear the rebbe saying to me: 'Let him be. He wants to listen; he is listening; you will know that he is listening.' "

These words spread quickly among all the chassidim, though no one could understand their import, and in the course of time were forgotten.

Decades elapsed. In 1813 the tzaddik passed away, and Reb Dov Ber, the son who succeeded him, passed away in 1827. After a great deal of persuasion by their chassidim, the leadership of the movement was assumed by the son-in-law of Reb Dov Ber, Reb Menachem Mendel, who was this same grandson of Reb Shneur Zalman of Liadi. And the very first discourse which he delivered as rebbe was a repetition of the discourse which had been delivered over thirty years earlier by his grandfather, and which was based on the words: "On three things the world stands." One of those present on this occasion was Reb Yitzchak Aizik of Homil, and as soon as the newly-inducted rebbe began to speak, the elder chassid recalled that occasion on which Reb Shneur Zalman had repeated this very discourse. He recalled too a little boy racing his way through the assembled chassidim ... But most clearly of all he recalled the words which in retrospect rang out clearly like a prophecy: "Let him be ... You will know that he is listening."

Reb Yitzchak Aizik's soul lit up.

"Now that's the kind of trick that only a rebbe can do!" he thought to himself.

This thought was cut short. The rebbe interrupted his lecture, turned for a moment to Reb Yitzchak Aizik, and said: "Do not suspect me of having what I have not. How can I help it if my grandfather orders me to repeat this discourse?"

When he had completed his presentation, the chassidim present were so overjoyed at the fact that they now had this personage as their rebbe that a happy song burst spontaneously from their lips, and they accompanied him joyfully to his home.

Only one riddle remained — the two cryptic sentences which the newly-appointed rebbe had directed in the middle of his *maamar* to Reb Yitzchak Aizik. So when the chassidim returned to their *beis midrash* they crowded around him inquisitively, and pressed him to let them into his secret. And it was then that the old man shared with them his treasured memory of the little boy — a mere child — who was listening to an abstruse philosophical dissertation while playing with his potatoes and his strings.

 ◆§ Thy Day Draws Nigh (i)

הֵן קָרְבוּ יָמֶיךָ
Your days are approaching (31:14)

In Berditchev there lived a man who was reputed to be a tzaddik, and who was known by his birthplace as "the *rav* of Merchov. His differences with Reb Levi Yitzchak of Berditchev were superficial; beneath them lay a warm friendship. When Reb Levi Yitzchak passed away the *rav* of Merchov was one of the many who came to his funeral, and as the bier was carried out of his home he followed it, then approached it and leaned over to whisper, as if to be heard by the deceased: שִׁבְעָה שָׁבֻעֹת תִּסְפָּר לָךְ – "Seven weeks shall you count."

And seven weeks from that day, the *rav* of Merchov passed away.

◆§ Thy Day Draws Nigh (ii)

Reb Menachem Mendel of Lubavitch used to give his grandchildren five kopeks every day as pocket money.

One Sunday in 1866 they came along on their usual visit, and he said: "Today I am going to give you thirty kopeks, for the whole week in advance. But if anyone of you wants to, he can come along every day instead."

All the grandchildren took their week's allocation in advance, except for Zalman Aharon and Shalom Ber, the sons of Reb Shmuel of Lubavitch. They decided to continue calling every day. On one of the days of that week the older brother came later than usual, and when he met his brother, Shalom Ber told him that he had already been to see their grandfather.

"Let us go again," said Zalman Aharon.

They arrived at their grandfather's house only to find it crowded with somber chassidim. The rebbe had just passed away.

❀ ❀ ❀

When later that day Zalman Aharon told his father, Reb Shmuel, that he had come too late to his grandfather's house, the father said with emotion: "What have you done, my son? Why, he gave your brother everything!"

Some sixteen years later, when after their father's passing in 1882 Reb Zalman Aharon absolutely refused to accept the leadership, and Reb Shalom Ber became rebbe in Lubavitch, the older brother once told a small group of elder chassidim that one of the reasons for his refusal was what he had then heard from his father — that his grandfather Reb Menachem Mendel "had given his brother everything."

◆§ *Thy Day Draws Nigh (iii)*

Reb Meir of Premishlan was clearly overjoyed that Reb Chaim of Zanz was visiting him, and showed him every mark of respect.

After a lively and learned debate Reb Meir said to his guest: "You, rabbi, are a member of a rabbinical court of repute. Tell me. Should Meir live in modest lodgings such as these? Would it not be proper that he dwell in a grander residence?"

"Of course it would be fitting for you to live in more beautiful and spacious lodgings," said the guest.

"If that is your opinion," said Reb Meir, "Then I will take your advice."

Reb Chaim suddenly realized that there had been some unsuspected intention lurking behind these simple words of his host. He now sought to correct what had been said: "What I meant was — more beautiful lodgings in This World!"

"It is too late," said Reb Meir. "I only wanted your agreement; and if you have already given it, then that is no doubt what will be."

And within a few weeks the tzaddik of Premishlan had departed to another abode.

◆§ *Thy Day Draws Nigh (iv)*

During the night of Yom Kippur, the Day of Atonement, Reb Yitzchak Meir of Ger would always study the Mishnah of Tractate *Yoma* in the hearing of an inner circle of elder chassidm. In the last year of his life tears appeared in his eyes in the midst of his study, and the expression on his face was completely transformed.

The chassidim were alarmed, and one of them, who was very close to the tzaddik, waited till all the others left, and then asked him why he was so morose.

"I suspect that I will not live out this year, God forbid," answered the tzaddik.

"Rebbe," asked the chassid, "why should you say such a thing?"

"Every year," explained the tzaddik, "on the eve of the Day of Atonement, immediately after the *Shemoneh Esreh* prayer, two guests call on me — the Prophet Eliyahu and another old man wearing a cloak. And they always speak to me with smiling faces. But when I welcomed them on their arrival tonight, they returned my greeting with faces clouded by sorrow. May God have mercy on us all!"

❦ ❦ ❦

On the fifteenth day of Shvat in the same year the tzaddik was in Warsaw, where he called on his old friend, Reb Yeshayahu of Prague. Their meeting was a happy one, and after a time Reb Yitzchak Meir told his host that he wanted to speak to him in private. For a long time they remained alone. After the distinguished guest later took his leave affectionately, it was clear to all who saw Reb Yeshayahu that his mind had been thrown into turmoil. He did not even explain his sudden metamorphosis to his immediate family; he said only that the tzaddik of Ger had insisted that he divulge his words to no man.

When a few weeks later word reached him of the passing of the tzaddik, he wept bitterly and said: "Now I can reveal the secret which the rebbe of Ger told me. He said that he had come to me in order to be farewelled from This World, for he would be leaving it within a few weeks. When I asked him what made him think so, he said that the Prophet Eliyahu had visited him that day, and had told him the exact *day* of his passing — the *day*, the month, and the hour."

❦ ❦ ❦

When during the same week these tidings reached Reb Shlomo of Radomsk, he broke out in tears, took hold of his beard, and said: "Look, my beard is already white."

Then he added: "I have it on the authority of my holy teachers that when the tzaddik of my generation passes away, I too will be called to heaven, and I will be given the honor of leading the congregation there in Friday evening's prayers of welcome to the *Shabbos* Queen" — for during his life in This World, Reb Shlomo had often led his own congregation in prayer with his mellow and melodious voice.

And so it was. That same week, on Thursday night, while he was sitting at his table engrossed in the sacred mysteries of the *Zohar*, his soul flew aloft and found its rightful place in the congregation of the righteous — in time for Friday evening's prayers of loving welcome to the *Shabbos* Queen.

☙ *Thy Day Draws Nigh (v)*

One of the chassidim of Reb Yitzchak Aizik of Zhidachov dearly wanted to make the journey to *Eretz Yisrael,* and went to consult his rebbe.

"Wait," said the tzaddik, "and make the journey with me."

Assuming that his rebbe intended to set out shortly for the Holy Land, the faithful chassid waited patiently. But not for long — for soon after, the tzaddik of Zhidachov passed away.

When the news reached the chassid, he said to his townsmen: "It seems that the hour has come for me to make my preparations for the great journey, for my rebbe told me that I would set out together with him."

He immersed himself tranquilly in the purifying waters of the *mikveh,* called for the wardens of the *Chevrah Kaddisha* burial society, pronounced the solemn confession of *Vidui,* and wrote out a will for his children.

And within a few days the whole community of Zhidachov learned that the faithful chassid had indeed set out on his last journey — together with his rebbe.

☙ *Thy Day Draws Nigh (vi)*

Reb Mordechai Dov of Hornisteipl was the grandson of Reb Yaakov Yisrael of Chercass, and the

וילך

great-grandson of Reb Mordechai, the Maggid of Chernobyl. The young man once set out to visit Chercass at the invitation of his grandfather, who had earlier asked him to begin leading a community of chassidim as their rebbe during his own lifetime.

When a day or two had passed since his warm welcome, Reb Mordechai Dov decided it was time to ask his grandfather for the purpose of his invitation.

"Come along with me to Bobbe's room," said the tzaddik.

And when the young man had greeted his grandmother, the tzaddik said: "I have a disagreement with your Bobbe, and so we agreed to abide by whatever you decide on the matter. Now here is the subject of the argument. Bobbe says that she should leave This World before me, because if she is left a widow and the chassidim will no longer come to our house, she will not be able to accustom herself to the loneliness. I claim that I should pass away first, because being left half a man, I will not find life pleasant.

"Now, young man," he concluded, "give us your ruling. We rely on your judgment."

Said Reb Mordechai Dov: "In fact Bobbe is right. Life for her as a widow would be harder to bear. But you, Zeide, hold otherwise, and I would certainly not want to contradict you. I would therefore say that when the time comes, the passing of you both should be in the same year."

And so it was. The *rebbitzin* — who was the daughter of Reb Menachem Mendel of Lubavitch — passed away in the month of Sivan 1876, while her husband, the tzaddik of Chercass, followed her in Elul, three months later.

◆§ *Brevity is the Soul of Wit*

עַד תֻּמָּם *Until their completion (31:30)*

Reb Simchah Bunem of Pshischah once entered the study of his rebbe, Reb Yaakov Yitzchak, who is better known as the Yid HaKadosh of Pshischah.

"Quote me some verse from the Torah," said the rebbe, "and I will give you an interpretation of it."

The *pasuk* that happened to come to mind was the last verse of the weekly Portion of *VaYeilech:* וַיְדַבֵּר מֹשֶׁה

ha'azinu בְּאָזְנֵי כָּל קְהַל יִשְׂרָאֵל אֶת דִּבְרֵי הַשִּׁירָה הַזֹּאת עַד תֻּמָּם – "And Moshe spoke in the ears of all the congregation of Israel the words of this poem, until their completion."

The chassid having quoted his verse, the rebbe now gave his interpretation — which he did by simply echoing its last two words: עַד תֻּמָּם ("until their completion").

Reb Simchah Bunem was overjoyed at this "interpretation."

But also present was another disciple, Reb Chanoch Henich of Alexander, who turned to his colleague and asked him: "What is the meaning of this joy? And what did the rebbe explain here?"

"Here, you're a clever fellow," replied Reb Simchah Bunem. "You work out the rebbe's meaning yourself!"

"It would seem," suggested Reb Chanoch Henich, "that this was the rebbe's meaning. If the word תֻּמָּם ('their completion') was intended to refer to the poem, then it should have appeared in the singular form — תֻּמָּהּ ('*its* completion'). Why, then, does the plural form appear? And we must answer that Moshe Rabbeinu no doubt went about among the Children of Israel, repeating over and over again the words of this poem, which sings of the historic covenant — past and future — of the Creator with His People. He repeated its words to his brethren until it entered their very hearts: indeed, עַד תֻּמָּם – 'until *their* completion,' until *they* were perfected."

"That's it!" exclaimed Reb Simchah Bunem.

סדר האזינו
sidra ha'azinu

◆§ *Fair Play*

אַסְתִּירָה פָנַי מֵהֶם
I will hide My face them them (32:20)

Reb Yechiel of Alexander and the son who was to succeed hm, Reb Yisrael Yitzchak, were once in an isolated village where they had gone for a rest cure. In the middle of the night the father suddenly took ill and was in danger of his life. There was no doctor for many miles around. The tzaddik thought his end was near, and wept, whereupon his son embraced him and *swore* that no harm would befall him.

Then he left his father for a few moments, walked out into the thick of the forest, and cried out: "Master of the Universe! Is this what you do to the rebbe of Alexander? In the forest, with no one at hand?! Do our Sages not teach us that 'The Almighty cares for the honor of tzaddikim'?"

He quickly returned to his father and found him feeling better.

"How were you able to swear?" asked Reb Yechiel.

"I relied on the words of Reb Yisrael of Ruzhin," answered his son. "In the Book of *Psalms*, King David pleads: עַד אָנָה תַּסְתִּיר אֶת פָּנֶיךָ מִמֶּנִּי, עַד אָנָה אָשִׁית עֵצוֹת בְּנַפְשִׁי — 'How long will You hide Your face from me? How long shall I take counsel in my soul?' These words the tzaddik of Ruzhin reads as a question and an answer, as follows: 'How long will You hide Your face from me?' And the supplicant answers his own question: 'So long as I can take counsel in my soul.' That is to say, when the supplicant can do nothing whatever to remedy his situation, and help can come from God alone, — in such a time the Almighty *cannot* hid His face.

"And here, out in the middle of the forest, when there was no way in which we could possibly take counsel and help ourselves, and no one could help us but God alone, I was perfectly certain that no harm would befall us. So that is why I swore as I did."

סדר וזאת הברכה
Sidra V'zos Habracha

◆§ *Attuned*

וְזֹאת לִיהוּדָה
And this was for Yehudah (33:7)

Reb Avraham of Sochatchov was once out on a journey on the first day of the month of Nissan with his nephew, Reb Yitzchak Menachem of Shidlitz. Strangely, his learned conversation throughout the entire day was related exclusively to one subject — the many Talmudic references to Yehudah, the son of the Patriarch Yaakov. His traveling companion found this something of a riddle.

Towards the end of the day the rebbe suddenly realized that the first of Nissan was a date mentioned in the Torah in connection with the dedication of the *Mishkan* in the days of Moshe Rabbeinu. This was the day on which the representative of the tribe of Yehudah had brought his offering as part of the dedication of the Sanctuary in the wilderness.

The riddle was solved — for both of them.

"So *that* is why I have been speaking about Yehudah all day!" exclaimed the rebbe.

◈§ *Mortal Remains (i)*

לֹא כָהֲתָה עֵינוֹ
His eye was not dim (34:7)

His eye was not dim: Even when he died. The body of Moshe Rabbeinu did not crumble, nor did his countenance alter *(Rashi).*

In 1943 word reached the Jewish community of Chechanov that the Nazis were about to desecrate the burial place of Reb Avraham of Chechanov, who had passed away in 1875, by plowing over the site and erasing it from mortal memory.

The wardens of the *Chevrah Kaddisha* burial society immediately met in secret with the elders of the community. They decided together that they would foil this plot, even if it cost them their lives. Late one night they went out in stealth to the old cemetery on the outskirts of the town, and opened the grave of the tzaddik in order to remove his last remains to another resting place. But as they moved aside the tablet that lay above the body they were dumbstruck. For though some sixty-eight years had passed since the burial, the holy body of the tzaddik lay intact and whole, as though he had been buried a moment before. Even the shrouds had not decomposed.

With brave hands trembling in awe they lifted the body from its resting place, enveloped it in a *tallis,* and bore it reverently to the grave which they had prepared in the new cemetery, between the two tall trees which were to serve as a sign.

The Nazi invaders soon heard of this exploit. They hunted and tracked down the townsmen, and dragged them out of the cave in which they had hidden for almost two weeks. Finally, after dreadful torture, their racked bodies *(May God avenge their blood!)* were hanged.

◆§ *Mortal Remains (ii)*

While troops of Nazis were on their frenzied rampage through the towns and villages of Poland and Galicia, they arrived at Lyzhansk. They first razed the town to the ground, and then turned to the old Jewish cemetery, where they found a number of aged Jews praying softly at the graveside of Reb Elimelech. This was the same tzaddik who until his passing in 1787 had been a source of inspiration to such luminaries as the Chozeh of Lublin, the Ohev Yisrael of Apta, the Maggid of Koznitz, and Reb Menachem Mendel of Rimanov.

The troops demolished the modest edifice which had been built over the gravesite, tore open the grave itself, but were shocked by what they saw — a countenance, as in life, which bespoke quiet joy and dignity.

Leaving the grave open they fled in sheer fright, and the aged Jews were left to resume their whispered prayers at the graveside of Reb Elimelech.

Glossary

All terms are Hebrew unless otherwise indicated.

AGUNAH: woman unable to remarry because she has neither a divorce nor evidence of her missing husband's death

AHAVAS YISRAEL: the love of a fellow Jew

AMORA (pl., *amoraim;* Aram.): authority quoted in the *Gemara*

APIKORES (pl., *apikorsim*): freethinker

ARENDA (Pol./Yid.): lease on inn or other source of livelihood commonly held by East European Jews; the leaseholder was called the *arendar*

ATZILUS: one of the supernal levels of Creation described in the Kabbalah

AV BEIS DIN: chairman of a rabbinical court

AVODAH: the service of God, whether in sacrifice, prayer, or self-refinement

BAAL TESHUVAH (pl., *baalei teshuvah):* a penitent

BAR-MITZVAH: religious coming of age on thirteenth birthday

BATLAN: impractical fellow

BEIS DIN: rabbinical court of law

BEIS HAMIKDASH: the Temple (First or Second) in Jerusalem

BEIS MIDRASH: communal House of Study

BERACHAH: blessing, benediction

BIKKURIM: First Fruits offered in Temple times

CHACHAM: sage

CHALITZAH: ceremony exempting a man from marrying the widow of his deceased childless brother

CHALLAH (pl., *challos*): braided loaf baked in honor of the Sabbath

CHAMETZ: leavened products forbidden for Passover use

CHANUKAH: eight-day festival commemorating the Maccabees' rededication of the Temple

CHAPERS (Yid.): kidnappers of children for conscription in the Czarist army

CHASSIDISM: Movement within Orthodox Judaism founded in 18th-century Eastern Europe by Reb Yisrael, known as the Baal Shem Tov. Stresses emotional involvement in prayer; service of God through the material universe the primacy of wholehearted earnestness in divine service; the mystical in addition to the legalistic side of Judaism; the power of joy, and of music; and the collective physical and moral responsibility of the members of the informal brotherhood, each chassid having cultivated a spiritual attachment to their saintly and charismatic leader — the rebbe or tzaddik.

CHAZZAN: cantor

CHEDER: elementary school for religious studies

CHEVRAH KADDISHA: voluntary burial society

CHEVRAH TEHILLIM: brotherhood for the communal reading of *Psalms*

CHUMASH: the Pentateuch

CHUPPAH: canopy under which the marriage ceremony is solemnized. Also, by extension, the ceremony itself

DARSHAN: preacher

DAVVEN (Yid.): to pray

DAYS OF AWE: the New Year period of judgment, from Rosh HaShanah to Yom Kippur

DAYYAN: judge

DEITSCH (or *Deitsch'l;* Yid.): nickname for the assimilationist Jews of the "Enlightenment" movement

DERASHAH: a sermon or discourse

DIVREI TORAH: discourse or conversation on Torah subjects

DVEIKUS: the ecstatic state of cleaving to the Creator

ERETZ YISRAEL: the Land of Israel

ESROG (pl., *esrogim*): the citron fruit used in the festivities of Sukkos

FERTZIGER (Yid.): coin

FARBRENGEN (Yid.): gathering of chassidim for mutual edification and comradely criticism

GABBAI: (a) attendant of a tzaddik; (b) master of ceremonies in synagogue

GALUS: exile; the Diaspora

GARTL (Yid.): belt worn in prayer

GEHINNOM: purgatory

GEMARA (Aram.): that portion of the Talmud which discusses the Mishnah; also, loosely, a synonym for the Talmud as a whole

GEMILUS CHASSADIM: the mitzvah of doing good deeds

GLATT KOSHER: ritually fit for consumption, without any query

GOY (pl., *goyim):* gentile

GRAF (Pol.): noble

HAFTARAH: the passage from the Prophets read in the synagogue after the Pentateuchal reading

HAKADOSH: "the holy" — traditionally suffixed to certain names

HALACHIC (Eng. adjectival form): referring to the *halachah,* the corpus of Torah law

HAMOTZI: blessing pronounced over bread

HASKALAH: the 18th cent. "Enlightenment" movement which sought to introduce Western culture into traditional Jewish circles

HAVDALAH: the Saturday evening ceremony by which the sanctity of the outgoing Sabbath is separated from the workaday week

HOSHANAH RABBAH: the seventh day of the festival of Sukkos

KABBALAH: the body of Jewish mystical teachings

KAPOTE (Yid.): black frockcoat, worn usually in honor of the Sabbath

KAVANAH: devout intent

KIDDUSH: blessing over wine, expressing the sanctity of the Sabbath or a festival

KIDDUSH HASHEM: sanctifying the Divine Name, especially through self-sacrifice

KITTEL (Yid.): white gown worn on certain solemn occasions

KOHEN (pl.: *kohanim*): priest; *Kohen Gadol:* High Priest

KOPEK (Russ.): small copper coin

KOSHER: ritually fit for use

KVATER (Yid.): person honored by bringing infant to circumcision

KVITL (pl., *kvitlach;* Yid.): note handed to tzaddik bearing name of supplicant and his mother's name, and the nature of the request

LAG BAOMER: minor festival celebrated by picnics

LAMDAN: scholar of repute

LASHON HARA: lit., "the evil tongue"; slanderous talk

LECHAIM: lit., "To Life!" — greeting exchanged over strong drink

LULAV: palm-branch used in ceremony on festival of Sukkos

MAAMAD: regular contribution made by chassid for maintenance of his rebbe's household

MAAMAR: chassidic discourse

MAGGID: preacher

MALACH: angel

MARA DE'ASRA (Aram.): the recognized halachic authority for a particular region

MASHIACH: Messiah

MASKIL: (pl., *Maskilim):* adherent of the Haskalah movement

MATZOS (pl, of *matzah):* unleavened bread eaten on Passover

MAZEL TOV: greeting of congratulation

MECHUTAN: the parent-in-law of one's son or daughter

MEKUBBAL (pl., *mekubbalim):* adepts of the Kabbalah

MELAMED: schoolmaster or tutor

MESHORERIM: choirboys accompanying a *chazzan*

MESIRUS NEFESH: self-sacrifice

MEZUZAH (pl., *mezuzos):* tiny parchment scroll affixed to doorpost

MICHYAH (Heb./Yid.): lit., "sustenance"; in Yiddish usage, a synonym for *arenda*

MIDRASH: (a) classical anthology of the Sages' homiletical teachings on the Torah; (b) a particular passage therefrom

MIKVEH: pool for ritual immersion

MINCHAH: the afternoon prayer service

MINYAN: quorum of ten required for communal prayer

MISHNAH: (a) the germinal statements of law elucidated by the *Gemara,* together with which they constitute the Talmud; (b) any paragraph from this body of law (pl., *Mishnayos)*

MISNAGED (pl., *misnagdim;* adj., *misnagdish, -er):* opponent of the teachings of Chassidism

MITZVAH (pl., mitzvos): a religious obligation; loosely, a good deed

MOHEL: circumcisor

MOTZAEI SHABBOS: the time of the departure of the Sabbath; i.e., Saturday night

NE'ILAH: concluding service of the Day of Atonement

NETILAS YADAYIM: ritual washing of the hands

NIGGUN: melody, usually wordless

NU, NU: untranslatable Yiddish expression meaning (among its scores of uses) something like "Well, well!"

PARITZ: local squire in Eastern Europe

PASUK (pl., *pesukim):* Biblical verse

PESSACH: the festival of Passover

PEYOS: earlocks

PIDYON (or *pidyon nefesh):* the contribution for charity which accompanies a chassid's request to his rebbe

PIDYON HABEN: ceremony of Redemption of the Firstborn

PILPUL: involved legalistic dissertation

PINKAS: communal register

POSKIM (pl. of *posek):* decisors; rabbis whose legal decisions are authoritative

RAV: rabbi

REBBE (Heb./Yid.): (a) a tzaddik who is spiritual guide to a following of chassidim; (b) a Torah teacher

REBBITZIN: wife of a *rav* or a rebbe

REB YID (Yid.): informal term of address to an individual whose name is not known

RIBBONO SHEL OLAM: Master of the Universe

ROSH HASHANAH: the New Year festival

SABBATH QUEEN: the Sabbath personified

SEFER TORAH: scroll of the Law

SELICHOS: penitential prayers

SEUDAH: meal, especially a festive one

SEUDAH SHLISHIS: the mystic Third Meal held at sunset on the Sabbath

SEUDAS MITZVAH: meal held in celebration of a religious obligation

SGULAH: spiritual remedy; talisman

SHABBOS: the Sabbath

SHABBOS HAGADOL: the Sabbath preceding the festival of Pessach

SHACHARIS: the morning prayer service

SHALOM: greeting — "Peace!"

SHALOM ALEICHEM: (a) greeting — "Peace be upon you!" (b) Friday evening hymn of welcome to ministering angels

SHAMMES: sexton in synagogue or beadle in attendance on rabbi

SHAVUOS: the festival commemorating the Revelation at Sinai

SHE'ELAH: legal query

SHEMA YISRAEL: opening words of the Jew's declaration of faith

SHEINER YID (Yid.): a fine, dignified Jew

SHEMINI ATZERES: one-day festival at end of Sukkos

SHEMONEH ESREH: prayer which is the solemn climax of each of the three daily services

SHIDDUCH: a matrimonial match

SHOCHET: ritual slaughterer

SHOMRIM: pious congregants who meet in synagogue before dawn for non-mandatory devotions

SHUL (Yid.): synagogue

SIDDUR: prayer book

STENDER: movable lectern

TACHANUN: prayer requesting forgiveness, omitted on festive occasions

TALLIS: shawl worn in prayer

TALMID CHACHAM: Torah scholar of standing

TALMUD: the basic compendium of Jewish law, thought, and Biblical commentary; comprises Mishnah and *Gemara;* Talmud Bavli: the edition developed in Babylonia; Talmud Yerushalmi: the edition of the Land of Israel

TEFILLAS GESHEM: prayer for rain

TEFILLIN: small black leather cubes containing parchment scrolls inscribed with *Shema Yisrael* and other Biblical passages, bound to the arm and forehead at weekday morning prayers

TEHILLIM: the Biblical Book of *Psalms*

TESHUVAH: repentance

THIRD MEAL: see *Seudah Shlishis* (above)

TIKKUN (pl., *tikkunim):* (a) refreshments for *farbrengen; (b) the task of uplifting the universe by revealing its hidden sparks of spirituality*

TIKKUN CHATZOS: midnight lament over the Exile of the Divine Presence

TISH (Yid.): lit., "table"; ceremonial Sabbath meal conducted publicly by a chassidic rebbe, characterized by spontaneous Torah discourses, and singing by all present

TREFAH: ritually unfit for use; opposite of kosher

TZADDIK: (a) a saintly individual; (b) specifically, a chassidic rebbe

TZEDAKAH: charity

TZITZIS: the fringes worn at the corners of the *tallis*

VAYIKRA: the Book of *Leviticus*

VIDUI: the confession recited on the Day of Atonement, and during the final stocktaking of a lifetime

VORT (Yid.): lit., "word"; a quotable and insightful morsel of moral teaching or Biblical interpretation

YECHIDUS: private interview at which chassid seeks guidance and enlightenment from his rebbe

YESHIVAH: Talmudic academy

YIBBUM: marriage with the widow of one's deceased childless brother

YICHUD: a union in the spiritual spheres, effected by devout divine service in This World

YOM KIPPUR: the Day of Atonement

YOM TOV: festival

ZAL: suffix — "of blessed memory"

ZECHUS: the merit of a good deed, especially as deserving a spiritual reward

ZOHAR: the basic work of the Kabbalah